OF
MARSUPIALS
AND MEN

OF
MARSUPIALS
AND MEN

ALISTAIR PATON

Published by Black Inc.,
an imprint of Schwartz Books Pty Ltd
22–24 Northumberland Street
Collingwood VIC 3066, Australia
enquiries@blackincbooks.com
www.blackincbooks.com

9781760643645 (paperback)
9781743822487 (ebook)

 A catalogue record for this
book is available from the
National Library of Australia

Cover design by Tristan Main
Text design and typesetting by Tristan Main
Index by Belinda Nemec
Cover images: Quokka, Rottnest Island: Lisa / Adobe Stock
Blue sky: merrymuuu / Shutterstock. Binoculars: fractuɪ / Shutterstock
Butterfly net: Dimedrol68 / Shutterstock. Helmet: Dja65 / Shutterstock
Landscape: Rex Nan Kivell Collection, National Library of Australia, NK7429/B

Printed in Australia by McPherson's Printing Group.

Contents

Introduction

'We are almost inclined to believe that Nature has been leading us through a mazy dance of intellectual speculation, only to laugh at us in this fifth continent.'

— Founders of the Philosophical Society of New South Wales, 1821

THE FIRST SCIENTIFIC EXPEDITION TO AUSTRALIA was led by a pirate.

Born in Somerset in 1651 (his exact birthdate is not recorded), William Dampier was a famed explorer, exotic food connoisseur – he introduced the terms 'chopsticks', 'cashew' and 'tortilla' to the English language and brought the first recipe for guacamole to the old world[1] – and an enthusiastic naturalist. Dampier took detailed notes of the plants and animals he encountered on his many travels and kept them in bamboo tubes sealed with wax.

But his main line of business was piracy, joining a crew of buccaneers that raided ships and forts across the Caribbean. After commandeering one vessel the crew pocketed 3276 pieces of eight

---

1   In the Bay of Panama, he described a fruit 'as big as a large lemon' with soft green flesh and skin like 'black bark' that was 'mixed with sugar and lime juice and beaten together in a plate'.

and threw a priest overboard. In another attack, the Chilean city of La Serena was put to the torch after its Spanish rulers failed to pay the pirates' ransom of 95,000 pieces of eight.

In 1687 Dampier was on board the pirate ship *Cygnet,* which sailed across the Pacific to plunder the East Indies, a voyage beset by illness and infighting; during the long ocean crossing, food supplies ran so low the crew openly discussed eating the captain. He was eventually overthrown in a mutiny and left behind in the Philippines with forty of his men, but remained mercifully uneaten. The ship continued under new leadership and on 5 January 1688 hit the shoreline of what is now the Dampier Peninsula, north of Broome, making the remaining crew the first Englishmen to set foot on Australia.

After he returned to England in 1691 Dampier's diaries were published as *A New Voyage Round the World*, which became a best-seller and made him something of a celebrity – enough for the British Admiralty to overlook the more unsavoury aspects of his résumé and give him command of the Royal Navy ship *Roebuck*, which set sail in 1699, heading back to the southern seas.

He made anchor on the coast of Western Australia on 6 August in an inlet he named Sharks Bay (now Shark Bay) because of the large number of sharks caught by his crew in the shallow waters. Dissecting one of them, he made another interesting and somewhat startling discovery: 'Its maw was like a leather sack, very thick, and so tough that a sharp knife could scarce cut it: in which we found the head and bones of a hippopotamus.'

Dampier followed the coast north and explored Timor and New Guinea before setting course for England. Unfortunately, on 21 February 1701, the *Roebuck* 'sprung a leak which could not be stopped' and sank in the middle of the Atlantic Ocean. Dampier and his crew made it ashore on Ascension Island, where they survived for five weeks on goat and turtle meat before hitching a ride home. On his return to London, Dampier was court-martialled for incompetence, but he returned to the sea, circumnavigating the globe twice and publishing *A Voyage to New Holland*, another popular page-turner. He died in London in 1715, although no one knows exactly when or how.

His identification error at Shark Bay – the bones he found most likely belonged to a dugong, which also inhabit the bay in large numbers – may have been the first of its kind, but being completely mystified by the animals of this apparently upside-down land was the universal reaction among the learned men of the age (Dampier also described 'a sort of raccoon' that was probably a wallaby).

Sir Joseph Banks, a giant of the natural sciences, said of the kangaroo: 'To compare it to any European animal would be impossible as it has not the least resemblance of any one I have seen.' French zoologist François Péron described Australia's wildlife as 'strange and incomprehensible'. Writing *The History of New South Wales* (one might say a tad prematurely) in 1817, James O'Hara noted that 'nature may be said in this country to have engaged in whim', and English cleric and noted wit Reverend Sydney Smith expanded on the theme:

> In this remote part of the earth, Nature (having made horses, oxen, ducks, geese, oaks, elms, and all regular productions for the rest of the world) seems determined to have a bit of a play, and to amuse herself as she pleases. Accordingly, she makes ... a monstrous animal, as tall as a grenadier, with the head of a rabbit, a tail as big as a bedpost, hopping along at the rate of five hops to a mile.

Reverend Smith's condemnation of the kangaroo as a species was not unusual in an era when the natural sciences were in their infancy and the men engaging in the new field were all God-fearing Christians. In their judgement, not only were Australia's animals different from those they were familiar with – they were objectively worse. John Washington Price, surgeon on the convict transport ship *Minerva*, wrote after arriving in Sydney in 1798:

> If we examine through the various regions of the earth, we shall find that all the most active, sprightly and useful quadrupeds have been gathered around man, and either serve his pleasure or still maintained their independence through their vigilance, their cunning or their industry. It is in the remote solitudes that we are to look for the helpless, deformed and monstrous works of nature …

Nature was, the logic went, a picture painted by God at the dawn of creation, and the job of the naturalist was to interpret his divine will as expressed in plants and animals. Creatures that didn't fit the established worldview were morally suspect. Kangaroos, thylacines (considered lowly scavengers) and the baffling platypus – which simply refused to fit neatly into the animal kingdom – were especially vulnerable to this kind of reasoning, known as natural theology. Writing about the koala (or 'New Holland sloth'), English naturalist George Perry observed:

> Whether we consider the uncouth and remarkable form of its body, which is particularly awkward and unwieldy, or its strange physiognomy and manner of living, we are at a loss to imagine for what

particular scale of usefulness or happiness such an animal could by the great Author of Nature possibly be destined.

It is worth pausing to remember that in 1800 it was possible for a gentleman of means to be an authority on multiple fields, from botany to geology to astronomy. Expertise was based on interest rather than formal training, and wealth and social standing provided the time and resources to pursue that interest. Over the next 100 years the picture changed completely as the frontiers of science expanded; the term 'scientist' was coined in 1834 and there were giant leaps forward in newly specialised fields such as biology (Darwin dropped his theory

The emu, or 'New genus of bird at Botany bay 1788', by Arthur Bowes Smyth, from his *Journal of a Voyage from Portsmouth to New South Wales and China in the Lady Penrhyn*, 1787–89. (Mitchell Library, State Library of NSW)

of evolution on an unsuspecting public in 1859) and chemistry (Dmitri Mendeleev came up with the periodic table ten years later). Meanwhile, patents were lodged for the electric light bulb, the internal combustion engine and the telephone. In short, there was a lot going on. Into this exciting mix was added an explosion of interest in the field of natural history, spurred by the arrival in Europe of exotic animals and plants from newly colonised places like Australia, a continent that both demanded explanations and, owing to its isolation, attracted those with a maverick streak.

After the arrival of the First Fleet in 1788, senior figures in the new British colony – governors, clergymen, ships' officers – recorded the continent's unusual flora and fauna. There were no trained naturalists on the First Fleet itself; some of the first paintings of birds around Sydney Cove were produced by George Raper, a seventeen-year-old midshipman on the *Sirius*, while the journal of Arthur Bowes Smyth, surgeon on the *Lady Penrhyn*, included the earliest drawing by a European of an emu.[2] But botany was the main game, with serious plant-lovers like Banks (who is credited with bringing 30,000 specimens back to England on the *Endeavour* in 1770), and Robert Brown (author of the landmark 1811 compilation *Prodromus Florae Novae Hollandiae*, which listed 2000 species of Australian plants – all new to science) dedicated to documenting every flower and shrub they could find.

---

2   The fleet's chief surgeon (and later surgeon-general for the colony), John White, took notes on the plants and birds around Sydney Cove and his diary was published with the catchy title *Journal of a Voyage to New South Wales with Sixty-five Plates of Nondescript Animals, Birds, Lizards, Serpents, Curious Cones of Trees and Other Natural Productions*. The book – Australia's first natural history publication – was a huge success and was translated into French, German and Swedish.

Arthur Bowes Smyth's pen and ink drawing of a kangaroo.
(Mitchell Library, State Library of NSW)

Australia's animals remained a curiosity. Shipfuls of furred and feathered creatures were transported to Europe, where they were inspected and displayed, first as stuffed specimens in museums and soon as living animals in zoos, private collections and travelling sideshows.

Into this picture stepped a remarkable band of enthusiastic amateurs who were inspired to get to know the weird and wonderful creatures of the new colony. Their backgrounds varied, but they shared a particular set of character traits: single-minded determination; courage, often to the point of recklessness (that anyone would volunteer to blindly poke around in a hollow log in the hope of disturbing a highly venomous snake is astonishing; the fact that multiple men fitted this description almost defies belief); resilience; resourcefulness; and, importantly, a growing love for the subject.

A touch of eccentricity also didn't hurt. Some achieved a level of fame, but most were driven by an insatiable and endearingly pure curiosity.

Over the next 150 years they would advance the knowledge of Australia's native animals, and the field of biology in the process. And they transformed public attitudes to those creatures, from scorn and embarrassment to wonder and pride. In the early decades of the colony, marsupials and gum trees were considered strange, exotic and hostile; rabbits, horses and oak trees were familiar and safe. At some point public opinion flipped, as academics Heather Aslin and David Bennett explain:

> The term 'exotic' is now often applied to the animals and plants introduced by the early British settlers, which in the wild state are now the feral and the unwanted ... The plants and animals that once made an alien country feel more like home for exiled British convicts and newly arrived settlers are now seen as out of place because the descendants of these settlers now consider themselves to be Australians ... Koalas, kangaroos, wombats, parrots, cockatoos, lyrebirds, even tree frogs and frillneck lizards, are now familiar and attractive icons of a homeland Australians take pride in.

Aslin and Bennett contrast European attitudes towards wildlife – a long tradition of regarding the animal kingdom as separate from humanity – with the perspectives of Australia's First Nations peoples. Indigenous people had advanced knowledge of the nation's animals long before Europeans arrived and played an indispensable role in assisting British and German naturalists locating and collecting specimens. Their contributions were rarely credited.

Joseph Banks, for example, had recorded the word 'gangurru', used by the Guugu Yimithirr people of far north Queensland for a specific large grey kangaroo, although Banks took it to refer to all species of kangaroo and wallaby. The Darug people who lived around modern-day Sydney were unfamiliar with the word 'kangaroo' until they heard it from European settlers, and assumed it meant all large animals; they were later heard referring to sheep and cows as kangaroos.

Another complication was that Indigenous people and the colonists thought about animals in totally different ways. Before the arrival of British convicts, Australia's animals were hunted for food, clothing and shelter, but they were also respected. Aboriginal people and Torres Strait Islanders knew that leaving a balance in nature assured an ongoing supply of resources.[3] Wildlife was also central to spiritual and cultural identity. For Australia's Aboriginal people, a particular area's animals, plants, land, air, water, spirits, songs and stories are all bound up in the idea of caring for country. Some animals were adopted as totems by particular groups, conferring extra layers of connection and responsibility. This deeply ingrained belief system was reinforced through stories, songs, dance and art over more than 2000 generations (for context, there have been only twelve or so generations since William Dampier stepped ashore), forging a deep connection with Australia's animals in a way that makes it hard to imagine an Indigenous version of the European naturalist.

---

3   This may have been learned through experience; hunting probably contributed to the extinction of Australia's megafauna, giant, lumbering creatures including 500-kilogram kangaroos, seven-metre lizards and Volkswagen-sized tortoises.

Thankfully, confusion and condemnation have largely been replaced by acceptance and affection. A century ago, three men could pose for a photograph in front of a car weighed down by thousands of koala skins. In 2019 a video shot on a mobile phone of a woman rescuing a koala from a bushfire became an international sensation. Quokkas on Rottnest Island – an island named by Dutch sailors who mistook the animals for giant rats – star in a flood of selfies on social media. Australians even regard the deadliness of the country's snakes, spiders, crocodiles, sharks, jellyfish, ants, shells (you get the idea) as a matter of national pride, along with the fact that international visitors still scratch their heads at our upside-down corner of the animal kingdom. In 2021, an advertising campaign urging Australians to 'holiday here this year' featured the tagline: 'This is a place that took a look at the rule book and said, "Na, here's a platypus".'

For that we can thank the strange cast of characters who broke new ground in their devotion to Australia's native animals, from the nineteenth-century artist whose pet wombat slept on his London dinner table to the twentieth-century scientist tasked with a top-secret mission to deliver a platypus to Winston Churchill at the height of World War II. And many more unusual, fascinating, inspiring and mostly unknown wildlife pioneers.

These are their stories.

I

Doing Nature's Good Work

'No country in the world is so favourably circumstanced for
acclimatisation purposes as Victoria, and it is within the power of its
inhabitants to enrich it by stocking its broad territory with the choicest
products of the animal kingdom borrowed from every temperate region
on the face of the globe.'

—from the first annual report of the Acclimatisation Society
of Victoria

T
O GRASP HOW FERVENTLY THE NOTION OF SETTING
exotic animals free in the Australian bush gripped some
influential Victorians in the mid-nineteenth century,
look no further than the monkey vs boa constrictor debate of
1862–1863.

At a dinner to celebrate the first anniversary of the Acclimatisation
Society of Victoria (ASV) at the Melbourne Mechanics Institute in
1862, the governor, his excellency Sir Henry Barkly, spoke enthusiastically in support of releasing monkeys into the forests of greater
Melbourne: 'It is desirable to acclimatise the monkey tribe if it can
be done,' Barkly told the assembled diners, adding that the primates
would be 'exceedingly useful, for the amusement of the wayfarer

'Acclimatisation': artist Edgar Ray's engraving of animals in Royal Park, Melbourne, from the *Illustrated Australian Mail*, 1862. (State Library of Victoria)

whom their gambols would delight as he lay under some gum tree in a forest on a sultry day.'

By the next year's dinner Barkly had been succeeded by Sir Charles Darling, who wasn't onboard with the monkey plan. But he had another bold idea, volunteering to source boa constrictors from the West Indies that could be let loose in Melbourne's parks. The giant reptiles, he declared, would provide an amusing distraction for hardworking city folk while controlling the existing population of smaller snakes – by eating them.

Darling recalled having seen boa constrictors 'introduced suddenly amongst a party, and made to rear their heads over a piano, and although a little alarm was at first created, the creature soon became an object of interest and curiosity'. The society's account of Darling's speech noted that 'he had also seen on one occasion a boa constrictor swallow a snake, and when only a little portion of the tail was left exposed he had himself pulled it out again, and sent it in a Seidlitz powder box by the steam packet as a present to a young lady in a neighbouring island.' Sadly, her reaction is not recorded.

Neither monkeys nor boa constrictors roam the Victorian bush today; neither idea got any further than these after-dinner speeches. But serious attempts were made to introduce alpacas, antelope, goats, glow worms, ostriches, deer, exotic bees and numerous species of bird and fish to Australia's parks, forests, waterways and farms. Most failed, but some of the exotic arrivals, such as rabbits, foxes, sparrows and the irredeemable cane toad, took to their new surroundings with an enthusiasm that changed the Australian landscape forever. Nowhere on Earth was this short-lived pseudoscience more enthusiastically embraced or more ruinous to the native flora and fauna. 'There was never a body of eminent men so foolishly, so vigorously and so disastrously wrong,' was the blunt assessment of farmer, naturalist and poet Eric Rolls in *They All Ran Wild*, his 1969 epic on Australia's introduced pests.

The idea of sending animals across international borders had been around for centuries – sheep first domesticated in the Middle East appeared in Britain in about 3000 BC, and the Romans imported lions, leopards, crocodiles, bears and elephants to battle to the death in the arena (Emperor Titus opened the Colosseum in 80 AD with 100 days of spectacle in which 9000 wild beasts were killed). But setting introduced animals loose in the wild, an idea known as acclimatisation, gained momentum as an organised movement in the 1850s. The first acclimatisation society, the Société zoologique d'acclimatation, was founded in Paris in 1854. Étienne Geoffroy Saint-Hilaire, professor of zoology at the Paris Museum of Natural History and director of its menagerie, was its founding president. He defined acclimatisation like this: 'the prospect was nothing less than to provide [the] fields ... forests and ... rivers with new guests; to increase and vary their alimentary resources, and to create other economical or additional products.' From the start, acclimatisation was tied to ideas of church and empire. The French enterprise had government backing, and while there were experiments with llamas, yaks and ostriches, the focus was largely on trying to establish sugar, spices and exotic fruit from the Caribbean in France's African colonies (without success).

The British acclimatisation movement was born of similar ideals but had two important differences. First, it never attracted large-scale government support and was instead the project of a small number of enthusiastic, wealthy and misguided individuals. Second, as historian Michael A. Osborne notes, while French acclimatisors believed that species from the tropics could easily adapt to different environmental conditions, the theory in Britain was that animals needed a familiar climate to survive and prosper – so antelopes used to living in South African grasslands could be deposited in English pastures and not notice the difference (at least during summer). These rival theories were soon to be put to the test in Australia.

British enthusiasts gathered at the Aldersgate Tavern in London in January 1860 for what has become known as the 'eland dinner' (named for the world's largest species of antelope). The meeting was organised by famed British Museum palaeontologist Richard

Owen, who served up roast African venison and dreamed of 'troops of eland gracefully galloping over green sward and herds of kudus ... added to the list of foods good for the inhabitants of not only England, but Europe in general'. A meeting in June that year formally established the British Acclimatisation Society. In England at the time was Edward Wilson, a Melbourne newspaper editor seeking treatment for failing eyesight caused by working until four a.m. before the days of electric lighting. He was to become the driving force behind acclimatisation in Australia.

Wilson was tall and earnest with muttonchop sideburns. Born in London in 1813, he boarded a ship to Sydney in 1841 after his partners in a calico-printing firm fleeced him of his savings and inheritance. The ship stopped in Melbourne and, attracted by the prospects of the young settlement, Wilson got off, tried his hand (unsuccessfully) at cattle farming for a few years, then bought *The Argus* newspaper for £300. His strident and utterly incorruptible personality was perfectly suited to running a newspaper and he waged war with the leaders of the new colony, sparring over issues including the end of transportation of convicts and Victoria's split from New South Wales, which happened in 1851.

Running *The Argus* was hard work. When Wilson took over, each edition was just four pages long and he didn't get a decent printing press for another six years. After gold was discovered in Ballarat in December 1851, Melbourne transformed from a colonial outpost to one of the most thriving cities in the British Empire. One thousand people arrived in Melbourne each day en route to the goldfields and they were joined by many Melburnians, who downed tools and walked away from their jobs to join the hunt

for buried riches. They included printers at *The Argus*, prompting
Wilson to ship out forty compositors from England. The investment proved worth it: the newspaper's circulation rose from 250
in 1849 to almost 20,000 in 1853.

Burnt out – or, as he put it, 'overfagged' – Wilson retired as
editor in 1856 and became a gentleman farmer, a lifestyle that gave
him time to pursue his other great passion: making Australia more
like England. Wilson wrote after a visit to South Australia: 'It is
England with a finer climate, with a virgin soil, with freedom from
antiquated abuses, with more liberal institutions, with a happier
people: and this is what I always thought and hoped Australia
would become.'

While Australia offered many advantages over Europe, in Wilson's mind there was one great deficiency: a vastly inferior offering
of native plants and animals. Australia was, he wrote, 'a country in
which all the natural productions are peculiar; almost all greatly
inadequate to the capacities of the country.' He had already released
nightingales in Melbourne's botanic gardens, and during his trip back
to England to have his eyesight treated he wrote regular letters to
The Times on the subject and absorbed the thinking of Saint-Hilaire
and other prominent acclimatisors; Eric Rolls describes Wilson as
Saint-Hilaire's 'most enthusiastic disciple'.

After returning to Australia, in February 1861 Wilson established the Acclimatisation Society of Victoria, with the stated
purpose of:

> the introduction, acclimatisation, and domestication of all innox-
> ious animals, birds, fishes, insects and vegetables, whether useful or

ornamental; the perfection, propagation and hybridisation of races newly introduced or already domesticated; the spread of indigenous animals from parts of the colonies where they are already known to other localities where they are not known.

Within a year Wilson had travelled to Sydney and Hobart to establish similar groups, sister societies were up and running in South Australia and Queensland,[4] and the Victorian chapter had dispatched emissaries to New Zealand. In its first annual report, the Victorian society proudly reported it had arranged for a pair of ostriches to be delivered from Paris, although both died on the voyage. Attempts to send lobsters and crabs to Tasmania were similarly unsuccessful, although eight English tench (a type of carp) had arrived in Victoria from Hobart.

The fundamental belief underlying acclimatisation was that all animals were created by God for the use of mankind. It was not only man's duty to exploit them – it would be downright rude not to. Wilson was scandalised when he discovered that of the 140,000 species of plants and animals identified by science, Great Britain had domesticated only thirteen:

It seemed to me that nature had furnished us with an inexhaustible variety, that it had been left to man to carry the good thing to the

---

4   The Queensland group's focus was on introducing foreign plants and grasses, including bananas, cotton, apples, pineapples, maize, olives, mangoes and macadamia nuts, to replace native eucalypts and grevilleas. The group imported sugarcane from Mauritius and New Caledonia, helping to kick-start one of the state's biggest industries.

good new place but that, by some unaccountable oversight, this had never been undertaken in a catholic and systematic spirit; and the consequence was that we were stupidly dragging on our lives in a half-furnished world.

(He wrote this to the *Colombo Observer* during a visit to what was then Ceylon, showcasing his inexhaustible passion for both acclimatisation and writing letters to newspapers.)

* * *

What made the Australian experience so singular was the accepted belief that the animals native to the continent were inherently deficient. Kangaroos bounded across the plains with seemingly no purpose, koalas just sat there – and what the hell even was a platypus? A Victorian Legislative Assembly committee observed in 1856 that Victoria had 'no animal fitted for man's use ... and many millions of broad acres lying utterly waste and unproductive'. The same committee noted that Britain was 'too full' to benefit from the introduction of new species. Even the local fish were assumed to be duds; Wilson advocated for the introduction of 'better kinds of fish [from] European seas'. In other colonies like North America, the local animals were feared; in Australia they were to be replaced. Sadly, the same attitude was extended to the humans who already lived on the continent, who were considered inferior and expected to soon 'die out'.

This idea of a largely barren land owned by no one and populated by strange, useless creatures may seem dispiriting, but acclimatisors were inspired by the task before them. In an 1864 lecture, Dr George

Bennett declared that the enterprise would 'impart life and beauty to our plains and forests, where at present animals are scarce, and it will fill our lakes and rivers with beautiful objects of nature'. The logical conclusion was to import familiar animals from the other side of the world. The species introduced to replace the 'useless' local creatures could be 'useful' in one of four ways, and these categories often overlapped.[5]

The first reason was economic, leading to the accidental creation of the Melbourne Zoo. The Zoological Society of Victoria, the first of its kind in Australia, was established in 1857 in a sweep of civic pride that included the foundation of the University of Melbourne, a museum of natural history and a public library. The meeting that founded the zoological society was originally convened to form a bird-lovers' club, but the attendees decided in a moment of inspiration to aim higher and create gardens modelled on the London Zoo, which had opened thirty years earlier. The Melbourne Zoo's original collection, comprising native fauna plus two monkeys, was donated by the society's first president, F.M. Selwyn, from his private collection. The animals were kept in Melbourne's Botanic Gardens while fences and paths were prepared on a patch of land beside the Yarra River in Richmond.

Over the next three years, animals including alpacas, goats and ostriches were added to the collection. In *The Zoo Story*, historian

---

5   There were some other unusual reasons. Rabbits and poultry were sent to
     New Zealand for the 'sustenance of such persons who were unfortunate
     enough to be shipwrecked there'. Camels were brought to Australia to help
     with excursions into the desert and were set free when the arrival of the
     internal combustion engine made them obsolete.

Catherine de Courcy notes that the zoo 'had more in common with
a farm of slightly unusual animals than with a nineteenth-century
European zoo'. The animals weren't intended for public display or
scientific study; the 'zoo' was really a holding area for creatures destined for acclimatisation. Although the Acclimatisation Society of
Victoria imagined imported animals roaming wild in their adopted
home, their plans also included vast pastoral runs featuring new
and interesting livestock they assumed would emulate the success
of the Spanish merino sheep imported from South Africa by John
and Elizabeth Macarthur in 1796.

After the Acclimatisation Society of Victoria was formed in
1861 it absorbed the zoological society and took over management
of the Botanic Gardens collection, moving the animals in police
vans to new lodgings at Royal Park – still the site of Melbourne Zoo
today – after the Richmond paddock was found to be too swampy.
Meanwhile, the Acclimatisation Society stepped up its attempts
to source new animals, distributing circulars to sea captains and
shipping companies and using its contacts with the French and
British societies.

* * *

In 1830 the *Sydney Gazette* and *New South Wales Advertiser* had
published a report in which a Mr Southey advocated importing
three new animals to support new local industries: alpacas, and
angora and Tibetan goats. The case was taken up with enthusiasm
by Thomas Embling, a doctor and politician who championed
causes including the eight-hour work day and the establishing of
public baths to improve the health of the working classes. In 1856

he chaired a Victorian parliamentary committee that recommended government funding for importing alpacas. Sadly for Embling, the report was laughed out of parliament. According to *The Argus*, more than £21,000 was spent on sourcing the animals from South America and the income generated from selling their wool added up to £175.

A major obstacle to bringing fine-wool-producing animals from South America to Australia was that it was illegal – Peru passed a law in 1845 banning the export of llamas to other countries, and Bolivia had similar bans. The Peruvian government explicitly rejected a petition by a group of NSW businessmen to allow the transport of llamas to Australia. But this was not the kind of thing to deter committed acclimatisors and private animal dealers.

One such dealer, Charles Ledger, moved to Peru in 1836 to work as a clerk for an English merchant firm and in 1848 began to breed alpacas. During a visit to Sydney he was asked by Governor Charles Augustus FitzRoy to bring some of the animals to New South Wales. To avoid the export ban, Ledger decided to drive a flock of 728 alpacas 1700 miles through Peru, Bolivia, Argentina and across the Andes into Chile, navigating narrow mountain paths and crossing regions no Englishman had previously visited. Two hundred animals died in one night 'from drinking out of a leech pond' and hundreds more were wiped out by a snowstorm. To avoid local authorities, Ledger divided the surviving animals into three groups and used three different routes before meeting at a pre-arranged rendezvous point. According to an account of his 'heroic' expedition in the *Sydney Morning Herald*, Ledger was captured twice but the 'indefatigable gentleman' eventually succeeded in nursing 336 seasick animals back to Sydney. Eighty died on the voyage and by the time he arrived in Australia in November 1858, interest in the alpaca venture had waned. The government bought the flock for a token sum of 1500 pounds, which all went to the Chilean merchants who had financed the project. Ledger wrote after submitting his resignation: 'On the faith of promises made in this country, I undertook every risk – did succeed – and am ruined!' The alpacas were put up for auction but failed to reach the reserve price and most were given away. (Ledger returned to South America and turned his attention to the seeds of the cinchona tree – the source of quinine, used to treat fevers and malaria, and cause of the bitter taste in a gin and tonic. Exporting the seeds was illegal, but Ledger smuggled some out to the Dutch government, who planted the seeds in Java and monopolised the world's quinine trade until US scientists developed a synthetic version during World War II.)

Even the most passionate Australian acclimatisor could see that alpacas weren't a sustainable industry, but the search for a source of funds for the fledgling colony beside gold and wool continued. Sir Samuel Wilson, a wealthy pastoralist, accepted a number of animals from the Society for Acclimatisation in 1866 including ninety-three angora goats, which arrived from Constantinople via London. These animals were seen as easy to look after and highly suited to Australian conditions. After some initial difficulties (including a number wandering away), by 1873 Wilson had a flock of over 100 goats and calculated that in forty years there would be more than seven million in Australia.

But breeding or farming goats presented unforeseen obstacles. When a farmhand at Wilson's property in the Wimmera tried to pick up the first for castrating, it leapt 'on to the top rail of the yard, ran along it as far as a shed, jumped on to the roof and stood bleating down at the helpless man.' Eventually the goats were returned to the society and sold at a low price. The society's camels were sold off in 1865; cashmere goats and alpacas were deemed unsuccessful in 1867; and a Ligurian bee experiment failed when the bees mixed with the common honey bee.

Four ostriches were ordered from London in 1865 in the hope of producing feathers for ladies' hats. More arrived from South Africa courtesy of Governor Barkly, but the climate in Melbourne and Sydney proved unsuitable and birds were sent to Victoria's Murray Downs, near Swan Hill, and to Townsville. Eventually one pair was sold to a buyer in New Zealand. Farms were later established at Port Adelaide and the NSW Riverina but the industry died out when the feathers became unfashionable.

Attempts to acclimatise European fish were more successful. There were some failed attempts to introduce English crabs and sponges, but thousands of English trout were distributed in streams around the colony, often in the early hours of the morning. In 1886 brothers Albert and Dudley Le Souef (later directors of Melbourne and Sydney zoos) travelled from Melbourne to Ballarat by train, picked up 3200 trout fry and caught the train back to Melbourne. Six hundred of the baby fish were liberated in Badger Creek near Healesville and others were sent to Gippsland and Camperdown. Carp was even more successful, but considerably less popular.

Other animals on the society's wish-list included giraffes, African river hog, the chinchilla – an adorable hamster-like South American rodent 'desirable for its fur' – Californian bighorn sheep, and South African gazelles 'in large numbers to turn loose in the country beyond the Murray, where they would thrive well and ultimately afford both excellent food and good sport'. Yaks were promoted as a source of rich milk that produced excellent butter (their tails could also be used as fly swats), while 'that interesting animal the beaver' was valued for its fur, which could be used to make 'some excellent and warm socks'. But above all these stood the eland. Native to the open plains of southern Africa, the giant eland stands 1.8 metres tall and weighs in at up to 700 kilograms. As well as being the world's biggest antelope, it is also the slowest, which no doubt added to its appeal, along with its reportedly delicious flesh. Introducing the eland, however, proved harder than anticipated. One was shipped from Africa but died on the way.

There was more success with the zebu, a species of humped cattle native to south-east Asia, brought to Australia by acclimatisation societies in the mid-nineteenth century, and water buffalo, which first arrived at Melville Island, near Darwin, on a boat from Timor in 1826 to be used for milk, meat and heavy labour. By the 1980s, that initial population of sixteen had exploded to 350,000 feral buffaloes, before a culling campaign cut the population in half. It's still a lot of buffaloes.

* * *

In July 1864 the Acclimatisation Society of Victoria held its second meeting, a lavish dinner to celebrate its early success (previously cited examples of failure notwithstanding) and to give a practical demonstration of one of the benefits of having a wide array of wild animals available to humans: 'To discover what, within the limits of the colony, was eatable — to range the kingdom of Nature in search of meat,' reported *The Argus* enthusiastically, rallying behind the movement created by its former editor.

The menu was in French, as was the custom for large important dinners at the time, and included such delicacies as 'Le fricandeau de wombat aux épinards' (thinly sliced wombat served with spinach), 'Le bandicoot en currie' (bandicoot curry) and 'Le pâté chaud de perroquets' (warm pate of parrot). Kangaroo, black duck, magpie goose and Murray cod were also part of the eight-course degustation.

The practice of eating animals – usually exotic ones – is known as zoophagy, another nineteenth-century fad that not coincidentally paralleled the acclimatisation movement. Strictly, the original idea was that animals from distant places could enrich the British palette. There were dreams of farming elands, alpacas and ostriches, among others, for human consumption. But the embrace of eating every living thing went beyond the field testing of potential livestock; nobody really believed that one day they would harvest paddocks of bandicoots for domestic production. But then if you weren't eating a bandicoot, what was it good for? And every animal had to be good for something.

The champions of the idea of eating their way through the animal kingdom were the Bucklands, senior and junior. Buckland senior was famed geologist William Buckland, who wrote the first full description of a dinosaur – a giant reptile he uncovered at Stonesfield and dubbed Megalosaurus. But if there was a subject he was more passionate about than palaeontology, it was zoophagy. His lectures at Oxford University were described as 'lively affairs' that included waving a hyena skull around and screaming at his students from atop his rostrum that 'the stomach rules the world'.

In 1825 Buckland was made a canon of Christ Church and married 28-year-old Mary Morland, also an avid fossil collector.[6] Her job was to label specimens but her talents were much more wide-ranging; she drew excellent illustrations of the creatures the couple discovered, edited her husband's writings, and in one memorable household experiment created a paste that covered the kitchen table while he fetched the family tortoise from the backyard – they were both delighted to discover that the tortoise's footprints in the paste matched those on a sandstone slab he had been puzzling over. Guests at the Buckland house were served meals including mice on toast, potted ostrich, hedgehogs and cooked puppies. When a stepbrother's horse died, Buckland pickled its tongue and served it at a luncheon party: 'the guests enjoyed it much, until told what they had eaten'. After one dinner, famous raconteur Augustus Hare recounted what is now the best-known story about Buckland:

> Talk of strange relics led to mention of the heart of a French King preserved at Nuneham in a silver casket. Dr Buckland, whilst looking at it, exclaimed, 'I have eaten many strange things, but have never eaten the heart of a king before,' and, before anyone could hinder him, he had gobbled it up, and the precious relic was lost for ever.

---

6   Around this time a young Charles Darwin enrolled at Cambridge University and joined the glutton club, which met weekly to taste-test exotic birds including a hawk and a brown owl. Darwin wrote the owl's flesh was 'indescribable' – not in a complimentary way – but it didn't deter him from going on to snack on animals he found on his famous voyages, including puma, iguanas and Galapagos tortoise.

Frank Junior – Francis Trevelyan Buckland – inherited his father's passion and gastronomic curiosity. From an early age he showed an insatiable enthusiasm for the natural world and in particular tasting samples of any animal he could get his hands on, including earwigs, squirrels and a panther that died at Surrey Zoo (he befriended a zookeeper, who dug it up). Years later he fondly recalled his days as a boy at Winchester College:

> I was looked up to by the other boys as the most experienced mouse-digger in the college. I used to skin the mice, run a bit of stick through them and roast them in front of a fire ... a roast field mouse – not a house mouse – is a splendid *bonne bouche* for a hungry boy.

Buckland Junior owned a bear cub named Tig, whom he dressed in a cap and gown and took to wine parties at Christ College in Oxford. (It was said Tig also rode a horse and drank champagne. Buckland gave the bear to a zoo after Tig escaped and terrified a shopkeeper by helping himself to all her sugar and sweets.) Buckland trained as a surgeon but was more successful as a natural history writer. His quest to eat his way through the animal kingdom continued throughout his life; at home with wife Hannah, whom he married in 1853, the menu included boiled elephant trunk, rhinoceros pie and porpoise head. (Buckland said it tasted like 'broiled lamp wick'.)

In 1860 Buckland junior founded the Acclimatisation Society of Britain, championing zoophagy as one of its key planks.

Edward Wilson was an enthusiastic devotee and returned to Australia with copies of Buckland's speech to the London Society of Arts, which he distributed widely. It made a passionate case for

acclimatisation and referenced a letter to *The Times* from Wilson
arguing that there was 'a great want in this country' for a domestic
animal that a family could raise and eat for a Sunday roast that was
smaller than a sheep and larger than a rabbit – 'for the new animal
the wombat was suggested'. This idea did not disappear quickly: in
the official guide to the Melbourne Zoo published in 1922, visitors
were informed that the wombat is 'very uninteresting and grumpy'
in captivity but that 'the flesh of the young is good eating, somewhat
resembling pork in flavour'.

Being hunted for sport was also considered a worthwhile purpose for an animal, and hunting was a respectable activity for a
gentleman. A sly fox or noble stag was a worthy adversary. Native
Australian animals not so much – what honour was there in shooting
an echidna? Various types of deer, partridge, quail and hares were
introduced in Victoria to provide 'for manly sports, which will lead
the Australian youth to seek their recreation on the river's bank and
mountain side rather than in the café and the casino'. Remember,
this was a time when being a naturalist and shooting animals for
sport were not incompatible.

The acclimatisation society released deer, hares, pheasants,
partridges and ducks on Phillip Island and game birds at Gembrook
and Wilsons Promontory, east of Melbourne, but was not directly
responsible for the biggest imported scourge in Australian history:
the rabbit. However, the society inspired, encouraged and celebrated
private acclimatisation efforts, including those by Thomas Austin,
a wealthy sheep farmer and member of the society. Austin was a
keen hunter and after migrating to Victoria from Britain held lavish hunting parties on his property at Barwon Park, near Geelong.

But he had a problem: there wasn't much to shoot at. He asked his nephew William Mack to send fresh game from England, and in October 1859 the clipper *Lightning* docked in Melbourne carrying twenty-four English rabbits, seventy-two partridges and five hares. What Austin did with the rabbits isn't entirely certain; he may have turned some loose immediately. Regardless, within three years any remaining in captivity had escaped and turned their attention to two activities at which they were exceedingly efficient: gobbling up the native grassland and producing more rabbits.

Less than six years later 12,608 rabbits were killed at Barwon Park – all progeny of the original batch. In another hunt at Colac, more than 4000 rabbits were killed in half an hour. But those efforts barely stemmed the tide. In 1865 rabbits burrowed into graves at the

Advertisement for the Eureka Patent Rabbit Extractor, c. 1891–1900.
(State Library of Victoria)

Point Ormond cemetery in bayside Melbourne and dug up human remains, a sign things were perhaps not going well. Not everyone took the hint – in 1869 the Queensland Acclimatization Society released rabbits on the Moreton Bay Islands (the same group, one of the most active in Australia, also released sparrows in the Brisbane Botanic Gardens).

Within twenty years, rabbits had overrun thousands of acres in Victoria and crossed into New South Wales. South Australia soon fell to the rabbit invasion and in 1901 the West Australian government built a 1824-kilometre fence – promoted as the world's longest – from the southern coast to the north to keep the rabbits out. The next year rabbits were spotted west of the fence line. A second rabbit-proof fence was built in 1908 and eventually a third was added. These were more successful, but by the early twentieth century ten billion rabbits covered four million square kilometres, making the Australian rabbit one of the fastest colonising mammals in history. The devastation caused by European rabbits munching through native vegetation and farmers' crops had an unintended consequence, dimming the English settlers' affection for animals from home over their native cousins. One writer in the *Queanbeyan Observer* described the rabbit as 'the biggest curse that has ever visited Australia'.

It was a similar tale for the red fox, imported from England in the 1850s for hunting (kangaroos, wallabies and dingoes had been the targets of earlier hunts but were seen as too boring). Credit for releasing foxes can be given to brothers Thomas and Andrew Chirnside, who conducted hunting expeditions on their Werribee estate before turning their attention to building a fine mansion which is now a popular location for family picnics. Within forty years foxes were spotted in Western Australia, and by the early 1900s they were established across most of mainland Australia, tormenting native animals including bandicoots, bilbies, numbats, turtles and ground-nesting birds and eating several species out of existence. In the 1990s credible evidence was found that foxes had crossed Bass Strait to Tasmania.

But rabbits and foxes evidently weren't enough. Eighteen species of deer were imported and released at sites around Australia. Some established wild breeding populations and today there are an estimated 200,000 wild deer in Australia, competing for food with native herbivores, trampling vegetation and helping to spread weeds.

The trail of destruction left by these animals is enormous and tragic. The number of successful hunts was not recorded.

The final, best known and, to modern sensibilities, most baffling reason for acclimatising foreign animals to Australia was to amuse and entertain the European human population – itself recently introduced. A member of the NSW Acclimatisation Society suggested the cashmere goat was 'a fine looking animal [which] would be very ornamental in a park, or a ruin, or the side of a rock, or in a churchyard'. Obtaining wool or cheese from the goat was seemingly an afterthought. Wilson's vision didn't stop at goats:

> The young people of [Australia], like the young people of other lands, will fall in love with one another, and will indulge in their evening rambles; and, as in other lands, probably they will occasionally fall a little short of topics for conversation. What debt of gratitude would then, so circumstanced, not owe to anyone who should provide them

with such materials as the light of the glow-worm and the song of the nightingale?

This idea was deeply Biblical: man was at the top of the natural order of things, and everything else was created to serve him, although in some cases it took some creative thinking to explain how.

In the view of Wilson and others, virtuous pastimes such as chasing rabbits for sport or taking an evening stroll under monkey-filled gum trees would improve the moral character of the new nation. Professor Frederick McCoy believed the melody of English songbirds would cut the crime rate. According to the professor, these 'delightful reminders of home' were capable of 'sweetening the poor man's labours, inspiring the poet with the happiest thoughts, and turning from evil even the veriest brute that ever made himself drunk or plotted ill against his neighbour'. George Bennett argued that the beauty of English birds illustrated why 'one may be allowed to constitute the superiority of one class of beings over another'.

English thrushes, blackbirds, larks and starlings were transported to Victoria in cages throughout the 1860s and released around the colony, with no thought given to their impact on native species. Thrushes were liberated at Yarra Bend, Geelong, Port Albert, Como and Preston and another three pairs were sent to Sydney. Starlings were released at Melbourne University. On 15 September 1863, eighty sparrows were liberated at Royal Park after a concerted push by Edward Wilson (of course), who argued they would help farmers by eating destructive grubs. Batches were sent to Victorian country towns including Castlemaine,

Beechworth, Heathcote and Tower Hill, and more were put on a ship to Hobart. By 1871 the ASV was receiving complaints about sparrows destroying fruit crops. They are now endemic across eastern Australia.

Even more successful were Indian mynas, which were set free at sites including the Botanic Gardens and Melbourne General Cemetery in 1862 in a bid to control caterpillars in Melbourne's market gardens. Mynas steal food from other birds and bully them out of their nests, and can also frighten off other tree-dwelling animals like feather-tailed gliders. They can go from one breeding pair to almost 13,000 birds in five years and are considered one of the world's most invasive species.

By the mid-1860s the acclimatisation movement was in trouble. Government funding had all been spent, donations dried up and there were few successes to boast of. The gardens in Royal Park were in poor condition, not helped by wallabies and escaped rabbits eating most of the flower beds. In 1870 the ASV made the historic decision to transform the gardens into a space for public leisure and education – in other words, a zoo. Under the direction of new ASV secretary Albert Le Souef, whose day job was usher of the black rod in the Legislative Council of Victoria, immediate efforts were made to improve the grounds for visitors and to acquire a wider variety of animals. These were largely native species – by 1875 the collection included thylacines, Tasmanian devils, wombats, a koala and assorted wallabies and kangaroos, which lived alongside the deer and livestock. Le Souef stepped things up when he bought two lions and some American black bears at a discount price. By now the ASV had been renamed the Zoological and Acclimatisation Society and

had turned its attention to establishing 'a good zoological collection'
for Melbourne. It had not entirely given up on acclimatisation; the
objects of the society remained unchanged and it discussed releasing
birds such as African guinea fowl into the wild at secret locations.
But the dream of large-scale acclimatisation was over.

Although it had lasted little more than a decade, the Australian
acclimatisation movement outlived its British counterpart, which
amalgamated with the Ornithological Society in 1866, just six years
after it was created. Acclimatisation movements were founded in
other parts of the world but interest never really took hold, although
there were some curious cases – including a concerted push to support large-scale farming of hippos in the United States' deep south
to supply a meat-hungry nation with supposedly delicious 'lake-
cow bacon' (the plan never took off). Eccentric drug manufacturer
Eugene Schieffelin, chairman of the American Acclimatization
Society, released sixty European starlings in New York's Central
Park in 1890, reportedly because he wanted to look out the window
and see all the birds mentioned by Shakespeare. Today starlings
gather in flocks of up to a million in the USA and can eat twenty
tons of potatoes in a day. Russians also tried acclimatisation, and
there were societies in China, Egypt, Holland, India, Italy, South
Africa and Switzerland.

One country that rivalled Australia for acclimatisation enthusiasm was New Zealand. While Australian animals were considered
odd, to the British colonists New Zealand didn't seem to have
many animals at all; there were no native mammals and not many
birds to be found when Captain Cook landed at Poverty Bay
on the east coast of the North Island on 6 October 1769. New

Zealanders got behind the idea of filling the country with introduced species, founding about thirty acclimatisation societies.
Deer and game birds were released, along with ferrets, songbirds
and some brush-tailed possums from Australia in a bid to start
a fur industry.

Even more than their Australian counterparts, New Zealand's
fauna had evolved in isolation and was totally unprepared for the
threat of introduced animals. Before the arrival of Europeans,
the kea – the world's only alpine parrot, which nests in holes in the
ground – was found across the South Island. Today fewer than 5000
remain as they have been ravaged by stoats, possums and humans
(between 1898 and 1929, when a bounty of 10 shillings per beak was
in place, more than 54,000 beaks were turned in). The number of
kiwis has dropped from twelve million to under 70,000; possums,
now considered New Zealand's number one pest, kill adult kiwi and
chicks, destroy eggs and steal their burrows.

Sir George Grey, twice governor of New Zealand, perfectly fitted the mould of the nineteenth-century acclimatiser – eminent,
independently wealthy, deeply religious, slightly eccentric and totally
untrained in the subject in which he lavishly experimented. In 1862
Grey purchased the island of Kawau, in the Hauraki Gulf north
of Auckland, and set about transforming it. He imported a bizarre
assortment of animals, including kangaroos, antelopes, zebras, elk,
emus, sheep and monkeys, as well as an array of exotic plants. Wallabies overran the island and ate most of the native vegetation; they
are still a serious pest.

Even more bizarrely, in 1900 four moose were released near
Hokitika, a small town on the west coast of the South Island. They

didn't breed but were seen wandering the streets in search of biscuits (which they had been fed during the voyage over) for the next fifteen years. A decade later the Southland Acclimatisation Society inexplicably introduced ten more moose in Fiordland, one of the world's great wilderness areas. Some were shot for sport in the 1920s and although there hasn't been a confirmed sighting since the 1950s, DNA evidence indicates a small population survives deep in the rainforest. A $100,000 reward offered for a photo of a New Zealand moose had not been claimed at the time of printing.

* * *

Acclimatisors saw themselves as scientists, but in the nineteenth century this was a much vaguer term than it is today. Even so, the scientific method had been established by Sir Isaac Newton more than 150 years earlier, yet acclimatisation societies paid no attention to it. Although the original objectives of the ASV included 'inquiry into the causes of success or failure' of acclimatisation efforts, there is no evidence they ever engaged in any scientific assessment of the impacts of introducing exotic species. Instead, they simply tried to introduce as many animals as possible. (Edward Wilson's motto was 'If it lives, we want it).' Darwin's *On the Origin of Species* was published in November 1859, just as acclimatisation was taking off, but was completely ignored by writers in this field despite its obvious relevance.

Rather than a science, acclimatisation is best understood as the eccentric pet project of some rich men with a love of nature (as they saw it) and a lot of spare time. There is a darker side to this pseudoscience that was tied intrinsically to notions of empire: just as it was assumed the 'inferior' Indigenous people would eventually die out and be replaced by superior European stock, the deficient and frankly baffling Australian native fauna were expected to face the same fate. No attempt was made to investigate the success or failure of efforts to introduce foreign species because no thought was given to the possibility that the European animals wouldn't thrive. Rolls observed that the failure of some species to adapt 'saved the world from these societies' worst enthusiasms'. That was certainly true of early attempts to introduce alpacas, goats and ostriches to Australia, as well as some of the more fantastical ideas such as monkeys and boa constrictors. But some of the exotic fish and most of the exotic songbirds became established.

Acclimatisation societies did do some laudable work. They undertook some of Australia's earliest conservation efforts, including lobbying for forest reserves in Queensland. Their motives for seeking to preserve native species were sometimes questionable: in declaring the ASV's commitment to 'preserving them from destruction', George Bennett noted the culinary potential of native fauna: 'kangaroo tail soup is not to be surpassed', while 'the monitor lizard, or guana [sic], if one could overcome the repugnance of its appearance, is delicate and excellent food'. He also noted that native species were worth keeping around to be traded for animals from other countries.

Attempts to introduce glow worms ran into basic practical problems. Wilson sent a number from England, but plans for a breeding program were cut short when it was realised they were all the same sex. According to a letter in the *Hobart Daily Post* in 1908, a box of glow worms did arrive from England in 1861 or 1862 addressed to Baron von Mueller, director of the Melbourne Botanic Gardens. Unfortunately, the 'little lamps' did not survive the trip. However, the box also contained European garden snails ('their slimy moisture was to have fed the glow worms') and they made it to Australia alive. Von Mueller took pity on the snails and put them in his garden. The descendants of these snails, and of others that immigrated inadvertently in imported house plants and shipping containers, became Australia's most widespread introduced pest.

Wilson attended his final ASV meeting in September 1864, then sailed to England, where he had a cataract operation and retired to Hayes Place in Kent. His generosity was legendary and he threw parties so local children could enjoy his small private zoo, which included kangaroos, emus and monkeys. On one such occasion an intruder reportedly broke into the property and was scared off by an ill-tempered emu, which kept part of the man's coat as evidence. Wilson died peacefully on 10 January 1878. His remains were transported to Australia and buried in Melbourne General Cemetery.

2

Animals for Sale

'The wonderful Kangaroo from Botany Bay (the only one brought
alive to Europe) [will be] on exhibition at the Lyceum in the Strand
from 8 o'clock in the Morning, til 8 in the Evening. Different from all
quadrupeds, let it suffice to observe that the Indigenous are delighted,
and the Connoisseur impressed with Wonder and Astonishment, at the
unparalleled animal from the Southern Hemisphere. Cost one shilling'

—Poster in London, 1790

H OW DO YOU GET A KOALA TO THE OTHER SIDE OF the world? It is a question without a simple answer today, so try to imagine the head-scratching 150 years ago. But animal traders of the nineteenth century were nothing if not persistent. Repeated attempts were made to ship koalas from Australia to England, each ending with the death of the precious cargo within days of setting sail. It was soon realised that a key to the problem might be that koalas eat only the leaves of certain gum trees, a food source that doesn't stay fresh for long at sea (koalas eat just thirty-five of the 600 species of eucalypt and can be very fussy, rejecting leaves even from their preferred eucalypt species if the trees didn't grow in their home range). It wasn't until 1880 that one survived the journey, and it was well into the twentieth century before live koalas made it to London in sufficient numbers to create viable captive populations. Even today, koalas can be found at only a small handful of zoos in Europe and North America.

One of the ASV's founding objectives was to facilitate 'the transmission of animals from the colony to England and foreign parts'. The society advised Governor Darling in 1864 that emus were 'suitable for introduction into many other countries' and that kookaburras, 'by the robust, jovial humour of their merry pleasant notes and quaint manners, would form most desirable additions to British parks'. Edward Wilson recommended the export of 'Various Marsupiata, from the larger species of kangaroo to the kangaroo rats'. Although 'their flesh ... with the exception of the bandicoot – which is superior to rabbit – is scarcely equal to that of most of other game', 'their skin furnishes a good kind of leather'. Moreover, Wilson suggested, 'From the peculiarity of form, and their eccentric movements, they would constitute a very interesting feature in parks; and from their speed they might furnish a valuable addition to objects of sport.' But Wilson also issued a word of caution: 'The transit of these animals is attended with great difficulty.'

The voyage from Australia to Europe could take a sailing ship four months in calm weather. Nevertheless, there was a constant movement of animals in both directions. This was an age of limited understanding of animal behaviour but boundless enthusiasm for sharing exciting newfound species. Of course, acclimatisors weren't the first to transport animals to and from Australia, and when they did, they were merely the crest of a much bigger wave. Much earlier, the first exotic animals introduced to the Australian continent by humans were dingoes, native dogs descended from south-east Asian wolves which scientists believe came with hunter-gatherers from Sulawesi – now part of Indonesia – about 4000 years ago. They had a severe environmental impact, replacing the thylacine as the top predator and driving it to extinction on the mainland, but they are now considered part of the natural landscape. The first animals sent overseas from Australia were probably sea cucumbers, traded by the Yolŋu people of Arnhem Land to regular visitors from the north along with turtle shells, pearls and canoes.

In 1788 Australia experienced its first influx of European animals; the First Fleet inventory included eighteen turkeys, twenty-nine geese, thirty-five ducks, 122 fowls, eighty-seven chickens, six horses, four cows, one bull, one bull calf, forty-four sheep, nineteen goats,

KANGAROO.

A boxing kangaroo pictured in *The Naturalist's Cabinet: Containing Interesting Sketches of Animal History*, vol. 1, by M. Thomas Smith (London: James Cundee, 1806).

thirty-two hogs, five rabbits, Governor Phillip's greyhounds, Reverend John Marsden's cats and an unspecified number of puppies and kittens. They didn't all make it to Australia, and some that did didn't last long; Arthur Phillip lamented in a dispatch to Lord Sydney dated 9 July 1788 that three sheep had been killed by lightning and all the cattle had taken advantage of the lack of fences to wander off. These problems foreshadowed the challenges of transporting animals on an industrial scale.

The colonisation of Australia coincided with an intense British fascination with exotic animals. In the late eighteenth century a well-to-do family could acquire a parrot, monkey, flamingo or zebra, or even a docile rhinoceros for the right price. The most famous menagerie was in the Tower of London, where animals including lions, leopards and, for a brief period, an African elephant (a gift from Louis IX of France) had been kept since the thirteenth century. Travelling menageries were a popular form of public entertainment in the provinces, with George Wombwell's the largest. At the peak of the trend, more than 500 animals circulated England in purpose-built wagons and were put on display at local fairs.

For animal dealers, the arrival of a new array of creatures from the far points of the globe presented a great business opportunity, and no animal aroused more excitement than the kangaroo. James Cook had brought dead kangaroos back with him to England on the *Endeavour*, and live specimens weren't far behind. In 1790 Alexander Weir advertised 'an extraordinary quadruped called THE CUNQUROO ... being the first that was ever brought to Britain' at his natural history museum in Edinburgh. The first living kangaroos to be seen in England were in the private collection of

Queen Charlotte, wife of George III, at Kew Gardens, and before the turn of the century Kendrick's Menagerie in Piccadilly boasted a kangaroo. There were six on display at rival Pidcock's Menagerie, where customers could also hire a cassowary for the evening and see a monkey riding a camel. A baby kangaroo born at Pidcock's in 1800 drew large crowds and was hailed as one of the 'greatest rarities every seen'. In 1805 the Reverend Thomas Smith was impressed by the 'prodigious strength' of a male kangaroo at Pidcock's:

> I saw this noble quadruped wrestle with the keeper for the space of ten or fifteen minutes, during which time he evinced the utmost intrepidity and sagacity; turning in every direction to face his opponent, carefully watching an opportunity to close with him, and occasionally grasping him with his fore paws, while the right hind leg was employed in kicking him upon the thigh and hip, with equal force and rapidity.

An illustration accompanying this description in *The Naturalist's Cabinet: Containing Interesting Sketches of Animal History* shows a shopkeeper squaring off with the kangaroo with fists raised – the first depiction of a 'boxing kangaroo'.

Smith remarked that 'these animals may now be considered as in some degree naturalized in England', referring to successful breeding populations at Kew Gardens and Great Windsor Park. Encounters with kangaroos became almost commonplace; in 1809 a young Irishman studying law in London wrote to his father:

> I was walking down Picadilly, when I met a porter carrying a live kangaroo, which he was conveying from Mr Pidcock's at the Exteter

'Change, to a person who had purchased it. The animal was fastened to his knot by the feet, and his head lay dangling over, very near the left ear of the fellow who was carrying him; this it seemed was a temptation not to be resisted by the kangaroo, who, after smelling at the man's ear for a long time, gave it a terrible bite, and nearly clipped it off.

The incident, recounted in Christopher Plumb's *The Georgian Menagerie: Exotic Animals in Eighteenth-Century London*, resulted in a street fight between the enraged porter and a drayman who ran to defend the kangaroo after it was thrown onto the footpath. 'A crowd speedily collected, a ring was formed, and the drayman after several severe rounds gave the porter a heavy drubbing. Then he took the kangaroo into his cart and … drove off to deliver it.'

In 1834 *The Times* published an article describing a woman waking with fright to discover 'a strange animal lying at her back, with one of its paws laid over her shoulder'. She tried to beat it away with a towel, and 'with one bound it sprang to the furthest corner of the room'. The creature was apparently a kangaroo that had escaped from Wombwell's Wild Beast Show.

* * *

Two black swans arrived in England on the *Buffalo* in 1800 and were presented to the Queen, but unfortunately one died soon after, and the other 'availed himself of the liberty they gave him … and was shot by a nobleman's game-keeper as it was flying across the Thames'. A living wombat was taken to England in 1805 by Matthew Flinders' naturalist Robert Brown, who gave it to anatomist Everard Home.

Another arrived on the *Investigator* in 1810. A pickled wombat and platypus had arrived in London in 1799, delivered in a cask of brandy, which promptly burst over the head of a woman who was carrying it over her head after it had been unloaded (transporting a living platypus would prove an even bigger challenge, as we shall see).

The presence of kangaroos in particular was seen as further evidence of British superiority over the kangaroo-less French, with whom Britain was presently engaged in the Napoleonic Wars. In 1802, during a brief period of peace, Joseph Banks presented two kangaroos to the Ménagerie du Jardin des Plantes in Paris, and two years later the expedition of Nicolas Baudin returned after almost four years exploring the southern coast of Australia (or 'Terre Napoleon', as it appears on Baudin's charts) with thirty-three large cases full of scientific specimens and seventy-two very seasick live animals including kangaroos, dingoes, long-necked tortoises, wombats, black swans and a lyrebird. Most of the Australian animals – plus others collected en route, including lions, ostriches, porcupines, monkeys, a hyena and a wildebeest – ended up in Empress Josephine's menagerie in France. Her collection also included dwarf emus from Kangaroo and King Islands, a species that was driven to extinction soon after; the last surviving Australian dwarf emu died in France in 1822. In 1803 a kangaroo appeared in the royal menagerie in Vienna. By 1830, Penny Olson writes, 'kangaroos (and wallabies) featured in public and private menageries, museums, in plays and circuses from England to Russia'.

By the first half of the nineteenth century, however, menageries were increasingly seen as unfashionable and the more enlightened embraced a modern feature of most Western cities: the zoo. The first modern zoo opened in London in 1828 with a vision of furthering public education and scientific understanding, and the animals from the Tower menagerie were transferred there three years later. Dublin Zoo opened in 1831 and Bristol, Amsterdam, Antwerp and Berlin followed in the 1830s.

The Australian acclimatisation movement took full advantage of the trend. Prominent Australian acclimatisors may have lamented the worthless local fauna, but they were happy to offer them to overseas collectors, who clearly found them more interesting. Wombats were shipped to France, dingoes to London and black swans to Copenhagen, Cologne, Java, Calcutta and Paris. The ASV sent Australian fish, ducks, dingoes and magpies to the London Zoological Society for research, and in 1865 alone the society dispatched animals to St Petersburg, Amsterdam, Rotterdam, Hamburg, Cologne, Copenhagen, Calcutta, Mauritius, Sicily, Rangoon and Java – mostly kangaroos, emus and black swans. Lords of the Admiralty in London made Her Majesty's ships available for the transport of specimens 'provided no expense be thrown on the department'. The British Foreign Office circulated a questionnaire on animals and vegetables suited to acclimatisation to consuls and governors around the world, and the ASV placed advertisements in newspapers in Cape Town, Rio, Lima and San Francisco.

In the 1880s Albert Le Souef travelled to Europe to inspect foreign zoos and took with him some kangaroos, emus, wombats and dingo pups. During his journey he traded them for new animals for the Melbourne Zoo including bears and badgers. Le Souef and his sons subsequently visited India, South Africa, the USA and Singapore to buy and exchange animals.

* * *

There are limited accounts of how animals fared on international voyages but it clearly wasn't well. Many died en route and those that made it alive had to endure cramped conditions and storms that could last for days – which must have been a novel experience for an animal that had spent its life bounding through open plains, burrowing under the ground or nesting in treetops.

The first annual report of the ASV noted the challenges of transporting wild animals:

> The usual course with private individuals – and even in the first instance with societies – who have animals to send is to take them down to the ship at the last moment and put them under the care of the steward, the cook or the butcher without knowing anything about his disposition or character, or the amount of other duties which he may have to attend to. Everything goes well as long as the weather is fine. But a storm arises, every man is called to his proper post ... in the meantime the dens and cages are washed by every sea, the animals tumble over each other and are at their wits end, and when the gale is over it is found that half of them are maimed or dead.

The ASV's solution was to provide 'proper care and attendance for the animals on board', and to ship animals in huge quantities to improve the odds of some making it to their destination alive. The ASV noted in 1864 that echidnas required great care on long voyages because they had to be fed 'on a milky food and eggs'. Salmon and trout ova were shipped in boxes on beds of charcoal, green moss and chipped ice. Songbirds, apparently more expendable, were sent in wire cages without an attendant. Seals were reportedly one of the hardest animals to transport by sea since they had to be kept in water tanks that allowed them to come to the surface regularly to breathe.

An account by famed American animal dealer Frank Buck hints at the huge casualties involved in transporting animals around the world for public display. An agent for Buck purchased 2000 exotic birds from a village market in Asia. Half had died by the time the bird dealer returned to Calcutta to ship them to San Francisco: 'Most of them were packed so tightly in the baskets and crates that it was impossible for them to move,' Buck recalled. 'Many of them had been in these baskets and crates for from ten days to two weeks.' Of the 300 he dispatched to California, only 125 arrived alive, or just 6 per cent of the original purchase.

In 1849 Tasmanian politician and botanist Ronald Campbell Gunn procured two thylacines caught in snares near Launceston for the London Zoological Society. Gunn wrote to the society informing it of the prized animals' travel arrangements:

Sir, I have shipped on board the barque Stirlingshire ... two living thylacines (male and female) ... and which I trust will reach you alive and well. Captain Gwatkin, whom I have known for some years, has promised his utmost personal care and attention to them during the passage home. I have put on board 12 sheep (together with hay for their sustenance) as sea stores for the thylacines, and have made every arrangement I could think of to ensure their safe arrival in London.

Both animals arrived safely and were put on display in the London Zoo.

In December 1891 an article in *The Mercury* newspaper noted 'a fine specimen of the Tasmanian Tiger' was on its way to London, and 'a number of opossums and wallabies are also on the vessel bound for the Old Country'. Between 1850 and 1926 London Zoo displayed twenty thylacines; the last arrived from animal dealer Bruce Chapman, who bought it from a Queensland zoo in exchange for an elephant. It was one of a pair; the other sadly died when a strike at London's ports forced the ship they were travelling on to stay at sea for an extra six months. A newspaper article describing the unfortunate incident informed readers that 'all the indigenous animals of Tasmania, including the devil, are much sought-after by dealers and zoo agents'. According to the digital Thylacine Museum, five Tasmanian tigers purchased by London Zoo died in transit. Thylacines were also displayed in zoos in Paris, Berlin, Cologne, Antwerp, Washington DC (which received a mother and three pups) and the Bronx Zoo in New York, as well as in Melbourne.

The Le Souef family experienced first-hand the problems of transporting animals over vast distances. In Paris in 1886 Dudley Le Souef bought zebras, reindeer and wild Barbary sheep for the Melbourne Zoo, but the real prize was an American bison, which died at sea despite the best efforts of Le Souef and the ship's doctor. Two years earlier Dudley spent a month in Singapore with a shopping list of animals including a rhinoceros and a tapir (a large mammal native to South America). He bought two tapirs and sent them on to Melbourne while he waited for a rhinoceros to come up for sale (during his stay he was driven out of one hotel by cockroaches and passed the time by capturing and preserving snakes). A month later he finally got his hands on a rhino, which made it as far as Sydney before falling ill and dying before it reached Melbourne. When Le Souef arrived home he discovered one of the tapirs had also died in transit and the other had passed away soon after arriving. The trip had taken three months and cost £400, but it wasn't a total failure – he did bring home some other interesting animals including a black panther, a leopard, a tiger and some orangutans, which were added to the zoo collection.

Two years later, Le Souef successfully brought a tapir back with him from Europe. A rhinoceros proved more of a challenge, but one was eventually purchased in Calcutta. It was loaded onto the SS *Bancoora* along with a young elephant, monkeys and parrots. On 13 July 1891 the steamship ran aground in a gale near Barwon Heads. The animals were rescued and put on a train to Melbourne, but the rhino died weeks later (in the time it was on display, attendance at the zoo doubled). The treacherous waters of the Southern Ocean didn't spare travelling animals. The ship carrying Ranee, Melbourne Zoo's first elephant, was hit by a severe storm on its way from India in 1883. She reportedly wrapped her trunk around an iron stanchion and held on.

* * *

Early arrivals at Melbourne Zoo provide a window into the process of procuring exotic animals. In 1883 an elephant arrived from the King of Siam in exchange for a selection of Australian native animals. According to a 1922 visitor guide, two polar bears were purchased in Europe after being 'captured in the Arctic regions in the summer of 1918' and a lion was promoted as having been caught in the wild as a cub. The zoo's donkey was donated by the Australian Aviation Corps, which had obtained it in Mesopotamia, while the ostriches were descendants of those imported by the ASV in the 1860s. Many of the large animals were bought from circuses or local collections – while Australia did not have the tradition of animal menageries seen in Europe, there were some; a Mr Stutt of Bourke Street, Melbourne, for some reason owned lions and bears (a plan by the ASV to buy them fell through). Meanwhile, locals left injured animals or pets they no longer wanted on the zoo's doorstep. By the early twentieth century the zoo looked a lot more like a modern zoo than a farm, although there were still some animals we would find surprising today, including dogs, hens, cattle, seagulls and a family of guinea pigs in a miniature Swiss chalet.

* * *

With local animal lovers and foreign zoos in the market for exotic animals, there was money to be made, and Charles Jamrach's emporium in London's East End was the biggest animal dealership in the world. An article in *The Strand* magazine in 1891 described a sense of wonder at entering the shop:

> We find ourselves in a bright, clean room, eighteen or twenty feet square, properly warmed by a stove placed in the centre. The walls, from floor to ceiling, are fitted with strong and commodious wire cages, in which birds of wonderful voice and hue and monkeys of grotesque lineament yell, whistle, shriek, and chatter. Great and gorgeous parrots of rare species flutter and scream, and blinking owls screw their heads aside as we pass.

Jamrach was born in 1815 in Hamburg, where his father, a harbour master and chief of the Hamburg River Police, started collecting wild animals that arrived in the port. Charles took over the London branch of the business after his father's death in 1840. The shop was conveniently located close to the Port of London, where shipping had surged to unprecedented levels in the seventeenth and eighteenth centuries; hundreds of ships lined up along the Thames, waiting to disgorge cargo from all over the world. As an 1879 edition of the magazine *Good Words* explained, 'Master of merchantmen ... before sailing, call on Mr Jamrach for a priced list of animals required and bring back as many of the things ordered as they can lay their hands on.'

Many of those things came from Australia. An 1887 edition of the *Illustrated London News* shows Jamrach in his shop, inspecting cages stuffed with kangaroos. The *Good Words* article described specimens for sale, including fifteen young flying foxes, a female wallaby, a kangaroo rat ('a kangaroo in miniature'), and birds including cockatoos, a pair of Australian king parrots 'looking very much like pompous flunkeys in their green coats and red waistcoats', zebra finches and an Australian nightjar. The author noted with disappointment there were no lions or tigers in the shop when he visited, but he did see four black panthers, a pair of pumas, two cheetahs, an eland, two tapirs and an ocelot. A rhinoceros had recently arrived from Burma, bound for London Zoo: 'How queer, if her sea voyage had not dulled her senses, the huge beast must have felt when she found herself in Ratcliffe Highway.' Indeed.

Jamrach's emporium also showcased artefacts from around the empire, including 'waddies, nullahs, boomerangs, spears [and] womeras from Australia'. There were also skins of various exotic creatures, including the kiwi – 'that queer bird that looks so much like an old gentleman', according to *Good Words*.

Our friend Frank Buckland was a regular Jamrach customer. In his four-volume *Curiosities of Natural History*, he recorded a visit in which the proprietor:

> took me upstairs and opened the door of a room, and there I saw such a sight as really made me start. The moment the door handle was touched, I heard a noise which I can compare to nothing but the beating of a very heavy storm of rain upon the glass of a green-house. I cautiously entered the room and then saw that was one mass, windows and walls, of living Australian grass parakeets ... such a number of birds I never saw before together in my life.

A second room contained as many birds as the first – 6000 in all. Jamrach explained that two ships had arrived from Port Adelaide stuffed with native birds and he had 'bought the lot'. On the same visit Buckland saw a zebra, llamas, black swans, a jaguar, emus, a kangaroo, possums, wedge-tailed eagles, a pelican, 'masked pigs from Japan', porcupines, camels and a yak. The *Good Words* article noted that prices were calculated according to popular taste but admitted surprise that a giraffe was so affordable: '£40 seems a low price for that fleet creature, or which 50 years ago there was only one live specimen in England'.

The birds that astounded Buckland weren't an isolated case. An article in *The Register*, a South Australian newspaper, describes ships with up to 30,000 parrots departing on a regular basis, with 400-gallon drums of seed to feed them. Some were destined for zoos and private ornithologists, but others for the booming millinery industry; the late nineteenth century was not a good time to be a bird. As new and interesting species were discovered around the globe it became fashionable for Victorian women to wear clothes adorned with feathers, and hats crowned with whole stuffed birds, sometimes with wings outstretched and mounted on springs and wires as if captured mid-flight. More extreme examples included twigs, leaves and stuffed mice or reptiles in large-scale natural diorama.

The best-known episode involving Jamrach occurred in October 1857, when a Bengal tiger escaped from his yard and picked up a small boy in its jaws, only letting go when Jamrach bludgeoned it over the head with a crowbar. The event is immortalised in a statue on London's Tobacco Dock. Jamrach's clientele ranged from public institutions like the London Zoo to businessmen such as American showman P.T. Barnum and private animal enthusiasts, including the Prince of Wales. One of the most colourful was poet and painter Dante Gabriel Rossetti. Rossetti was born in London in 1828, the son of an exiled Italian patriot. At age twenty the promising artist and his Oxford undergraduate friends began calling themselves the Pre-Raphaelite Brotherhood, 'to do battle against the frivolous art of the day'. Rossetti became a national celebrity and, following the death of his wife from a morphine overdose in 1862, moved to a large house at 16 Cheyne Walk, Chelsea, which he shared with poet Algernon Charles Swinburne and a rotating cast of other artists. Life in the house was interesting, not least for the complicated love triangle involving Rossetti, painter William Morris and his wife Jane. Swinburne was a bizarre figure, later nominated five times for the Nobel Prize for Literature, noted for skipping about the house reciting poetry at the top of his voice and drinking himself to unconsciousness. But what brings this unusual home to our attention is Rossetti's peculiar fixation with the wombat.

The first Europeans to encounter wombats were the crew of the *Sydney Cove*, which was shipwrecked in Bass Strait in 1797. They were also the first to taste them – sailors survived by eating large numbers of wombats on the surrounding islands. Matthew Flinders was part of the relief party and took a live wombat back to Sydney as a gift for Governor John Hunter. When it died six weeks later, Hunter mailed it to Sir Joseph Banks in London, where it was stuffed and mounted in a bizarre squirrel-like pose, crouched on its hind legs; it can still be viewed at the Great North Museum in Newcastle Upon Tyne.

As engaging as wombats are, Rossetti is perhaps the only person to describe the marsupial as 'the most beautiful of God's creatures'. (Lieutenant David Collins, deputy judge advocate of New South Wales, described the newly discovered animal as 'a squat, thick, short-legged, and rather inactive quadruped'.) British professor John Simons, an authority on exotic animals in Victorian London, details in his book *Rossetti's Wombat* how the artist spent hours admiring the wombats at Regent's Park Zoo (the first had arrived in 1830, and one was born in captivity in 1856). His Chelsea garden was already filled with interesting animals, including armadillos, kangaroos, peacocks, a kookaburra and a raccoon. A zebu had to be given away after uprooting the tree it was tethered to and chasing a visitor around the garden. Some accounts suggest he may have kept a penguin in the house, but a bid to purchase an African elephant was shelved when Rossetti balked at the £400 price. In September 1869 he bought a wombat from Jamrach for eight pounds, and it became his obsession. The wombat arrived while Rossetti was in Scotland, and he wrote:

> *Oh! How the family affections combat*
> *Within this heart; and each our flings a bomb at*
> *My burning soul; neither from own nor from bat*
> *Can peace be gained, until I clasp my wombat!*

Rossetti's sister wrote back with verses in Italian describing the wombat as 'irsuto e tondo' (hairy and round). After Rossetti arrived home he wrote to his brother: 'The wombat is a joy, a triumph, a delight, a madness.'

Named Top by Rossetti, the wombat lived indoors and had the endearing – or annoying, depending on your point of view – habit of following people around the house and nibbling at their trousers. Rossetti would place him in a tall silver serving platter in the middle of the dining table, where he would slumber while London's Bohemian elite discussed art and politics. On one occasion he awoke and took advantage of the guests' lively conversation to gnaw on a box of cigars.

Sadly, Top fell ill and died less than two months after arriving. Rossetti had him stuffed and displayed in the entrance to the house. The grieving artist painted a self-portrait with the wombat, with the accompanying verses:

> *I never reared a young wombat*
> *To glad me with his pin-hole eye,*
> *But when he most was sweet and fat*
> *And tailless, he was sure to die!*

I never reared a young Wombat
To glad me with his pin-hole eye,
But when he most was sweet & fat
And tail-less, he was sure to die!

Dante Gabriel Rossetti laments the death of his wombat, 1869. British Museum via Wikimedia Commons.

Jamrach was the biggest name in town, but at the height of the trade in 1895 there were 118 animal dealers in London. Jamrach's great rival was German merchant Carl Hagenbeck, who also emerged from the port of Hamburg. Like Jamrach, Hagenback inherited his animal trading business from his father. By the time Carl took over running the family firm just before his fifteenth birthday, its collection included lions, panthers, cheetahs, monkeys and gazelles. Carl added to the animal collection whatever came along – including in 1863 five large bears – and expanded his business internationally. He dispatched collectors to all corners of the globe and soon had agents in most major international ports to collect animals for sale to European zoos, circuses and private menageries. Between 1866 and 1886 he imported more than 1000 lions, 150 giraffes, 300 elephants, 400 tigers, 600 leopards, 800 hyenas, seventeen rhinos, tens of thousands of monkeys and more than 100,000 birds.

Hagenback became the leading supplier to the booming American market, and travelled there with 'ethnographical shows' which showcased animals and people from remote regions. One famous tableau included a Lapp family with reindeer and sled in the backyard of Hagenback's home – 'All Hamburg came to see this genuine "Lapland in miniature".' Other entrepreneurs cashed in on the fad; more than 35,000 indigenous people from around the world, including Australia, were displayed in these cruel human zoos, alongside mentally and physically disabled people, for spectators to gawk at. Twenty were lured from Palm Island and far north Queensland by Barnum and Bailey Circus recruiter Robert A. Cunningham to be put on display across North America and Europe, while three Badtjala people from Fraser Island were taken to Germany in 1882 and toured cities including Hamburg, Leipzig, Berlin, Dresden and Lyon, throwing boomerangs and spears, participating in mock fights and climbing tall poles.

A poster printed in Frankfurt in 1885 announced the appearance of 'Male and Female Australian Cannibals' in Cunningham's touring show. The poster proclaimed:

> The first and only obtained colony of these strange, savage, disfigured and most brutal race ever lured from the remote interior wilds where they indulge in ceaseless bloody feuds and forays to feast upon each other.

(There is no credible evidence any Indigenous Australians killed people for food.) Shockingly, these touring shows continued until 1940 and were not confined to Europe and the USA; in the late nineteenth century an Aboriginal family was displayed at Melbourne Zoo. 'We're horrified today, but it's a different era,' current Zoo director Michael Tanner told *The Age* in 2012. 'I think we have to learn from our history and move on from that.'

* * *

Phillip T. Robinson, author of *The Pygmy Hippo Story*, argues that by the turn of the century public opinion had turned against big-game hunters and an expectation had developed that traders would embody 'a deep love of nature and animals' and contribute to 'larger projects of conservation and education'.

A letter to Hagenbeck from Bronx Zoo director William Hornaday in 1902 revealed his acute awareness of evolving attitudes about the treatment of animals:

> We must keep very silent about 40 large India rhinoceroses being killed in capturing the four young ones. If that should get into the newspapers ... there would be things published in condemnation of the whole business of capturing wild animals for exhibition. There are now a good many cranks who are so terribly sentimental that they affect to believe that it is wrong to capture wild creatures and exhibit them – even for the benefit of millions of people ... in my opinion the three young ones that survive will be more benefit to the world at large than would the 40 rhinoceroses running wild in the jungles of Nepal and seen only at rare intervals by a few ignorant natives.

Albert and William Jamrach inherited their father's business after his death in 1891, but after flourishing for several years it suffered a sharp decline. In 1903 a lion that cost £100 twenty-four years earlier was selling for twenty pounds. The price of a tiger had fallen from £300 to eighty pounds. By 1908 the number of animal dealers in London had fallen to thirty-two. Albert Jamrach died in 1917 and the business closed its doors two years later. Charles Hagenbeck died in Hamburg in 1913. Ironically, although he had engineered and profited enormously from the animal trade, his biggest legacy was in revolutionising the treatment and display of animals. In 1907 he opened a zoological garden at Stellingen, near Hamburg, where animals were exhibited in uncovered pits that imitated their natural habitats and separated them from the public by moats rather than steel bars.

* * *

Throughout these years there was also a smaller animal trade in Australia. A taxidermist in Sydney's Hunter Street had a sideline selling wild animals, and in the 1850s the Sir Joseph Banks Hotel at Botany Bay assembled a collection of creatures, including a Bengal tiger, grizzly bear, an Indian lop-eared goat and, according to an article in the *Sydney Morning Herald*, 'eight pairs of beautiful birds never before seen in the colony'. Owner William Beaumont also imported a male and female elephant, which lived in the hotel's 'pleasure gardens'. They were the first elephants on the Australian mainland (a male had arrived in Hobart on a ship from Calcutta in 1851; it was sold at auction and displayed at various hotels before being put to work pulling a plow near Adelaide).

One major international dealer who spent at least part of his career in Australia was Ellis Joseph. He was born in India and moved with his parents to the United States as a baby. At age thirteen he realised he could make money trading animals after buying some green parrots while on holiday in Panama and selling them in San Francisco. By the turn of the century he was shipping large numbers of birds between Australia and the US. In 1916 he tried to send a platypus to America but the animal died seven days into the voyage. He tried again in 1922, putting five male platypuses on a steamer to San Francisco in a remarkable portable hutch designed by naturalist Henry Burrell (more on him later) that included a water-filled chamber and a dry sleeping den connected by a ramp lined with rubber squeegees to help the animals dry off after a swim. Despite the effort put into their comfort, only one platypus survived the journey.

It was the first monotreme to be put on display outside Australia. Upon its arrival in New York City, zoo director William Hornaday declared ecstatically:

> This most strange and wonderful of all living animals has been carried alive from the insular confines of its all-too-distant native land and introduced abroad ... No matter what evil fate may hereafter overtake the platypus, nothing can rid us of the fact that New York has looked upon a living *Ornithorhynchus paradoxus* and found it mighty interesting.

The platypus survived at the zoo for just forty-nine days.

Joseph returned to Australia with raccoons, foxes, skunks, ocelots, bison, monkeys, bald eagles and most famously 'Casey', a young male chimpanzee he had captured in what is now Ghana in west Africa (where all four species of chimp are now endangered). Joseph went on tour with the chimp, the first to be seen in Australia, billing it as the so-called 'missing link'. On 9 April 1910 Broken Hill's *Barrier Miner* reported:

> He is extremely intelligent, answering readily to his name, and performs various tricks. He also shakes hands with visitors with an air of good fellowship that is nothing short of laughable ... His ceaseless activity is simply wonderful, and must give rise to envy in the minds of any gymnasts who may be among the audience. Casey plays the piano, wheels prams, nurses babies, smokes, writes, plays the mouth organ, and does a hundred other things.

After touring Australia, Joseph exhibited Casey in New Zealand, where he sold him to showman Thomas Fox, although it seems Casey didn't take to the new arrangement and gave 'his new proprietor several maulings', according to the *NZ Truth*. Their relationship evidently didn't improve and Casey escaped from Fox's house in the Sydney suburb of Marrickville in 1914. According to a newspaper report, Casey 'created such a scare that Mrs Emily Russell, 42, of Meeks Road, Marrickville, dropped dead'. The *Sydney Morning Herald* described Casey's escape, his pursuit by Fox (carrying an iron bar), Fox's wife (armed with hot water) and two policemen, and his eventual capture (after being shot in the foot) as 'probably the most exciting event in the history of Marrickville'. Mrs Russell's grieving husband sued Fox for £1000 but, the *Herald* noted, admitted under cross-examination that the 'deceased was of stout build, and somewhat excitable'. Fox pleaded not guilty but was ordered to pay £450.

In Western Australia, two English trappers set up a trading business in the remote Kimberley region. Walter Payne and Jack Wallace were bird specialists but also caught kangaroos. In 1906 they landed in England with forty-five kangaroos, twenty wallabies and more than 6000 assorted parrots and lorikeets and set up what they called the Little Zoo on a farm near Bath. Payne looked after the animals while Wallace made annual trapping trips back to Western Australia. A 1908 description of the Little Zoo in the journal of London's Foreign Bird Club describes two magnificent aviaries containing 'a feast for the eyes', including kookaburras, sacred kingfishers, numerous types of doves and pigeons, cockatoos, owls and hawks. Housed in the same enclosure were 'kangaroos of different varieties, apparently very happy in their environment'. There were also some 'very fine' emus on display, along with the cases used to transport them from Australia:

> Mr Payne pointed out to us how the cases had been enlarged as the birds grew during the journey. He informed us that when they left the depot at Wild Dog Creek, N-W Australia, they were only the size of ordinary fowls, but we saw them as they stood over five-foot high.

The same journal includes a number of ads for the zoo, promoting the sale of animals and birds including a pair of young kangaroos bred in Bath, a male agile wallaby, a 'very tame' sulphur-crested cockatoo, frillneck lizards, a pair of emus and 'boomerangs (a few) and native art (various)'. The advertisement concluded: 'We are the

only firm in Europe that visits Australia annually for the purposes
of collecting birds and animals. Therefore make your purchases
direct from the trappers and save the dealer's profits.' It was a good
pitch but evidently an unsuccessful one; the Little Zoo appears to
have shut down by 1911.

More successful was John Roach, a former convict who had
been sentenced to seven years' transportation for stealing a coat.
After serving his sentence, Roach opened a shop in Hunter Street,
Sydney, which also served as a museum, housing around a hundred
stuffed animals and other curiosities. But his main business was
selling birds. An advertisement in the *Sydney Morning Herald* in
January 1845 alerted settlers to his interest in live birds and eggs,
and informed 'Captains of vessels and Gentlemen about to leave
these shores for Europe, India, or the neighbouring colonies that
he always has on hand Black Swans, Emus, Kangaroos, and many
other varieties of Birds and Animals for sale'.

Australian birds were big business, and not just for commercial
animal dealers. Museums and private collectors were stuffing their
cabinets with specimens from around the globe, and they were waking
up to Australia's avian riches. Obtaining them required enlisting an
army of passionate, memorable and occasionally misguided collectors, who are the focus of the next chapter in our story.

3
Birds on the Brain

'From their incapacity for running and their total inability to fly, the parent bids are very easily captured, and when taken with the hand offer no other resistance than a smart peck with the bill.'
— John Gould, on catching little penguins

'BIRD LOVERS ANNOYED' SCREAMED THE NEWSPAPER headlines after an unusually acrimonious bush campout in October 1935. The source of the unrest, which prompted ten of the eighteen campers to pack up their tents in protest, was George Mack, a Scottish-born bird expert and director of the National Museum in Melbourne. While the other seventeen members of the Royal Ornithologists Union observed the birds around the camp at Marlo, on the mouth of the Snowy River, shared stories and enjoyed nightly lectures, Mack had a different agenda. This became clear as the bird lovers watched a delightful scarlet robin tend its nest, an activity that ended abruptly when Mack took out his shotgun and killed it. All in the name of science.

The incident was a turning point in the study of birds in Australia, effectively ending more than a century in which birds were collected in their millions – when 'collecting' meant certain death for the birds, and for the collector more often than you might expect. After the campout the museum defended Mack's 'destruction' of the scarlet robin as 'repulsive but necessary' for the acquisition of scientific knowledge, although there is no record of the museum ever having received the bird. A week later the Royal Ornithologists Union banned collecting at its annual camp.

The large-scale killing of animals, including marsupials, for private and institutional collections had rarely been questioned during the nineteenth century. This was far from a uniquely Australian phenomenon; competition was fierce to obtain animals across the globe. French American zoologist Paul Belloni Du Chaillu gained worldwide fame when he returned from an expedition to West Africa in the 1860s with pickled gorillas, confirming the species was more than a myth. Also on board were a collection of bats, an African pygmy squirrel and thirty-nine species of birds not previously known to science. The first director of the Melbourne Museum, Frederick McCoy, acquired three of Du Chaillu's gorilla specimens and used them in a display intended to disprove Darwin's theory of evolution.

Animals were just one arm of a wide-ranging nineteenth-century collecting craze. The press in Victorian England declared an 'epidemic' as all classes hoarded coins, stamps, matchboxes, biscuit tins, military medals, thimbles, books and the many other weird and wonderful items that became available through the travels of British explorers and colonialists.

The general collecting mania collided with an explosion of interest in the rapidly expanding field of natural history. A young Charles Darwin was an enthusiastic participant in Britain's 'beetle craze'.

The 'fern madness' that gripped Britain from the 1850s to the 1890s was given a scientific name: pteridomania. The discovery that plants could be grown indoors in glass terrariums led to a national obsession that drove plant species to the brink of extinction. No sooner had it died down than orchid fever swept the nation. One plant imported from the Philippines sold for 235 guineas, the equivalent of almost $25,000 today.

Fossil collecting briefly became all the rage; the Mantellian Museum in Brighton, England, established by self-taught paleontologist Gideon Algernon Mantell, had more than 20,000 specimens. Meanwhile, women excluded from most collecting clubs combed British beaches for seashells and seaweed – children's author Margaret Gatty spent fourteen years describing more than 200 varieties for her two-volume *British Sea Weeds*. In the USA, future president Theodore Roosevelt opened his own museum at age nine to showcase his collection of more than 100 seashells, minerals, pressed plants, a seal skull and other natural objects.

But nothing inspired nature lovers like harvesting birds and their eggs. Americans were especially enthusiastic. The Smithsonian bird collection grew from 3696 specimens in 1850 to more than 81,000 in 1880. Charles Batchelder, president of the American Ornithologists' Union from 1900 to 1905, declared there was not 'much of a dividing line between ornithologists and sportsmen'. Not to be outdone, British bird enthusiasts saw Australia as the next great hunting ground, with hundreds of species that were yet to be catalogued. This sentiment found expression in Australia: Eric Rolls cites David Carnegie's report of his thirteen months prospecting in the Great Victorian and Gibson deserts: 'Of the bronzewings, which at sundown, and before sunrise, lined the rocks literally in hundreds, we shot as many as we wanted. How thick they were can be judged from the result of one barrel, which killed fourteen.'

Horace William Wheelwright quit his job as a lawyer in the United Kingdom in 1852 to try his luck on the Victorian goldfields. When that didn't work out he made a living as a professional shooter, living in a tent on the outskirts of Melbourne. In 1861 he wrote *Bush Wanderings of a Naturalist, or Notes on the Field Sports and Fauna of Australia Felix*, under the pseudonym 'An Old Bushman'. The book provided first-hand accounts of similar bird hauls, along with observations of dozens of animals, reptiles, insects and fish, plus instructions on how to catch joeys for pets, cure kangaroo hams and make platypus tobacco pouches. At one small waterhole Wheelwright and his partner bagged more than 200 birds in March and April 1858. He described a typical haul near Mordialloc from 22 December 1854:

> At night we brought home to my tent 16-and-a-half couple quail, three-and-a-half couple scrub quail, one rail, 11 couple snipe, three nankeen cranes, one red lowry, five black ducks, three shovellers, three coots, two black cockatoos, two moorhens, seven shell paro-quets. I do not quote this as anything extraordinary, and I have no doubt it has often been beaten.

Wandering the bush with a loaded shotgun gripped by bird mania was a dangerous activity. South Australian explorer John Horrocks was headed north into the outback in 1846 when he stopped to shoot a particularly beautiful bird. To get the shot he had to persuade Harry, the camel he was riding, to lie down. As Horrocks reloaded his rifle, Harry lurched sideways and set off the gun. The blast ripped off Horrocks' right middle finger, entered his left cheek and took out a row of teeth from his upper jaw. Horrocks died of his wounds four weeks later. Before his death he ordered Harry's execution. The local mayor was asked to carry out the sentence, but he bungled the shooting and another man had to finish Harry off. The bird, presumably, flew away.

For many, the danger was worth it. Collecting animals was a profitable exercise. Wheelright sold snipes in Melbourne for two shillings and sixpence each, which was no small sum. But nothing compares to the empire created by an Englishman who became a giant of Australian natural history despite spending just eighteen months in the colonies. John Gould was described as an 'egotist', a 'queer fellow' and had a string of strained personal relationships throughout his career. But he was an extraordinarily skilled ornithologist, had a brilliant business mind and benefited from exceptional timing. His emergence coincided with unprecedented public interest in natural history and the arrival in England of interesting new specimens from around the Empire. New methods of taxidermy had become widely available by 1830 and the invention of lithography created a way to illustrate birds and animals that brought them to life like never before. As a result of this combination of factors, Gould remains one of the most influential figures in Australian natural history.

Gould was born into a poor household in 1804 at Lyme Regis in Dorset, England, a seaside resort that was popular with fossil hunters. He was the son of Elizabeth Clatworthy and John Gould

Senior, a gardener who specialised in growing cucumbers. When John Jr was fourteen his father was offered a job in the Royal Gardens at Windsor Castle and John Jr was apprenticed to the head gardener. He didn't particularly take to gardening but the job introduced him to the art of taxidermy, an area Gould found a lot more interesting – and profitable; he displayed an early entrepreneurial spirit by catching and stuffing birds and selling them at nearby Eton College. He was also very good at it – the British museum still has a pair of magpies Gould stuffed in the first year of his apprenticeship.

A giraffe brought Gould to prominence. This was no ordinary giraffe – in England in 1829 there was no such thing as an ordinary giraffe. Before King George IV received one as a gift from the Pasha

Portrait of John Gould, c. 1870. (Walker & Sons; State Library of Victoria)

of Egypt in 1827 it's doubtful anyone in Britain would have seen a live giraffe; a camel that was painted with spots and paraded through London in 1810 doesn't count. When the king's favourite pet died, Gould – newly appointed as curator and preserver at the Museum of the Zoological Society of London – and a colleague were given the job of stuffing the three-metre tall 'camelopard' (as giraffes were sometimes known in those days), plus a crane and two lemurs. It was a massive assignment that required removing the giraffe's insides, creating a fake skeleton of wood and iron rods, filling the skin with straw and hemp and sewing it back up again in a shape that still looked like a giraffe. The result was a resounding success, and at age twenty-five Gould had earned a reputation as one of the country's pre-eminent animal stuffers.

In 1829 he married Elizabeth Coxen, who was working as a governess for a prosperous family in the shadows of Buckingham Palace. The match transformed Gould's career in two ways. First, Elizabeth was a gifted artist, and would eventually play a role that rivalled Gould's own producing the major works that created his legacy. Second, she had family connections in Australia. Elizabeth's brothers had emigrated to New South Wales and correspondence with them alerted Gould to the continent's native curiosities, and to the untapped possibilities of doing business there.

The next year the couple moved into Broad Street, Soho, in London's West End, and Gould published his first major work. *A Century of Birds from the Himalaya Mountains* contained descriptions and lavish illustrations by Elizabeth of 100 specimens that had come into Gould's possession at the Zoological Society. The book was a commercial and critical success and established a publishing process that Gould was to repeat over a career that produced twenty-one major works, including the seminal *Birds of Australia* and *Mammals of Australia*.

Gould's publications weren't the sort of books you could pick up at the local bookshop. *Birds of Australia* was published over a period of eight years in seven volumes, each the size of a small suitcase. It features 681 large colour plates, each coloured by hand and accompanied by several pages of descriptive text. Only 250 copies of *Birds of Australia* were printed but it was one of the most important and influential scientific works of the nineteenth century, and one of the most laborious.

The elaborate production was financed by subscribers; Gould made valuable contacts through the society and wasn't shy about approaching them. The list of subscribers to *Birds of Australia* included Prince Albert and the kings of Prussia, France, Denmark and Belgium. After enough subscribers were secured, Gould would write the text and draw sketches of each specimen. The quality of Gould's drawings is a subject of much historical debate, but everyone agrees they were well short of publishable standard. However, he cared deeply about producing accurate depictions of his subjects, which was now possible using lithography. Gould's sketches were accompanied by explanatory notes to guide Elizabeth and a small team of artists (briefly including Edward Lear, who would later write *The Owl and the Pussycat*). They used a special greasy crayon to draw refined versions of Gould's initial sketches in reverse on a slab of smooth limestone. This was sent to a lithographic printer, who printed copies that were filled in by expert colourists, so each subscriber received in effect an original artwork.

Gould's fame was further enhanced when he was asked to examine and classify 450 birds brought back to England by another naturalist and collector: Charles Darwin. The *Beagle* docked in Cornwall in October 1836 after a five-year voyage that included sixty-one days in Australia, during which time Darwin visited Sydney, Hobart Town, King George's Sound in Western Australia and the Blue Mountains.

Gould's main interest was in some finches Darwin had collected in the Galapagos Islands, which turned out to be the most famous birds in history, not that anyone – Darwin included – realised that when the box containing them was delivered to the Zoological Society on 4 January 1837. Gould saw immediately that the finches' beaks seemed specialised for their individual habitats on different islands, and that the birds shared many traits with species from mainland South America. Within a week of receiving the birds, Gould had identified eleven different species, a discovery cited by Darwin twenty-two years later in *On the Origin of Species* as a key piece of evidence for his theory of evolution by natural selection.

Gould accepted the job of writing the birds volume of *The Zoology of the Voyage of HMS Beagle*, in collaboration with Darwin, but he didn't finish it. He had more important business to attend to – in Australia. Gould was so eager to get his *Birds of Australia* project off the ground that he started publishing it before he left England, using bird skins and pickled specimens – a decision he quickly regretted, recalling the twenty published plates and refunding his subscribers. Gould and his party – wife Elizabeth, eldest son John Henry (age seven – his three youngest children stayed behind in London), fourteen-year-old nephew Henry Coxen and expedition collector John Gilbert (much more on him later) – set sail on 16 May 1838 on the *Parsee*. Gould made the most of the four-month journey, collecting thirty species of birds on the open ocean, mostly by shooting them from the deck of the ship then using a small rowboat to scoop the dead birds out of the water (a process that may explain why the journey took longer than usual).

The *Parsee* docked in Hobart on 18 September 1838, its arrival noted in the *Hobart Town Courier*: 'Mr and Mrs Gould are now in the Colony to which they have come at great expense and sacrifice of comfort.' They came with letters of introduction to Governor Sir John and Lady Jane Franklin. John was a national hero in England for his exploits as an Arctic explorer; during one expedition into the Canadian tundra in the 1820s he survived by eating lichen and famously boiling his own leather boots.[7] Mr and Mrs Franklin were both natural history enthusiasts and they accompanied Gould on a trip to Port Davey, in the state's remote south-west wilderness. They didn't make it to the harbour due to bad weather but Gould made the most of the situation by returning to the boat in Recherche Bay with a live penguin. Collecting around Hobart was more successful – Gould found several new species in the city streets. After visiting Launceston he split up with Gilbert and sailed to Sydney in February 1839.

Gould stayed for three days with George Bennett, curator of the Australian Museum, then headed to the home of Elizabeth's brother Stephen Coxen in the Hunter Valley. Elizabeth wasn't with him – she had other pressing matters to deal with, namely

---

7   Sir John perished in the Arctic in 1847, along with twenty-four officers and 105 sailors, while attempting to find the fabled Northwest Passage.

preparing for the birth of another child. Gould returned to Hobart for the birth of his son, named Franklin Tasman, but less than a week later he hitched a ride on a sheep transport from Launceston to Adelaide. The city had been founded just three years earlier and the large number of chattering lorikeets in the middle of town made collecting ludicrously easy. Echoing the accounts of Wheelwright and others, Gould wrote:

> The incessant clamour kept up by multitudes of these birds baffles description … they feed together in perfect amity, and it is not unusual to see two or three species on the same branch. They are all so remarkably tame that any number of shots may be fired among them without causing the slightest alarm to any but those that are actually wounded.

Gould joined naturalist Frederick Strange (more on him too, shortly) on official surveys, accompanied renowned explorer Captain Charles Sturt on an expedition to the Murray Scrubs (now known as the Mallee) and visited Kangaroo Island. In three months he added more than 500 birds and forty quadrupeds to his collection, including shooting the last pink robin seen in South Australia. He then returned to Hobart, packed up his belongings and left with his family for Yarrundi, the Hunter Valley station owned by Elizabeth's brother, where they would spend the next four months. Meanwhile, specimens collected so far were packed in boxes and shipped back to England.

Gould didn't actually spend much time at the Coxen property. He was much more interested in exploring and collecting. Immaculately dressed in a suit and top hat, with his gun and collecting bag slung across his arm, he presented an arresting sight. He wrote that 'a successful mode of procuring specimens is by wearing a tail of a full-plumaged male in the hat, keeping it constantly in motion, and concealing a person among the bushes'. While these advanced tactics were required to snare a lyrebird, other 'stupid' birds were easily subdued with a whack on the head with a stick. In *The Bird Man*, her definitive biography of Gould, Isabella Tree notes that Gould had no qualms about using the 'distinctly unsportsmanlike' tactic of shooting birds in their nests.

Regardless of the morals, it worked. Gould bagged new species including the little eagle, black-breasted buzzard, red-backed king-fisher, black-eared cuckoo, Australian egret and red-chested quail, as well as two new types of kangaroo. He marvelled at a huge flock of bronzewing pigeons and brought down eight with one shot. On 11 December 1840 Gould was mesmerised by a crimson chat: 'As may be supposed, the sight of a bird of such beauty, which, more-over, was entirely new to me, excited so strong a desire to possess it that scarcely a moment elapsed before it was dead and in my hand.' Gould went a step further by putting some of his specimens in his stomach, taking a particular liking to rosella pie and the 'delicate' flesh of baby emus.

During an expedition to the Liverpool Ranges he first encoun-tered vast flocks of small green birds, which the local Darug and Tharawal Aboriginal people called the 'betcherrygah'. Gould was instantly charmed by 'the most animated, cheerful little creatures you can possibly imagine'. The birds elicited a unique response – rather than blasting them to smithereens, he wanted to take them back to England alive. This was based on business acumen rather than animal welfare: Gould (accurately) envisaged the birds as pets in parlour room cages delighting the upper classes. He captured twenty in the hope of getting a specimen alive to Britain but none survived the journey back to Yarrundi. Fortunately, Gould's other brother-in-law, Charles Coxen, had bred some budgies in captivity. He gave four to Gould and two made it to London alive, the first live budgerigars seen in Britain. Within decades they were being packed into ships in enormous numbers.

On 9 April 1840, almost nineteen months after arriving in Hobart, Gould and his family left Sydney, bound for home. They arrived in London four months later and immediately set to work on the gigantic *Birds of Australia*. It would take eight years to complete the seven volumes featuring 328 species that were new to science. Two-hundred and eighty-three subscribers signed up.

A year after their return to London, with production in full swing, disaster struck. After the birth of an eighth child, Sarah, Elizabeth contracted puerperal fever, an all-too-common ailment in the days when doctors routinely walked from an autopsy to the delivery room without washing their hands in between. She died on 15 August 1841, aged thirty-seven. The *Australian Dictionary of Biography* is matter-of-fact: 'It would appear that the strain of motherhood, together with the executing of approximately 600 drawings for publications, had sapped her vitality.'

When part fifteen of *Birds of Australia* was published three years later, Gould named a beautiful multicoloured finch *Amadina gouldiae* after Elizabeth – the only time he ever applied either his name or hers to a bird. His description of the species read:

It is therefore with feelings of no ordinary nature that I have ventured
to dedicate this new and lovely bird to the memory of her, who, in
addition to being a most affectionate wife, for a number of years
laboured so hard and so zealously assisted me with her pencil in my
various works, but who, after having made a circuit of the globe
with me, and braved many dangers with a courage only equalled by
her virtues, and while cheerfully engaging in illustrating the present
work, was by the Divine will of her Maker suddenly called from this
to a brighter and better world.

Gould worked even harder to distract himself from his misery. He
employed a new illustrator and new plates rolled off the presses. Close
to the completion of the project, Gould controversially sold most of
his collection of Australian birds, eggs and nests – 1800 specimens
in total – to the Museum of Natural Sciences in Philadelphia after
the British Museum knocked back his £1000 asking price.

Gould had plans to return to Australia, but he moved on to an
obsession that consumed the rest of his life: 'How vivid, then is my
recollection of the first hummingbird which met my admiring gaze!
With what delight did I examine its tiny body and feast my eyes on
its glittering plumage!'

Hummingbirds are indeed remarkable creatures. The world's
smallest birds, they have proportionally the second-largest brain, can
fly backwards and beat their wings 100 times a second. Gould first
saw a living hummingbird in 1857 in Philadelphia, and published his
five-volume *Monograph of the Trochilidae, or Family of the Hummingbirds*
in 1861. But he didn't wait for those milestones to stage a display of
the birds as part of the Great Exhibition of 1851 in London. A huge

hall at Regent's Park Zoo housed twenty-four glass cases containing 320 of the tiny, brightly coloured and very dead birds mounted on twisted branches.

Since Gould didn't know what hummingbirds looked like alive, he just made it up. The result was a macabre assortment of stuffed birds in unnatural poses, including wings outstretched at various angles. Fortunately, no one in the audience knew what a living hummingbird looked like either – and they loved it. More than 80,000 people saw the exhibition, including Charles Dickens and Queen Victoria, who wrote in her journal: 'It is impossible to imagine anything so lovely as these little humming birds, their variety, and the extraordinary brilliance of their colours.'

Gould continued publishing, issuing *The Handbook to the Birds of Australia*, *The Birds of Asia*, *The Birds of Great Britain* and, finally, *The Birds of New Guinea and the Adjacent Papuan Islands*. The final parts of *The Birds of Asia* and *The Birds of Great Britain* were published after his death in 1881 at age seventy-six. In his final months he was in constant pain but continued working while lying on his back and taking opium. After his death Gould's remaining collection of more than 12,000 bird skins, including 5378 hummingbirds, was sold to the British Museum for £3000.

Gould's impact stretched well beyond his own lifetime. He was one of the first to promote Australia's native animals, writing that the koala was 'a remarkable creature' and marvelling at elegant and noble members of the kangaroo family. He is still regarded as Australia's – and one of the world's – greatest ornithologists. Thousands of Australian children have learned about the natural world through membership of the Gould League, formed in 1909 with the pledge

Portrait of Ludwig Leichhardt by Samuel Calvert, 1862. (State Library of Victoria)

'1. I hereby promise that I will protect native birds and not collect their eggs; 2. I also promise that I will endeavour to prevent others from injuring native birds and destroying their eggs'. Whether they were aware of the irony is not known. And in his own lifetime, he inspired – and employed – many other collectors. In fact, Gould had at least eighteen collectors working for him in Australia, and several of them deserve to be examined in more detail.

* * *

John Gilbert was Gould's primary assistant in Australia (and the only one to be paid a salary), contributed enormously to Gould's success and deserves to be recognised in his own right as one of our greatest natural history collectors. No portrait of him exists but he was described as somewhat short but very strong and active, with a dark complexion, and as a 'pleasing and bright companion' with a beautiful tenor voice (after spending the day collecting he often regaled his companions with a song). He is recognised in the names of at least thirty-two animal and twelve plant species, including two marsupials, two molluscs, four birds and three types of fish. Gilbert is credited with finding the 'type' specimens (those which formally act as the name-bearer for any given scientific name) of at least 8 per cent of all forms of recent Australian birds and mammals. (Gould described about 350 new species, but many of those were specimens collected by Gilbert.)

Little is known of Gilbert's childhood or early life other than that he and Gould both studied as gardeners and both worked stuffing animals for the Zoological Society in London. Gould was eight years older than his protégé and he was impressed enough to write a reference when Gilbert applied for a position in 1834 at the Shrewsbury Natural History Society.

It appears Gilbert had a short-lived marriage before he took the job; he was fired after allegedly trying to install his second wife in his rooms at the museum. Gould was undeterred, signing up his former apprentice as chief collector for his Australian trip in 1838 on a salary of £100 (wife no. 2 was left behind and disappears from history at this point). When Gilbert left England, local landowner and duck enthusiast Thomas Eyton offered to buy his personal animal collection, including eighty-two birds and an 'almost perfect skeleton of an armadillo (with the exception of the toenails)'.

Gould and Gilbert explored together for three months – the only time they would do so – before Gould asked Gilbert to travel to Western Australia in February 1839. It appears to have been a spontaneous decision, since Gilbert left without any of his belongings. When he arrived at the Swan River Colony, very little scientific fieldwork had been done in the area, and in the twenty-eight months he spent there (in two visits) he single-handedly established a base of knowledge of the state's animals. He visited King George Sound, Cape Leeuwin and Rottnest Island, as well as exploring around Perth and Fremantle, sending a large number of the 'extraordinary novelties' he found back to England along with detailed descriptions. After an initial ten months in Western Australia he returned to Sydney to meet up with Gould, only to find his employer had departed for England three weeks earlier and the personal belongings he had left with Gould had been stolen.

Gilbert had every right to be upset but he showed only mild annoyance – writing to Gould, 'I must say I thought you would not have left before the time expired which I stated you might expect me' – before sailing to Port Essington, 300 kilometres north of present-day Darwin on the tip of Arnhem Land, on a relief ship headed north after the fledgling settlement had been flattened by a cyclone. (The British government had established Port Essington in 1837, imagining it would rival Singapore as a trading post, but it was beset by problems and abandoned in 1849.) His mind was quickly back on the job; three days after landing he wrote to Gould: 'I have been out once and saw so many beautiful species of birds that I knew not which to shoot at first.'

Gilbert stayed in the Top End for nine months, exploring further into the interior than any white man had gone before and visiting islands in the Van Diemen Gulf. In the process he recorded more than 200 new bird species, including the malleefowl. In 1841 returned to England via Singapore, and upon his arrival Gould promptly commissioned him to return to Australia to collect more specimens; four parts of *Birds of Australia* had already been published and Gould knew what he was missing for the remaining volumes (Gilbert was also tasked with finding new subscribers). Gilbert didn't need much persuading; he wrote in his journal that he was 'dreaming every night of kangaroos and native pheasants'.

He set sail on the brig *Houghton-le-Skerne* on 1 February 1842 – the last time he would see Gould – and by July was back in Fremantle. He carried a long list of instructions – Isabella Tree explains that:

> in addition to his beloved birds, Gilbert was expected to send Gould
> fish ... as many shells as possible; plans, ornamental shrubs, and pieces
> of bark for drawings; all the sponges and corallines possible; reptiles
> and insects; the skins and crania of all quadrupeds, great and small;
> even some live specimens for Lord Derby's menagerie.

Gilbert spent the next seventeen months in Western Australia, collecting 432 specimens of birds, 318 mammals and scores of insects, molluscs, animal bones, eggs, reptiles and plants, many of them new to science, including the elusive noisy scrub-bird, one of Australia's most endangered and primitive birds. He visited the Augusta area and spent almost two months on the Houtman Abrolhos Islands, a chain of 122 coral atolls and associated reefs west of Geraldton, home to interesting wildlife (Gilbert souvenired sea birds, kangaroos and sea lions) and more than fifty shipwrecks, including the

Batavia, probably Australia's most notorious, and certainly its most gruesome, maritime disaster.[8]

In January 1844 he set off on a collecting trip to the Darling Downs region in Queensland. This was where Gilbert came across 'a totally new parrot – without exception the most beautiful of the whole tribe I have ever yet seen in Australia'. He had found the elusive paradise parrot. The striking bird – a stuffed specimen in the Australian Museum has a turquoise chest, blue head, a long bronze-green tail and flashes of red on the rump and wings – nested in tunnels burrowed into termite mounds and spent much of the day on the ground feeding on grass. Landclearing and the destruction of termite mounds to obtain material for tennis courts in the early 1900s sent the bird on the path to extinction. The last recorded sighting was in 1927.

Gould's initial instructions were for Gilbert to return to Port Essington to continue collecting but he changed his mind, writing to say that his focus was now on preparing his new work, *Mammals of Australia*, and urging Gilbert to come home within the next twelve months. Gilbert never received the letter because by the time it arrived he had already departed on a doomed (from Gilbert's point of view, at least) overland expedition. On 10 September 1844 he wrote to George Bennett that 'a journey of this description offers a glorious opportunity of unmasking the hidden novelties of tropical Australia'. Eight days later the motley company departed, led by one of the most curious and controversial figures in Australian colonial history.

---

8   After the 1629 wreck the ship's commander sailed to Jakarta for help and merchant Jeronimus Cornelisz established a brutal rule on the islands, murdering more than 100 men, women and children.

Friedrich Wilhelm Ludwig Leichhardt was a self-taught naturalist with a delicate constitution, poor eyesight and little sense of direction who arrived in Australia in 1842 with the expressed intention of exploring the undiscovered interior. The son of Prussia's royal inspector of peat spoke six languages and had an unrivalled passion for the natural sciences, although despite being known as 'Doctor' he never achieved any formal qualifications. He was hailed as a hero in his lifetime and a villain (by some) in the decades since, and his demise remains one of Australia's greatest unsolved mysteries.

Leichhardt studied in Sydney and explored the Hunter Valley and Moreton Bay districts, collecting plant and rock specimens and ensuring he would be in the right place when a senior position became available at a major museum (it didn't). He hoped to join a mooted official expedition by surveyor general Thomas Mitchell to Port Essington but Governor Sir George Gipps vetoed official funding for the project in July 1844 because it was 'so hazardous and expensive'. Undaunted, Leichhardt leapt at the chance to become the first European to cross Australia from its east to north coasts, raising private funds and assembling a party of ten volunteers, including a 24-year-old Englishman named John Roper, a fifteen-year-old ship's boy named John Murphy, a 44-year-old convict named William Phillips, a 'negro cook' named Caleb and two Indigenous men – Harry Brown and Charlie Fisher, a native policeman from Brisbane. Gilbert signed on as the expedition naturalist and quickly realised he was the most experienced and competent member of the party.

The trip was expected to last five or six months. It took well over a year. Many of the details were not exposed to a shocked

Budgerigars illustrated by John Gould, c. 1837. (State Library of Victoria)

public until 1941 with the publication of Alec Chisholm's *Strange New World: The Adventures of John Gilbert and Ludwig Leichhardt*. Chisholm was an Australian journalist and bird lover who passed through London en route to a bird conference in Berlin in 1938. Chisholm placed an advertisement in the *The Times* asking for any information about Gould and his assistant and hit on a treasure trove of 'Gouldiana', including Gilbert's diary, which Leichhardt had dutifully kept for six months after the expedition and returned to Gould in London, apparently not having read it. It seems Gould didn't read it either, but he passed it down to his grandchildren, who were alerted to Chisholm's notice in *The Times*. Drawing largely on the diary, Chisholm described Leichhardt as 'an imposter' who fell apart under the strain of leading the expedition – 'his brain, it would seem, was unable to function to any extent over more than a brief period' – and who afterwards claimed all the glory for himself.

Other accounts are more flattering, acknowledging Leichhardt's energy, perseverance and accomplishments, including a journey of almost 5000 kilometres on foot, and his remarkably (for the time) accurate maps and records of the expedition. He was admired for exploring for science's sake, not personal wealth. But his singularity of purpose wasn't compatible with good personal relationships; he was labelled by others in the party as jealous, selfish, suspicious, reticent, careless, slovenly, wholly unfitted for leadership and 'very lax in his religious opinion'. A school textbook in the 1960s described him as 'an eccentric, gluttonous, gangling German'.

The party set off on 18 September 1844 and Leichhardt declared they were striving 'buoyant with hope, into the wilderness of Australia'. 'Many a man's heart,' he wrote, 'would have thrilled like our own, had he seen us winding our way round the first rise beyond the station, with a full chorus of "God Save the Queen" which has inspired many a British soldier – aye, and many a Prussian, too – with courage in time of danger.' But things went off script from the start. Bullocks threw their loads, horses wandered off and many of the party's provisions were lost within days. By November Caleb and a squatter named Pemberton Hodgson had quit the expedition, covering the distance back to Darling Downs in two days. The same journey had taken the expedition five weeks travelling in the other direction.

In January 1845 Leichhardt and Harry Brown got lost in the bush for four days after pushing ahead of the party and had to survive by capturing a pigeon (which was eaten whole, bones, feet and all) and a sleeping lizard that was 'roasted and greedily eaten'. Within four months every member of the party except Gilbert had become lost at least once, and Leichhardt twice. Meanwhile, Gilbert was taking copious notes on birds, fish, shells and plants seen along the way. The mystery of why there were so many coastal species so far inland was resolved when the party realised they were much closer to the ocean than they thought. By June they were months behind schedule and out of tobacco, sugar and salt.

On the night of 28 June the camp was attacked by an Aboriginal raiding party. A volley of spears took Roper's eye out, but he saw enough to later write:

> The whole body rushed upon us with their waddies, and how it is that our brains did not despatter the ground is to me miraculous. These rascals had crept up on us under cover of the tea-trees: the tent in which Calvert and I were being first in their road, the whole body attacked us; poor Gilbert, hearing the noise, was rushing from his tent with his gun, when a spear thrown at him pierced his breast, and, penetrating to his lungs, caused haemorrhage; the only words he spoke were these: 'Charlie, take my gun, they have killed me', when pulling the spear out with his own hands, he immediately dropped upon the ground lifeless.

Leichhardt wrote in his diary that the spear 'had terminated poor Gilbert's existence', while Roper noted the additional tragedy that Gilbert never finished a hat he had started making using pleated cabbage-tree leaves the previous afternoon, concluding: 'It is impossible to describe the gloom and sorrow this fatal accident cast upon our party. As a companion none was more cheerful or more agreeable, as a man, none more indefatigable or more persevering.' Gilbert was buried the following day in a shallow grave. After a eulogy from Leichhardt the earth was smoothed over and a large fire was built on it to deter the attackers from returning.

Roper, and later Leichhardt, portrayed the attack as unprovoked. However, Gilbert's diary tells a different story. He wrote the day before he died that Charlie Fisher and Harry Brown had told the explorers they had scared off an Aboriginal party trying to kill their bullocks. Gilbert didn't buy that story: 'I am inclined to think that the real cause was that our blackfellows surprised them at their camp, and as I know Charlie would not be very particular in his treatment of a native woman if he caught one.' It seems likely the raid the next day that claimed Gilbert's life was a revenge attack.

Ten months later, on 17 December 1846, the remaining seven members of the party, including Roper and botanist James Calvert, who each suffered multiple stab wounds in the attack, staggered into Port Essington, stunning the locals, who had given up all eight for dead, having not heard from them for over a year. Utterly exhausted and covered in boils, they had somehow climbed down the forbidding Arnhem Land escarpment to arrive at their destination. Leichhardt later wrote of his companions: 'The very sight of them disgusts me. I expressed even two days before arriving at Port Essington my ardent wish, not so much of being at the end of my journey, as being rid of companions who did take so little trouble to please me.'

He proceeded to Sydney, where he was greeted as a hero – receiving gold medals from the British and French geographical societies – and promptly set about planning a second expedition that would traverse the entire continent from east to west. A party of eleven departed on 7 December 1846 but they were also beset by slow progress and poor leadership – one said Leichhardt could get lost on George Street, Sydney – and in May they made the wise decision to turn back. Despite heavy criticism, Leichhardt left again in March 1848 with 'two friends, two hired labourers and two blackfellows', plus fifty bullocks, twenty mules and seven horses. On 3 April they made it to Roma, 500 kilometres west of Moreton Bay – and 3800 kilometres from Perth. They were never seen again. Leichhardt was thirty-four.

A number of attempts were made to discover what happened to the explorers but their disappearance remains a mystery. One Darwin university lecturer has theorised they were assassinated by the British colonial government using a sack of poisoned flour. A more likely explanation is that they became lost and died of starvation in the vast desert interior. The site of Gilbert's death is also unknown, although a probable site in the remote Western Cape York Peninsula is now marked by a small plaque and visited by dedicated Gilbert admirers. A memorial to him in St James Church in Sydney reads: '*Dulce et decorum est pro scientia mori*', which translates as 'sweet and seemly it is to die for science'.

Gilbert's birds were sent with his diary to Gould in London, along with several mammal skins. The British naturalist was dismayed to learn of Gilbert's fate but relieved his animal collections had survived. Of the dozens of new specimens Gilbert had found in Australia, Gould bestowed his name on one in *Mammals of Australia*: *Potorous gilberti*, or Gilbert's potoroo.

* * *

Gilbert wasn't the only Gould collector to die in the field. In fact, two others suffered the same fate, and the death of one was even more dramatic. Breathless press coverage of Frederick Strange's murder provides us with most of what we know about the self-taught naturalist. When it comes to his collecting career, about the only thing everyone seems to agree on is that he was terrible with money. His brief entry in the *Australian Dictionary of Biography* is less than complimentary: 'We know that Strange was semi-literate from a note he sent Gould and that he mismanaged his affairs and was financially incompetent.'

Strange seems to have battled to make ends meet all his life, rising from humble beginnings and never benefiting from the connections that freed the likes of Gould and Gilbert from financial strain. Falling behind on his debts and relentless self-promotion didn't endear him to his peers. Judging by his portrait, he also faced the lifelong handicap of not having a chin. These challenges make his achievements in natural science even more impressive.

Born in Norfolk, probably in 1816, he obtained a position as a seaman on one of the first ships bound for the new colony of South Australia. After disembarking he found employment as a fisherman and helped carry out land surveys before accompanying Captain Charles Sturt on an expedition in September 1838 to the Gawler River, where he was involved (although it is not clear how directly) in transactions of 'a somewhat notorious and unsavoury' nature. In 1839 Gould visited South Australia and joined Strange on field trips in the Mallee. By September Gould had moved on but Strange began sending him specimens, including cranes and dozens of eggs. In November that year Strange was with Sturt and the South Australian governor when they ran out of water on a trip along the Murray

River and only survived by 'bleeding' a horse to obtain life-saving liquid. Strange returned with a splendid fairy wren.

In 1840 he moved to Sydney and set up shop as a natural history collector, offering live birds for sale and marrying Rosa Prince in January 1841. The couple had either four or six children (sources differ) and operated a boarding house at 8 Bridge Street, near The Rocks. Among their guests were fellow collectors John MacGillivray and John Gilbert, who hunted for wallaroos with Strange at Broken Bay.

Strange was an enthusiastic – some might say obsessive – collector of shells. He picked up interesting specimens on beaches and dredged the ocean floor around Sydney and Moreton Bay. In 1849 he was on board the HMS *Acheron* as it mapped part of the New Zealand coast and was the first to obtain and describe many of the country's shells, as well as exploring inland during a nine-month voyage. In 1852 he sailed to England and sold his collection of thousands of shells, plus an array of previously unseen butterflies and the only living specimen of the giant water lily in Europe.

Strange's other notable achievements included collecting the type specimen of Albert's lyrebird near the Richmond River in New South Wales, discovering the yellow-footed rock wallaby in South Australia's Flinders Ranges and bringing what are thought to be the first living kiwis to Australia on his return journey on the *Acheron*. He also supplied Gould with fossils, lizards, fish and thousands of insects. In August 1854 Strange presented to the Australian Museum a 'portion of skin of an Aboriginal preserved by the natives of Bribie Island'. His name is immortalised in a genus of carnivorous snails, *Strangesta*.

But he could never escape money problems, and his desperate ploys evidently drove his colleagues, and Gould in particular, to despair. As well as animals and eggs, mail from Strange regularly included requests for money. He sent bills to Gould to cover his debts and, on one occasion, the cost of two hats. But Strange went too far when in 1847 he requested £200 in credit from Edward Smith-Stanley, the thirteenth Earl of Derby, a former politician and renowned animal collector. Strange promised to bring five rare live bird specimens to London to add to the Earl's collection in exchange, but Gould shut the scheme down, writing: 'I find you have written to Lord Derby and asked him to send you a letter of credit for 200 pounds, which rather astonished him and which he will not do.' (Lord Derby had an extensive collection of Australasian birds and animals, supplied mostly by Gould. In 1851 he bequeathed more than 700 mammal skins and skeletons to a new Liverpool museum, including 128 marsupials and twenty monotremes.)

However, Strange did find enough money to purchase a boat he called *Vision*, on which he set sail with nine companions for the Great Barrier Reef on 29 September 1854 for the purpose of searching 'for specimens of natural history'. On 14 October the boat arrived at Middle Percy Island and the next day Strange went ashore with a party including botanist Walter Hill, first mate William Spurling, a cook named Henry Gittings and Deliapy, an Aboriginal interpreter (spelling of his name varies in different accounts of the episode). The group came into contact with local Indigenous people, who were deemed friendly, before Hill left to explore the mountainous interior of the island while Strange and his colleagues collected shells on the beach. When Hill returned he saw Spurling's body 'stripped naked, thrown amongst the mangroves and quite dead'. as the *Sydney Morning Herald* reported, 'with a deep wound in the neck as if stabbed with a knife'.

Deliapy emerged from behind some rocks to inform Hill that an islander had, apparently without warning, speared Strange in the leg. The naturalist, who was the only member of the party carrying a firearm, shot his assailant then 'immediately expired'. Spurling and two other members of the party were also murdered. Hill and Deliapy hid and waited until dark to return to the boat and, after three days of unsuccessful attempts to signal to any other survivors, they sailed to Moreton Bay.

The colonial authorities dispatched a ship, the HMS *Torch* under the command of Lieutenant William Chimmo, to investigate. Spurling's skeleton was found in the mangroves but Chimmo concluded that the bodies of the other three victims, including Strange, had been thrown into the sea. He took three Aboriginal men prisoner, along with their families – three women and four children – and confined them to the *Torch*, which set sail for Sydney, stopping at Port Curtis near Rockhampton to bury Spurling's remains. What happened to the Aboriginal prisoners remains in dispute.

The men were put on trial in Sydney amid public outrage in 1855 and, after numerous remands and reappearances, the case was thrown out – either through lack of evidence or because the accused men didn't speak English and no one could find an interpreter, or possibly both. They were ferried back to Port Curtis and then home to Middle Percy Island. At least, that was what the magistrate ordered. According to some reports they were executed at Moreton Bay, while an article in the *Capricornia* newspaper in 1898 claimed they jumped ship at Gladstone and were murdered by local Aboriginal people. The most likely explanation is that all ten – or at least those who hadn't already died in custody – were set free at Port Curtis and the authorities washed their hands of them; the promised journey home never happened. Given the rough frontier justice of the time, the chances they lived out their lives in peace are not high.

Despite, or perhaps because of, Strange's lifelong financial struggles, he made the smart decision of taking out a life-insurance policy. But the Trafalgar Life Assurance Association in London refused to pay the £1000 benefit, leaving his wife destitute. Five years later a landmark decision in the British courts forced the company to pay the full claim plus interest, setting a benchmark that underpins all modern insurance law. Ironically, this is perhaps the biggest legacy of a man who, despite his shortcomings, established a fine career as a naturalist and, in Gould's words, 'sacrificed his life in pursuit of natural history'.

* * *

One other Gould collector was killed by 'the treacherous natives' (in Gould's words), but the death of Johnston Drummond, who supplied several specimens for *Birds of Australia*, had none of the heroic martyrdom associated with Gilbert and Strange.

One of Drummond's guides, a Noongar man named Kabinger, discovered that the collector was sleeping with his wife and drove two glass-tipped spears through him as he slept at a campsite on the Moore River in Western Australia in July 1845. Drummond's brother John, a police inspector, then shot and killed Kabinger. John Drummond was suspended, then reappointed four months later at a lower rank.

The Drummonds were a celebrated and occasionally controversial family in Western Australia. James Drummond, father of Johnston and John and four other children, was a giant in the field of botany and inspired young Johnston's passion for collecting. In 1829 James and his wife Sarah had packed up their six children and sailed from Scotland to the Swan River settlement, eventually settling in the Toodyay Valley, north of what is now Perth. Drummond was appointed an honorary government naturalist and his sons ran the farm while he collected seeds, roaming far and wide including to Albany, the Stirling Range, Rottnest Island and King George Sound (where he partnered with John Gilbert) and an attempted 91-kilometre overland expedition that was abandoned when James went blind (he recovered).

He was a familiar sight in the colony, with a face framed by bushy white whiskers and pockets bulging with seeds, which often filled his upturned hat as well. Evidence of his standing is a letter from Sir Charles Darwin in 1860 asking for advice on fertilising the red leschenaultia (a striking flower native to Western Australia). He also produced groundbreaking work on First Nations peoples' use of local plants for food and cultural purposes – he described the taste of one nut as 'disgusting ... resembling train oil'.

James Drummond died in his home on 27 March 1863, aged seventy-six. His specimens are now kept in Australia, Britain, Europe and the United States. His son Johnston left little lasting legacy, due partly to the scandalous nature of his death, as well as to the fact he was just twenty-five when he died.

*   *   *

The last of Gould's collectors we will examine died of natural causes, although it's likely he contributed to his own demise. John MacGillivray was a zealous and brilliant collector but the one activity he was even more enthusiastic about was drinking alcohol, a predilection that overshadowed his achievements as his eventful career, marked by three voyages from England to the South Pacific and a fraying relationship with one of history's most famous biologists, gradually ran off the rails.

MacGillivray was born on 18 December 1821 at Aberdeen, the eldest of twelve children of British ornithologist William MacGillivray. John studied medicine but showed more interest in natural history, and before his course was completed he was appointed as naturalist on the HMS *Fly*, which sailed from England in April 1842 under the command of Captain Francis Blackwood. The ship arrived in Hobart in August and the crew spent the next three years charting the north-east coast of Australia, surveying the Great Barrier Reef and New Guinea, with stops at Port Stephens, Port Essington, Adelaide, Melbourne and Singapore.

It also rescued the survivors of British merchant ship *Lady Grey*, which was wrecked on Alert's Reef, and stopped long enough in Sydney for MacGillivray to meet and marry Williamina Paton Gray in 1848. She would bear him a son and two daughters. There are scant records of MacGillivray's activities on the voyage but we know he supplied the Earl of Derby with a vast collection of animal skins and some live specimens, including several kangaroos.

He returned to England in February 1846 and fortunately wasn't on the *Fly*'s next journey to Australia, when a sailor loading a gun for a salute in honour of Queen Victoria 'had his right hand completely blown off, to which the attention of the bystanders was called by his exclaiming "Look here" at the same time extending his mutilated limb'. The sailor, aged twenty-three, was entitled to a pension on his return to England but official records noted he would be 'comparatively useless for the rest of his life'.

MacGillivray's next expedition was the most celebrated of his life, largely because he was partnered with a brilliant young scientist named Thomas Henry Huxley, who joined the crew with the official title of assistant surgeon and naturalist. The voyage was led by Captain Owen Stanley, a scientist, keen amateur artist and future namesake of the Owen Stanley Range, now famous for the Kokoda Track. Stanley's mission was to survey eastern Australia and the Torres Strait, and to draw new charts of New Guinea and the Louisiade Archipelago to the east. The HMS *Rattlesnake*, a 28-gun frigate, left Plymouth in December 1846 with a crew of 180 men and provisions including flour, raisins, peas, oatmeal, salted meat, sugar, chocolate, tea, tobacco, soap, vinegar, lemon juice, wine and 20,000 pounds of bread. As well as the two precocious young scientists – MacGillivray was twenty-five and Huxley twenty-one – the crew included two other collectors and overall had a distinctly scientific bent; more than half of those onboard kept a private shell collection.

MacGillivray and Huxley initially got on well, but their friendship deteriorated to the point that Huxley later referred to his senior colleague as a 'disreputable scamp' and 'the primary mud volcano', a particularly evocative insult. MacGillivray's instructions were to collect Australian and New Guinean plants and animals for the Royal Botanic Gardens and the British Museum, but he also gathered many more animals that were shipped to London (most ended up with Gould). At sea he recorded the movements of passing birds – he noted that a young albatross remained with the ship for twenty-four days, covering more than 2500 miles – and shot down interesting birds, which he skinned and preserved in spirits. It didn't always go to plan. One excursion to recover shot specimens ended abruptly when MacGillivray and two shipmates were thrown from their small boat into the sea, and the incident almost ended in disaster when a second boat lowered to rescue the men became tangled in ropes, along with another sailor. The men were eventually rescued with mostly minor injuries – although one had his cheek cut open by a ship's hook. And there was a further casualty: 'My best gun,' MacGillivray wrote, 'having none of the natatorial properties of the birds it was intended to destroy, went down to the realms of Father Neptune.' The gun had been a gift from Gould.

The *Rattlesnake* stopped in Sydney – now a thriving city of 50,000 – three times over the next year, surveying the harbour before sailing north to the Great Barrier Reef. MacGillivray's liking for alcohol was already a talking point among his colleagues, who later joked about him drinking alone in his cabin and talking to his reflection in the mirror in a thick Scottish accent, but he was in his element in the field, taking the opportunity to explore thirty-seven islands while the *Rattlesnake* was at anchor. He had no reference books with him but his knowledge of the local flora and fauna was unmatched as he hunted down everything from rare tropical birds to insects, plants and shells, adding to the albatrosses, puffins, shearwaters and petrels he had collected at sea. On the Barnard Island Group off north Queensland he shot 'a new and splendid rifle-bird', and two live possums 'of a rare and singular kind' were obtained from local

Indigenous people in exchange for two axe-heads. The possums were kept in a hen coop on the ship.

Wearing an old straw hat, sunburnt and unshaven, MacGillivray blazed through the bush in search of new specimens:

> We started heavily laden with provisions, water, arms and ammunition, besides boxes, botanical paper and boards, and other collecting gear, and although taking it very easily, the fatigue of walking in a sultry day, with the thermometer at 90 degrees in the shade, afforded a sample of what we had afterwards so often to experience during our rambles in tropical Australia.

When he couldn't go ashore, MacGillivray dredged the sea floor for undiscovered creatures, adding more than 900 specimens of molluscs to his collection, including 230 different species, not to mention scores of fish, sea snakes, starfish and endless shells. His enthusiasm sometimes got him into trouble. On Goose Island he stood on a venomous red-bellied black snake, but 'fortunately [it] was too sluggish to escape before I had time to shoot it'. He headed into the interior of Great Keppel Island but 'found little of interest, having spent most of my time in extricating myself from the mazes of a mangrove swamp into which I had forced myself after some birds'. At Cape Upstart he found himself in a similar predicament after chasing some bowerbirds. His clothes were pierced by a sharp stinging grass and he was pursued by clouds of mosquitoes 'as if to test the powers of human endurance'. To make matters worse, he was out of gunpowder. He tried using sand in his gun instead – 'which I had somewhere read of as a substitute but, although used under the most favourable conditions, the experiment proved a complete failure'.

MacGillivray also devoted significant attention to the appearance, customs, weapons, housing, canoe design and construction and, especially, languages of the Indigenous peoples encountered along the voyage. His notes on local dialects were one of the most important achievements of the expedition, even if some of his descriptions are hard to read today (the word 'savages' is used liberally). Impromptu meetings with Indigenous tribes were a regular occurrence for the *Rattlesnake* crew. Huxley drew sketches while MacGillivray tried to understand the local languages: 'My principal informant was called Wadai, a little withered old man with a shaved head, on which someone had stuck a red night-cap which greatly took his fancy.'

By the time the *Rattlesnake* returned to Plymouth in October 1850 the men were glad to see the back of each other, and the ship. Relationships had deteriorated over years at sea and two tragedies had befallen the expedition. The first began in April 1848, when the *Rattlesnake* had sailed out of Sydney with an added mission – accompanying the *Tam O'Shanter* 1900 kilometres north to Rockingham Bay in far north Queensland. The *Tam O'Shanter* was carrying explorer Edmund Kennedy, his Aboriginal tracker Galmahra, known as Jackey Jackey, eleven other men, twenty-nine horses, a flock of sheep and provisions for an overland expedition to Cape York and the Gulf of Carpentaria. From the gulf, Kennedy planned to chart a course overland back to Sydney, filling gaps in maps drawn by previous explorers. After disembarking at Rockingham Bay on 24 May, however, Kennedy and his party disappeared. It later emerged that the expedition had run into trouble from the outset, getting lost in the thick rainforest and running low on food. Kennedy was eventually speared to death in an attack by the local Yadhaykenu people; Jackey Jackey and two of the crew were the only survivors of the trek. Back in Sydney, MacGillivray attended an inquiry into the fate of Kennedy's expedition: 'I shall not easily forget the appearance which the survivors presented on this occasion – pale and emaciated, with haggard looks attesting the misery and privations they had undergone, and with low trembling voices, they gave their evidence.'

The *Rattlesnake*'s second calamity followed an acrimonious trip to New Guinea, the final leg of the expedition – and arguably the most important, given there were few charts of the islands and no Europeans had set foot on many of them. Surveying the Louisiade Archipelago and its surrounding coral reefs was difficult and tedious, especially for the naturalists on board; over several months the ship barely made landfall, and when it did Stanley forbade anyone from venturing beyond the beach unless it was to find fresh water, fearful of the thick jungle and the 'treachery of the natives'. (A group of enterprising Indigenous men had almost succeeded in hijacking the *Rattlesnake* at Fitzroy Island, boarding the ship at 3.30 a.m. and tossing lighted bark below deck. When crew members emerged 'they were instantly knocked on the head with boomerangs and rendered insensible'. The ship's mate averted disaster for the expedition when he cleared the deck with a sword.)

MacGillivray was bored out of his skull and Huxley, who had dreamed of uncovering the mysteries of the New Guinea interior, was outraged. In June he commented on the accidental death of Stanley's dog by suggesting it committed suicide by walking into the ocean: 'The skipper and his dog had this in common, that they liked one another and were disliked by everyone else.' He accused Stanley of cowardice and described surveying – the actual point of the trip – as 'an elaborate waste of time and opportunity'. Stanley deemed the voyage a success because no one had been eaten, but soon after leaving New Guinea to return to Sydney he began to feel unwell. He died in his bed in Sydney in March 1850, aged thirty-eight.

Back in London, MacGillivray had been commissioned to write the narrative of the voyage and further enraged Huxley, who provided the illustrations, by missing the production deadline. He wrote to friend John Thomson: 'I have done all I can, but MacGillivray has lied to me so thoroughly, that I am altogether disgusted.' But Huxley grudgingly admitted that the naturalist had done a good job when the book was finally published ten months later. Dedicated to Owen Stanley's mother, the two volumes came in at just under 800 pages, including a series of scientific appendices.

Now battling debt, drinking and family problems, MacGillivray needed a job. He wrote to Rear Admiral Sir Francis Beaufort requesting the position of naturalist on an upcoming voyage back to the south seas with testimonials from prominent scientists, including John Gould. Evidently impressed, Beaufort appointed MacGillivray as the naturalist on the HMS *Herald*, which arrived in Sydney in February 1853.

The boat visited Lord Howe Island and New Zealand but events took a bizarre turn when captain Henry Denham abruptly called off the crew's work in Fiji and set a course for Solomon Islands in the hope of finding a missing colonial entrepreneur named Benjamin Boyd, who had become one of Australia's biggest landowners through ventures including operating steamships between New South Wales and Hobart, establishing his own bank and collecting a whaling fleet – all run from his private town, Boydtown, on the New South Wales south coast. But his golden run couldn't last. A scheme to coerce and import 192 villagers from what is now Vanuatu and New Caledonia to work on his pastoral stations was considered a form of slavery by contemporary critics. After parliament effectively voided Boyd's contracts with his workers, he abandoned the scheme and the men, leaving them to find their own way home. His finances collapsed and his bank was exposed as a little more than a vehicle for financing Boyd's grandiose schemes.

In 1849 Boyd tried his luck unsuccessfully on the Californian gold-fields before sailing for the South Pacific with the dream of establishing a 'Papuan Republic'. In October 1851 he reached Guadalcanal, the largest of the Solomon islands, and after going ashore to shoot game was never seen again. After hearing shots fired, his sailing companions searched for his body but found nothing and presumed he had been murdered, and probably eaten, by the locals. They set sail for Sydney, only for their yacht to be shipwrecked in a storm off Port Macquarie.

Denham had been told by American whalers in Fiji that they had seen Boyd's name carved into trees on Guadalcanal, but a month-long search found no sign of the trees, or Boyd, and discussions with islanders convinced Denham that the missing man was in fact dead (and possibly delicious). The *Herald* returned to Sydney and Denham penned an article in the *Sydney Morning Herald* explaining the unsuccessful search. The same day a rival newspaper, *The Empire,* published an article by an anonymous member of the *Herald*'s crew that attacked Denham's leadership, accusing him of putting his men at risk and allowing most of the crew to contract scurvy. The author of the article was never revealed but after an inquiry MacGillivray was expelled from the service with a dishonourable discharge.

He was deeply in debt and drinking heavily, and his wife died in March 1856 while sailing back to Sydney from London. MacGillivray stayed in Australia, unsuccessfully applying for the vacant post of curator at the Australian Museum. He was secretary of Sydney's Horticultural Improvement Society and contributed to the 1857 edition of Cox and Co.'s *Australian Almanac*, providing advice on preserving birds, reptiles, fishes, insects and plants. He settled in Grafton and was collecting birds and mammals for museums in Sydney and Melbourne until his death in 1867, aged forty-six.

Huxley's career took a different turn after he disembarked the *Rattlesnake* in November 1850. On the voyage his attention was captured by jellyfish, snails and tunicates, a type of marine invertebrate also known as a sea squirt. His paper 'On the Affinity and Affinities of the Family of the Medusae' confirmed his status as a rising star in the world of biology and he was elected a fellow of the Royal Society before his twenty-seventh birthday. Three years later, the society awarded him its Royal Medal. He is best known as a fierce proponent of Darwin's theory of evolution, famously locking horns in a fiery public debate with Samuel Wilberforce, the Anglican Bishop of Oxford, at the Oxford University Museum in 1860. When Wilberforce sarcastically asked Huxley if he was descended from an ape through his grandmother or his grandfather, Huxley replied that he would rather have an ape than an ignorant bishop for a grandparent.

* * *

Despite his apparent omnipresence, not every Australian collector worked for John Gould. Naturalists were scouring the country from soon after the British penal settlement at Port Jackson began to grow into a colonial outpost in a very distant, very foreign land. One of the most prominent early collectors arrived in Sydney in January 1800 – eight months later than scheduled, amid a scandal that gripped the new settlement, kicking off a surprisingly action-packed career for a man whose primary passions were insects and birds. At different times John Lewin was shipwrecked, became stranded on a South Pacific island for almost a year during an attempted coup, and produced Australia's first illustrated book – although most of the copies mysteriously disappeared. Along the way he helped change attitudes towards the strange continent and laid the foundations of the stage Gould would step onto with such fanfare a few decades later.

Lewin was the son of William Lewin, author of *The Birds of Great Britain*. William's two sons, John and Thomas, assisted in colouring the book's 232 watercolour plates and completed the work after their father's sudden death in 1795. Around 1797, John secured passage to New South Wales on the HMS *Buffalo* with his wife, Maria. Wealthy silversmith and entomologist Dru Drury sponsored Lewin as a natural history artist and collector, providing him with bottles, nets, a beating sheet for collecting caterpillars, a long-barrelled gun for small-game hunting, fifty-two copper plates for etching, books on insects and birds and a set of gold scales to measure any precious metals he might find.

The morning of 8 June was perfect for sailing – so good that the ship set sail at ten a.m. with favourable winds at its back.

Unfortunately, Lewin wasn't there. He had gone back to London to collect an unknown item and returned to the dock to discover that he had, in the most literal sense, missed the boat with his distraught wife on board.

Lewin booked a ticket on the next available ship, the convict transport *Minerva*, which left London on 4 August and stopped to collect Irish convicts in Cork, where it was delayed for more than a year. Lewin was still waiting when the *Buffalo* arrived in Sydney on 3 May 1799 amid rumours that Maria had had affairs with two officers during the voyage. The allegations were the talk of the town, which must have come as a shock to Lewin when he finally arrived eight months later, particularly the stories that Maria had allegedly confessed that her husband was impotent. Mrs Lewin sued a member of the *Buffalo*'s crew for spreading the malicious rumours and won, the court awarding her £30 in damages.

Lewin's reputation had recovered enough by March 1801 for Governor King to assign him on an expedition to Bass Strait on the *Bee*. Unfortunately, the *Bee* was so bad at sea that it was turned around after two days and returned to Sydney. In July he joined a more successful overland expedition with Colonel William Paterson to the Hunter Valley, where he collected many 'new and beautiful birds'.

In November he returned to sea aboard the *Norfolk*, which was sailing to Tahiti to buy and sell pork. Lewin hoped to find insects and possibly gold. Both plans went out the window when the ship was wrecked in a storm in March 1802, stranding the crew on the island's northern coast. Making matters worse, they found themselves in the middle of a civil war between Tahiti's King Pomare I and the surrounding islands. The shipwrecked sailors joined the crew of a second ship (also in Tahiti to collect pork) and local missionaries in barricading themselves in a mission house; the *Norfolk*'s cannons were salvaged and positioned on the second floor to aid in their defence. Fortunately, they were not required after England threw its support behind the king, allowing him to prevail and the sailors to return to Sydney. We don't know if they had any pork with them.

Lewin next captured public attention when he was summoned to paint a strange new animal that had been brought to Sydney in 1803. The female 'colah', 'coloo' or 'coola' – all attempts to write down the local Aboriginal pronunciation – was apparently alive when drawn by Lewin sitting on a log with a joey perched on its shoulders, but later died and was sent to England preserved in spirits. In a letter to Sir Joseph Banks, Paterson described Lewin's watercolour as 'very bad'. The scale and biological accuracy of his depiction are questionable, but Lewin's sketch was historically significant as the first drawing of a koala to reach England. Versions of it are now in the State Library of New South Wales and London's Natural History Museum.

Lewin's first book, the catchily titled *Prodromus Entomology: Natural History of Lepidopterous Insects of New South Wales, collected, engraved and faithfully painted after nature*, was published in 1805. The first edition contains colour plates of eighteen moths found in and around Sydney, which were etched by Lewin and sent to his brother Thomas in London for printing. It is one of Australia's first natural history books and the first book about Australia containing plates engraved here.

A second, more ambitious, work followed in 1808. *Birds of New Holland* also contained eighteen plates – Lewin's never-fulfilled vision was to eventually record every species found in the colony. He used the subscription model that would later be adopted by Gould and persuaded fifty-five colonial families to sign up, ordering sixty-seven copies. Governor Bligh and his predecessor, Governor King, ordered two copies each. Lewin's brother Thomas added six more subscribers in England, including Sir Joseph Banks. A copy was also presented to King George III. Sadly and mysteriously, the Australian subscribers never received their copies. No official reason was ever provided; some have speculated they were destroyed in a fire at a publishing warehouse, but more likely they were lost in some mishap on board the ship that was carrying them to Australia, the *Buffalo* (again).

Lewin tried to fix the problem by publishing a second edition of *Birds of New South Wales*, compiled from discarded prints and plates from *Birds of New Holland*. It is considered the first illustrated book ever produced in Australia. Only thirteen copies are recorded and they were published on a range of paper stock, with Lewin using whatever he could get his hands on. No two copies are exactly alike. From a scientific point of view, the book has a number of problems. The descriptions are very basic and contain factual errors – bird lengths are mostly too long, but occasionally too short. The illustrations are problematic – birds' feet don't actually grasp the branches they are sitting on, some are smudged, and in one copy the legs of a spotted grossbeak are the wrong colour – and the names used by Lewin were mostly discarded over the ensuing decades. But aside from its historical significance as Australia's first illustrated publication, the book was a major scientific achievement, containing four species that had not been previously recorded.

In 1810, at age forty, Lewin made a surprising career change when he was appointed Sydney coroner. He also joined Governor Macquarie on a trip over the newly blasted road over the Blue Mountains in 1815. Lewin, who by now considered himself an artist more than a naturalist, produced twenty-one watercolour paintings from the expedition, including the view from Pitts Amphitheatre, near present-day Katoomba, and a painting called *The Plains, Bathurst*, which is now held in the Mitchell Library in the State Library of New South Wales. He is credited as one of the first artists to attempt to portray the landscape on its own terms, without reference to European conventions. Lewin was offered the chance to sail with Phillip Parker King on the *Mermaid*'s six-month expedition to Van Diemen Gulf, but declined. His exploring days were over.

Lewin's last major public contribution came in 1817, when he was commissioned by Governor Macquarie to paint botanical specimens collected on John Oxley's inland expedition to explore the course of the Lachlan River. He also took private commissions and produced hundreds, if not thousands, of drawings of natural subjects, including insects, birds and other animals, portraits of Aboriginal people, and a coat of arms for the Supreme Court. He died of a severe illness on 27 August 1819, aged forty-nine. His wife, Maria – who was herself a talented artist and had assisted John by colouring some of his plates – returned with their son William to England, where she arranged for the publication of new editions of his books, expanding the audience of an artist who was, in many ways, ahead of his time.

* * *

An entire volume could be dedicated to the multitude of full-time and part-time naturalists who roamed the countryside in search of specimens during this period. Many were enthusiastic amateurs, while others were attached to government-sponsored expeditions, tasked with recording the plants and animals along the way, and pocketing as many of them as they could. Some left detailed records; of others we have only a tantalising glimpse.

Sidney William Jackson, born in Brisbane in 1873, was a short-limbed, stocky man, physically resembling a large barrel on legs, who spent weeks at a time in the bush collecting birds' eggs using an ingenious combination of leg spikes and rope ladders to raid nests thirty metres above the ground. Entirely self-trained, he was also a skilled photographer and taxidermist, a practical joker and a talented ventriloquist. Contemporaries described a personality that might receive more sympathy from those with an understanding of mental health today. Alec Chisholm – noted critic of Ludwig Leich-hardt – wrote in *The Emu*, the journal of Australian ornithology, that Jackson was warm but reclusive, 'an odd mixture' who was 'apt to be completely downcast one moment and thoroughly joyful soon afterwards'. He added that Jackson had a 'childlike fascination for those trivial gadgets', such as pieces of tin cut into novelty shapes, that 'alarm or embarrass unwary people'. In 1906 Jackson sold his collection of nearly 2000 eggs, representing 500 different bird species, to wealthy pastoralist Henry Luke White, who bequeathed them on his death in 1927 to the Melbourne Museum, along with another 11,000 eggs and thousands more skins and bird nests.

* * *

Ludwig Becker was a popular choice as naturalist for the Victorian Exploring Expedition, Burke and Wills' disastrous attempt to traverse the continent from south to north. Born in Germany, Becker arrived in Tasmania via London and Rio de Janeiro in 1851. The enthusiastic, kind and likeable scientist had a luxuriant red beard, smoked a carved meerschaum pipe, spoke English 'badly but very energetically' and was described by Lady Caroline Denison, wife of Van Diemen's Land lieutenant-governor Sir William Denison, as 'one of those universal geniuses who can do anything ... a very good naturalist, geologist ... draws and plays and sings, conjures and ventriloquises and imitates the notes of birds so accurately'.

Becker arrived in Victoria at the height of the gold rush and spent time on the Bendigo diggings, where he took meteorological observations and produced sketches that were exhibited in Melbourne. He wrote papers for the Philosophical Institute of Victoria and illustrated works by fellow members Ferdinand von Mueller and Frederick McCoy. He also procured a lyrebird egg and was one of the first to try to raise a chick. Becker became an expert on the bird and corresponded with John Gould (of course) about it. In the introduction to her 1979 book on Becker, Marjorie Tipping wrote:

> He was a diligent observer of nature's treasures. Probably no one in Australia equalled him in his capacity to study and enjoy, with an almost childlike simplicity, the fruits of collecting. He was astonished and delighted with everything he found in the new world and freely gave of his time and knowledge to the organisations to which he belonged to extend the boundaries of knowledge.

He was appointed expedition artist, naturalist and geologist on the Burke and Wills venture on a salary of £300, and with detailed instructions to collect specimens, keep a diary and produce daily maps and illustrations. The party consisting of nineteen men, twenty-four camels, twenty-two horses and more than twenty tonnes of stores, including eighty pairs of shoes, a stationery cabinet, twelve dandruff brushes, an oak table (with two chairs) and a Chinese gong, left Royal Park in Melbourne on 20 August 1860. Becker sent his first dispatches from Swan Hill in September, consisting of his diary entries, five sketches and a bottle containing three snakes.

At fifty-two, Becker was the oldest member of the party. That was to tell against him as expedition leader Robert O'Hara Burke made little effort to hide his frustration as Becker struggled to keep up with his demanding schedule. Burke told Becker and the expedition botanist, who was somewhat confusingly named Hermann Beckler, that they would have to walk all the way to the Gulf of Carpentaria because the horses and camels were needed to carry stores. Becker wrote in his diary on 1 October that he had just marched twenty-four miles, pulling three camels loaded with supplies, without food or rest, and was in fear of fainting until he scrounged 'a few drops' of water from a shallow clay pan.

Burke ran out of patience after the expedition reached Menindee on 15 October and formed an advance party to push on to Cooper's Creek. Becker had quit by this time but was still with the others left behind at Menindee. They remained there for three months, during which time Becker sent forty drawings and assorted natural history specimens to Melbourne – plus a request for two bird guides, including one of John Gould's – but never received any replies. His sketches include beautiful drawings of the landscape, a meteor seen on 11 October, shells, birds, lizards and a 'parasite found in the arm-pit of a gecko No. 2'. He also passed the time by writing a monograph on 'the plague of Australia, the fly'.

A letter sent by Becker from Menindee on 11 January 1861 was to be the last he wrote. The supply party finally packed up camp and headed north on 16 January, reaching the Bulloo River in southern Queensland, 13 kilometres south of Cooper's Creek, in April. Becker didn't make it any further, succumbing to malnutrition and dysentery on 28 April. News of his death was received with shock and sadness by the Royal Society. At its 1862 meeting, Dr Mueller moved 'that this meeting records its profound grief in the great loss sustained by the Society in the death of Dr Ludwig Becker, one of its earliest, most enthusiastic, ingenuous, and self-denying members'. Royal Society president and Victorian governor Sir Henry Barkly paid tribute to 'one of our earliest and most indefatigable contributors ... whenever the history of the Burke and Wills expedition is written, the name of Ludwig Becker will, like theirs, rank with those of Cunningham, Kennedy, Leichhardt, and the rest of that noble band who have sacrificed their lives in the cause of science'. (The rest of the expedition fared no better: in all, seven members lost their lives, including Burke and Wills.)

* * *

Being appointed as a naturalist on an official expedition conveyed a level of status and prestige on a collector – the kind Frederick Strange never achieved. Allan Cunningham achieved that and more as he accompanied high-profile journeys of exploration at sea, then on land, then struck out as an explorer in his own right. Cunningham's primary area of interest was in botany but he also made observations about animals, including the first by a European of a remarkable reptile: the frillneck lizard. Cunningham and his brother Richard – also a collector, albeit with a shorter and more tragic career – were born in England in 1791 and 1793, respectively. Allan worked briefly in a lawyer's office but by 1808 he was stationed at the herbarium at Kew as a clerk to the curator of the Royal Gardens. There he came into contact with Sir Joseph Banks, who recommended him for a posting in Rio de Janeiro and, two years later, in New South Wales.

Cunningham arrived on in December 1816 and almost immediately joined John Oxley's expedition to the Lachlan River marshes, returning with 450 plant species. His next major break came when John Lewin passed up a spot on the cutter *Mermaid*; Cunningham took his place and would spend much of the next five years at sea, embarking on four separate voyages and sailing as far afield as Arnhem Land, Rottnest Island and Timor, and returning with hundreds of plant species. The trips weren't without drama; on the second expedition the *Mermaid* ran aground at Bowen and started leaking badly, forcing a major delay to complete running repairs. The ship was also overrun by rats and cockroaches.

The final voyage, meanwhile, included an unexpected passenger: a teenage girl was found hiding in the forward hold several days after leaving Sydney. At a hastily arranged kangaroo court, she declared herself in love with the boatswain and revealed she had secretly followed him on board. By the time she was discovered it was too late to turn the ship around, so she accompanied the explorers north through the Great Barrier Reef and as far as Mauritius before the *Bathurst* returned to Sydney in April 1822, eleven months after setting sail. What the girl did on board is largely a mystery. She receives only a few brief mentions in expedition diaries, and Cunningham is the only one to give her a name – Sarah Chambers. She was the only woman ever to sail on the English surveying voyages of the Australian coast.

In May 1830 Cunningham visited Norfolk Island, where his camp was raided by a band of escaped convicts. Cunningham and three servants were sleeping in tents on Phillip Island, six kilometres south of Norfolk Island, where they planned to spend a week investigating the local vegetation, and at about five a.m. 'I was suddenly awoke in my bed by three men rushing into my tent, and in an alarming boisterous tone desiring me to rouse up, as they had taken the settlement, and had put the commandant in gaol'. In what must have been a terrifying encounter, Cunningham was threatened with his own gun before the raiding party disappeared into the night with all of his food and equipment, including his hat and shoes, his tent and twelve gallons of fresh water. Two hours later a party of soldiers from the Norfolk Island settlement landed in pursuit of the escapees but no trace of them was ever found; it was presumed they perished at sea. Cunningham learned from the soldiers that the convicts had intended to kidnap him and force him to navigate a path to New Zealand, but the plan was abandoned when they discovered he did not own a compass.

Cunningham understandably decided to return to Sydney, but his Norfolk Island drama wasn't over. On 31 August he loaded his remaining belongings and four crates of live plants onto the *Lucy Ann*, but his departure was delayed overnight by a storm. Cunningham woke the next day to find the ship had been washed out to sea.

Winds blew it within sight of shore nine days later and Cunningham and a small crew rowed over giant waves for four miles in a whaling boat to catch the ship, board it and steer it to Sydney.

Before sailing for England in 1831 he was offered the post of superintendent of the Sydney Botanic Garden but declined, recommending his brother Richard instead. Richard had followed a similar path to his brother but until this point hadn't journeyed past Kew Gardens, where he had worked for eighteen years – much of that spent cataloguing the specimens his brother sent back from Australia. He arrived in Sydney on 6 January 1833 along with a selection of vines from the wine districts of France and Spain, which he distributed throughout the colony as he performed valuable collecting work, including a lengthy excursion to New Zealand, where Māoris treated him kindly after remembering his brother's visit years before.

Richard became lost while collecting near Wollongong early in his time in Australia, and perhaps this should have set off alarm bells when he was a late addition to Major Thomas Mitchell's 1835 expedition to follow the course of the Darling River. Ten days into the trip Richard wandered away from the party. He was never seen again. A search by members of the expedition turned up his hat, his dead horse and some scraps of clothing.

Two years after his brother's death, Allan Cunningham returned to Australia to take the job he had declined six years earlier. His original instinct was correct – he hated it. Growing vegetables for the governor's dinner table was an aspect of the job he particularly detested, and he quit after several months to return to his true love: collecting plants. He sailed to New Zealand again but returned to Sydney in October 1838 seriously ill with tuberculosis. Cunningham

died in June 1839 and was buried in Sydney's Devonshire Street
Cemetery, where Central Station stands today. Five years later
the grave was opened. His remains were removed and placed in a
ten-inch-long lead casket, which was then inserted into a marble
obelisk. It now stands in a pond near the tea rooms in Sydney's
Royal Botanic Garden – something to contemplate next time you're
enjoying a morning coffee in the gardens. A more fitting legacy is
the large number of plant species named after Cunningham by his
colleagues, including the hoop pine (*Araucaria cunninghamii*) and
myrtle beech (*Nothofagus cunninghamii*), one of the dominant trees
in Australia's cool temperate rainforests, as well as a lizard, Cunningham's skink. There is a plaque dedicated to Richard – provided
by Allan – in St Andrew's Scots Church in Rose Bay.

* * *

One more collector deserves our attention, although she was largely
anonymous in her lifetime despite her enormous contribution to
Australian natural history collecting. This was due to a number
of factors, not the least of which was her gender and what many
considered an inelegant and even strange manner. Amalie Dietrich
ignored expectations of women in colonial times and conventions
of personal appearance, abandoned her daughter and travelled with
only a dog as a companion. She had a brilliant mind, was small in
stature but reportedly 'tough as an old boot'. In his opening address
to the Science Congress at Canberra in January 1939, University
of Melbourne history professor Ernest Scott rated her the most
remarkable of the colonial collectors, declaring that 'the little German woman' surpassed even the great John Gould.

Dietrich spent almost ten years exploring the Queensland bush after arriving in Australia on assignment to collect for a private museum in Hamburg. Born Konkordie Amalie Nelle on 26 May 1821 in Siebenlehn, a small village in Saxony, she left school at age fourteen to help in her father's leather workshop. Amalie learned a love of nature from her mother and in 1846 married Wilhelm Dietrich, a chemist ten years her senior, who introduced her to the world of science; Amalie travelled through Europe collecting plants and sending them back to Wilhelm for study.

The business model collapsed when Amalie discovered Wilhelm was having an affair with the nanny hired to look after their daughter, Charitas Concordia Sophie. Amalie took the girl and went to live with her brother, but after a year she had deposited Charitas with her estranged husband and was wandering through Belgium and Holland collecting specimens, which she kept in a cart pulled by a dog named Hektor. In Hamburg she was introduced to shipping magnate Johann Cesar VI Godeffroy, who employed naturalists across the South Pacific to fill his new museum. In 1863, Dietrich became his first and only female collector.

The clipper *La Rochelle* departed Hamburg on 17 May 1863 with 451 immigrants in steerage and one passenger in the first-class saloon: Amalie Dietrich. Her luggage for the 81-day voyage included one magnifying glass, one microscope, six insect cases, four boxes for reptiles, three casks of salt, 100 glass phials and two boxes of poison. After arriving in Brisbane in August, Dietrich began enthusiastically collecting around Moreton Bay. Donning a large straw hat and veil to ward off flies and mosquitoes, she was overcome by joy at the array of new plants she encountered:

What freedom I have here in collecting! Nobody can set any bounds to my eagerness to collect ... the discomforts which the heat and the mosquitos bring me are soon forgotten in the feeling of infinite happiness that enters my soul when I find with every step treasures which no one has got before me ... When I walk through the wide region unconstrained, then I think no king can feel as free and happy as I am, and then I feel as if Godeffroy had given me the whole large continent as a gift. In all areas something new, something unknown!

Dietrich sent 600 plant specimens from the Moreton Bay area back to Hamburg before spending time in Gladstone and Rockhampton, often working in oppressive tropical heat. She also spent time in Bowen, where she became acquainted with a small group of eager scientists. In 1868, Bowen had a population of 1000 that included 100 Germans and a motley crew of scientists including Eugene Fitzalan, an Irish-born botanist who collected plants in Brazil before moving to Melbourne and then Queensland, Frederick Kilmer, harbourmaster and marine algae collector, and local naturalist John Rainbird. Dietrich set up a small zoo in the town; the main attraction was a tame white-breasted sea eagle she had purchased from local Indigenous people. She also used a small boat to collect fish, coral and many previously unrecorded species of sea cucumbers from offshore reefs and nearby islands.[9]

---

9   Sea cucumbers, or holothurians, are found in oceans around the world. There are about 1100 described species.

Researcher Hannah McPherson, who followed in Dietrich's footsteps around Europe and is trying to catalogue many of her specimens that remain unclassified, concludes:

> During her time in Australia, Dietrich collected approximately 20,000 plant specimens ranging from trees, shrubs, ferns, grasses to mosses, lichens and algae. She collected marsupials, fish, sea slugs and coral and her entomological collections include hundreds of beetles, many butterflies and the first significant collection of Australian spiders.

Dietrich's contribution to knowledge of Australian birds was even more profound. By 1870 there were about 600 known species of Australian avifauna, of which 266 – almost half – were collected by Dietrich. Ray Sumner, author of *A Woman in the Wilderness*, the definitive Dietrich biography, concludes: 'This was possibly the largest collection of Australian birds by a single person.' On the outskirts of Mackay she obtained a pair of spotted bowerbirds and their bower, which became a prized exhibit at Museum Godeffroy. There seemed no limit to the natural objects she could souvenir. Her insect collection included termites, ticks, stick insects and grasshoppers, plus native wasps and their nests. She found dozens of types of frogs and lizards, and at Fitzroy River she dissected a crocodile 6.7 metres long. In 1867 she won a gold medal from the Hamburg Horticultural Society for a collection of fifty varieties of Australian woods.

Dietrich spent countless hours drying plants, stuffing her bird specimens with grass, preserving animals in spirits and labelling everything for shipment back to Germany. Dozens of cases containing her specimens were placed on ships; one batch in November 1870 contained seventeen cases and four casks. It was followed in December by four bags and a turtle. She collected enough specimens to fill the display cabinets at Godeffroy's museum and sustain a lucrative business selling duplicates – up to forty of each species – to other museums and private collectors.

There were some mishaps along the way. In one letter to her daughter she recounts being rescued by Aboriginal people after almost drowning in a swamp while trying to collect a water lily. Another describes the agony of being bitten on the inside of her throat by a 'giant ant', which she killed by drinking scalding hot tea.

A description of her considerable achievements must also record her role in one of darkest chapters of Australian natural history. Interest in new and interesting plants and animals from the south seas was matched by a fascination with the Indigenous peoples of Australia and the Pacific. In this era, that included collecting and sending back to Europe Aboriginal artefacts – Dietrich obtained spears, clubs, shields, fishing gear and a large ironbark canoe – and worse. Twisted and ugly interpretations of 'science' such as eugenics and phrenology demanded skeletons for study, with a premium placed on skulls of allegedly 'primitive' people. Renowned anthropologist Charles Mountford promoted a lecture tour about the Indigenous people of Arnhem Land in 1945 under the title 'Australia's Stone-Age Men' and proceeded to remove hundreds of skeletons from sacred sites. Most ended up in the Smithsonian Institute in Washington, DC, and were only returned in 2010. Many skulls have been returned in recent years – not always without resistance – but the remains of as many as 900 Indigenous Australians remain in museums and institutions in the US, UK, France, Germany and elsewhere. And the issue is not only with international institutions. In February 2013, the University of Melbourne found bones and skulls of 400 people, most of them Indigenous, in a storeroom in the anatomy department. They were collected by Richard Berry, a former anatomy professor and dean of medicine, who worked at the university from 1905 until 1929. Professor Berry took skulls from burial sites and souvenired unclaimed bodies from the coroner's office after becoming obsessed with finding a correlation between head size and intelligence (he didn't).

In the 1860s, these perversions of Darwin's theory were yet to materialise, and interest in Indigenous remains was merely voyeuristic and dehumanising. Museum Godeffroy enthusiastically participated in what was at that time a respected branch of Western (white) science, assembling a collection of fifty-three skeletons and 375 skulls, including eight acquired by Dietrich near Bowen. Her most shameful act came when she was invited to the home of one of Rockhampton's leading families and is said to have asked one of the staff to shoot an Aboriginal man so she might have him as a specimen. Mercifully, the request was refused. Details of the incident are sketchy, but the Zoological Museum in Hamburg displayed the tanned skin of an Australian Aboriginal person collected by Dietrich.

Dietrich returned to Germany in March 1873, taking her favourite pet sea eagle and a wedge-tailed eagle with her, along with 'a quite considerable number of chickens' to serve as eagle food. The *Hamburger Abendzeitung* newspaper published an account of the voyage that noted the challenges of travelling with two large birds of prey:

> the birds were fastened to the deck with a footchain, not in a special
> cage, and thus of course in a position to perform many tricks which

were not very pleasant to various passengers. Once Mrs Dietrich saw how the sea eagle held the mate's coat with one claw and as a splendid pastime tore it into many narrow strips with its beak.

On arrival in Germany, the birds were donated to the Hamburg Zoo. After that little is known of Dietrich's life, although some reports suggest she worked at Godeffroy's museum. While visiting her daughter in 1891 she contracted pneumonia and died. In 1879 Godeffroy was declared bankrupt. He was forced to close his museum and his collection was split up and sold. The development may have helped save Dietrich's specimens, which have survived two world wars and are still housed today in scientific and cultural institutions across Europe and Australia. Professor Frederick McCoy purchased birds, fish and insects collected by Dietrich for the National Museum of Victoria, and some of Dietrich's plants are in the National Herbarium in Melbourne's Royal Botanic Gardens.

Despite the ugly ethnographic stain on her career, Dietrich's achievements are undeniable, including a discovery that would have a lasting impact for natural history, medicine and Australian culture. In 1866 she found a 223-centimetre brown snake near Rockhampton that was unknown to science. A year later Wilhelm Peters, a reptile specialist and director of Berlin's Museum of Natural History – where the snake is still kept in a large glass jar – read a paper titled 'On Bats and Amphibians' that described six new species, including the brown snake from Rockhampton, which he named *Pseudechis scutellatus*: the coastal taipan. The snake, and its many venomous cousins, would become the obsession of a unique group of thoroughly Australian naturalists.

4
The Snake Men

'The bite resembles the sting of a wasp or bee, and if no remedy is used the puncture becomes soon inflamed, and the immediate parts, finger or hand, gradually begin to swell, such swelling extending, according to the strength of the poison, up to the shoulder. In about half an hour the most violent headache sets in, the veins on the temple throbbing as if to burst, gradually the spine becomes affected, and the injured limb (if bitten in the arm for instance) grows quite stiff; the skin around the puncture has turned quite blue by this, and the usual drowsiness makes its appearance'

— Gerard Krefft, 'Remedies for Snake-Poisoning', in the *Maitland Mercury & Hunter River General Advertiser*, 9 May 1868

WITH NO EXISTING MANUALS OR FIELD NOTES, there was one reliable way to learn the effects of being bitten by a broad-headed snake in 1868: first-hand experience. The author of the self-inflicted account cited above also refers to being bitten by a death adder, and presumably took the advice of his own article in the *Sydney Morning Herald* four years earlier: 'The most essential thing after a person has been bitten by a venomous snake is not to despair, and not to consider himself doomed.'

This level of dedication may seem extreme, but very little was known about snakes well into the nineteenth century, when other parts of the animal kingdom were very familiar. The belief that nature was ordered by a divine creator extended to a prevailing view that animals that slithered along the ground were morally inferior, a lack of legs being a clear demonstration of their defective character. Modern understanding of poison did not emerge until the mid-1800s, and snakebite in Australia remained rare, at least for humans. So it is not surprising that knowledge about the continent's deadly snakes – today a subject of global fascination – remained worryingly low. The deaths of farm animals prompted settlers to take the issue seriously, but they were presented with an immediate challenge – which snake is which? Applying names to different species didn't necessarily solve the problem; a 'black snake' could describe any number of species and the tiger snake was known in some places as the brown-banded snake and in Tasmania as the carpet snake – a name applied to a different, harmless reptile on the mainland.

Figuring out which snakes were dangerous was the main concern, and this was achieved largely by allowing – or encouraging – captured snakes to bite domestic animals. Policemen, who were responsible for rounding up stray dogs and other creatures, often supplied the test subjects and the venue. *The Argus* of 8 November 1861 records an experiment at Richmond police barracks in which snakes of various species 'caught during the last few days within the neighborhood of Melbourne' were enticed to bite nine dogs and two chickens. Some of the animals were treated with an antidote while others were left to die. The results were mixed – two dogs died but one had received an antidote and one had not, while at least one dog that had been

A group of Australian snakes by Samuel Calvert, c. 1868. (State Library of Victoria)

bitten and received no antidote was 'quite well'. Neither chook made it. The two antidote purveyors, Underwood and Shires, 'expressed their willingness to be bitten by any of the snakes whenever the committee might wish', but the committee decided not to take them up on the offer.

The article didn't go into detail about what the antidote was, but treatments for snakebite in the nineteenth century included regular sips of coffee, tea or brandy, and injecting ammonia – mostly found today in fertiliser and household cleaning products – directly into the veins. Other cures peddled by showmen included chlorinated lime, suction caps, gunpowder, petrol, toad urine, iodide swabs and pigface plant juice.

In the 1869 edition of the *Australian Medical Gazette*, contributor J.P. Murray recounts the tale of 'a young Hindoo woman' in a state of lifelessness from snakebite, quoting from 'a reliable source': 'I forced her jaws open and poured down her throat three medium-sized leaves of [the native herb] Aristolochia indica, reduced to a pulp, with ten black peppercorns, diluted with a graduated ounce of water.' After about ten minutes the woman started to show signs of life, upon which 'I instantly directed her husband, with the aid of my own servants, to drag her about for the purpose of, if possible, increasing the circulation'. It apparently worked: 'In a few minutes she gave a deep inspiration, accompanied by a kind of shriek, manifesting the return of consciousness. This was followed by an exclamation: "A fire is consuming my vitals!"'

Fortunately, a small but dedicated group of Australians were not inhibited by the negative stereotyping of snakes, and if understanding them meant sticking your hand into a hollow log to find out what happened, that was something they were prepared – one could almost say excited – to do. For them, snakes had a strange appeal. In Murray's words:

> At first sight one might feel astonished at seeing so many labourers engaged in so unproductive a field, but there is a peculiar glamour, so to speak, about the subject – a blending together of the horrible, the marvellous and the deadly – that attracts while it appals; the moral counterpart of that strange fascination exercised by the serpent itself upon its victims.

The pioneer in this field was Johann Ludwig Gerard Krefft – zoologist, firebrand and author of the passages cited at the start of this chapter. He was Australia's first snake expert and the central figure in one of the most bizarre episodes in the new colony's scientific history, when he had to be physically removed as director of the national museum.

The son of a confectioner, Krefft was born on 17 February 1830 in what is now Germany and worked on a farm before migrating to the United States in 1850. Two years later he was on the Victorian goldfields. His first public venture into the world of natural science was an expedition to the lower Darling and Murray rivers with generously bearded and controversial Polish naturalist William Blandowski.

Blandowski was the youngest of thirteen children and worked as a mining engineer and spent time in the army before departing

Snake-bite experiments in the Melbourne Gaol, illustrated by Hugh George for *The Australian Sketcher* in 1877. (State Library of Victoria)

Hamburg in May 1849 on the *Ocean*, a three-masted sailing ship bound for Adelaide. His exact motivations are unknown, but he had expressed an interest in natural history and the bustling animal trade at the giant Hamburg port may have inspired a trip across the globe. Four months later the ship arrived at its destination, having changed its name to the *Wolga* en route to avoid a Danish naval blockade. After collecting plants and making some geological observations in South Australia, Blandowski tried his luck on the Victorian goldfields, where he successfully demonstrated a new kind of water pump. He may also have visited Sydney and Cape York, but pinning down his exact movements is difficult, in part because nobody could agree on how to spell his name; Blandowski, Blandowskie and Blandowsky are among the recorded attempts.

We do know he was a founding member of the Geological Society of Victoria in 1854 and soon afterwards set out on collecting expeditions in central Victoria and the Mornington Peninsula, where his companions noted his eccentricities. Assistant Alfred William Howitt wrote to his sister Annie: 'One constant theme is that the horses are lost. Suppose him standing over the fire deep down in the consideration of some philosophical chimera, or perhaps of nothing, when suddenly he rouses up [and] stares across the gully, turns round as if on a pivot and shouts out: "Gentlemans the horses am walk off".' Blandowski set to work on his grand work *Australia Terra Cognita* ('Australia the known land'), which was to feature 200 plates detailing 4000 objects of natural history, grouped under five headings: geological views, fossils, vegetation, birds and Indigenous people. The work was never finished, but Blandowski achieved long-awaited recognition when he was tasked with running the new Melbourne Museum. Sadly, it didn't last.

In 1855 the new governor, Charles Hotham, decided the fledgling museum was an expense the colony couldn't afford and all of Blandowski's collections were to be transferred to the University of Melbourne and its professor of natural history, Frederick McCoy, who was happy to take them despite objections raised at a public meeting. Amid the furore, a party consisting of Blandowski, Krefft and two others left Melbourne on a six-month expedition to explore the Murray and Darling rivers.

The trip ran overtime and over-budget. Blandowski's style of leadership didn't help; he left his companions while he took unplanned breaks and eventually packed up early and returned to Melbourne. Nevertheless, the expedition's haul added up to 17,400 specimens, filling twenty-eight boxes – but the university wasn't happy. McCoy declared many of the items were duplicates and the animal skins were in poor condition. He publicly questioned one of the expedition's genuine achievements, the discovery of two specimens of the rare pig-footed bandicoot.[10] The fallout reached its bizarre zenith when Blandowski presented a report of his findings to the Philosophical Society, revealing nineteen new fish species that he had named after society members. The 'objectionable' pages were removed from the report, robbing us of all nineteen names, but we know they didn't consider it an honour; one was reportedly described as a 'slimy, slippery fish. Lives in mud.'

---

10   At least one of the now-extinct creatures was eaten by Krefft. He wrote in his diary: 'I am sorry to say that my appetite more than once overruled my love for science.'

The 'fish scandal' was the subject of newspaper editorials and cartoons and the burned bridges were never rebuilt. Blandowski became embroiled in ugly disputes over claims of unpaid debts and ownership of the documents from the expedition, which the society claimed were government property. Krefft wrote to the society distancing himself from Blandowski's 'mad pranks and insults' and declaring that his descriptions weren't even scientifically accurate:

> For instance the 'Bleasdaliae' described as living in filth and slime or some such stuff is a fish often and most always caught in clear water. Mr Blandowski knows nothing of the habits of these fishes whatsoever, as he was never present when the natives caught them, which I can prove by my own diary.

Krefft also took Blandowski to court seeking unpaid wages, and won.

Blandowski, meanwhile, was awarded a £475 payout for his work on the expedition but had to hand over his papers before packing up his belongings and returning to Germany in 1859 (he was able to keep many of his illustrations after they were deemed not to be of high scientific value). It was a messy end to an at times distinguished decade in Australia. After returning to Germany, Blandowski resumed work on his opus on Australia's natural history, spending large sums on paintings and engravings, but was unable to find a publisher. He died in 1878 in a mental asylum. For Krefft, the court battle was a harbinger: he may have won, but he was about to embark on his own brawl with the scientific establishment that would end in strikingly similar circumstances.

The next year, Krefft won the job of assistant curator at the Australian Museum in Sydney after a power struggle between New South Wales governor William Denison, a strong Krefft supporter, and the museum trustees, who were suspicious of his lack of traditional qualifications and probably his German heritage. In 1861 the head curator, Simon Pittard, died of tuberculosis and the position was advertised in Australia and Europe, drawing a wide range of applications, including from John MacGillivray, well known for his work on the HMS *Rattlesnake*, and a man named William Jones, who appeared to have no qualifications beyond 'these past two years and more I have been perambulating the recess of the bush contemplating the beauties the wonders and the wisdom of God manifested in the work of his Creation'. Krefft won the full-time position, although he wasn't formally appointed until 1864 and the trustees didn't shelve their reservations about him and his abrasive personality.

In November 1866 Krefft explored the Wellington Caves near Dubbo, where fossils of extinct Australian animals had been uncovered thirty years earlier. After a seven-day journey by horse and cart, Krefft spent four days in the caves working by candlelight then returned to Sydney by hitching a lift on a passing mail coach, abandoning his colleagues where their cart had become bogged, near Orange. Krefft reported that the cave deposits included thylacines, Tasmanian devils, bandicoots, kangaroos, wallabies, wombats and two of the megafauna *diprotodon* (a rhinoceros-sized wombat) and *thylacoleo*, a savage-looking marsupial lion. After a closer look at the fossils, Krefft took issue with the idea that *thylacoleo* was as vicious as it had been portrayed and wrote to the British naturalist Richard Owen, who had examined the original specimens found in the caves in the 1820s and '30s.[11] Owen didn't budge, even when Krefft put large quantities of cave fossils in the post. It may not have been a coincidence that Krefft soon began championing the ideas of Owen's great rival, Charles Darwin.

In the meantime, Krefft continued his groundbreaking work on snakes, publishing *The Snakes of Australia: An Illustrated and Descriptive Catalogue of all the Known Species* in 1869, which expanded the number of known Australian snakes from about twenty in 1854 to more than seventy, largely through the work of the museum's new assistant curator and collector, George Masters, who was an expert marksman and also known to grab venomous snakes with his bare hands. Thousands of insects, birds and fish also made their way into Masters' collections as he travelled extensively in New South Wales, Queensland, Tasmania, Western Australia, South Australia and Lord Howe Island (he was supposed to hand them all over to the museum but kept many for his private collection).

Enthusiastic citizens also donated snakes to the museum, including a 'Captain P', who brought a python from Ceylon (now Sri Lanka) that had devoured the ship's pet monkey at sea. Krefft's volume opens with a detailed description of snakes that doesn't assume any prior knowledge – 'snakes are naked, that is, they are not supplied with any external covering such as hair or feathers' – and dispelled some common myths, including a belief that death adders could use their tails like clubs to attack people.

---

11   The fact the femur of a giant kangaroo had originally been identified as being from an elephant gave Krefft's argument extra weight.

In 1868 Krefft staged a fight between a snake and a mongoose at the museum to entertain the visiting Prince Alfred during his royal tour. The mongoose killed the snake and the prince took the victor home to England, along with 'a large and varied collection of colonial birds and animals', including 'a very fine wombat'. Krefft discovered the Australian lungfish when he was served one for dinner in 1870 and identified and named at least thirty Australian species, including the freshwater crocodile and cassowary.[12]

Krefft clashed regularly with the museum establishment, writing that 'the three families living in the museum quarrelled from morning til night' (at this time it was standard practice for museum staff and their families to live in the building). He reserved particular venom for trustee Sir William Macleay and a man named Michael O'Grady, who was employed as a porter. Krefft accused O'Grady of extorting money to help raise his 'eight or nine children' and 'a drunken wife'.

His vocal support for Darwin's theories was another source of tension between Krefft and the scientific establishment in Sydney and Melbourne – Melbourne Museum director Frederick McCoy was a staunch creationist who implored the public to visit his newly acquired gorillas to observe how different they were from humans. Krefft was one of Australia's earliest champions of evolutionary theories and in a letter to Darwin in 1873 he described the Australian Museum trustees as 'mere collectors ... and the greatest drawback

---

12   With bone-like structures in their fins, the lungfish represents a 'missing link' between the first creatures that lived in the oceans and land-based animals. They are thought to have remained unchanged for 140 million years. Krefft wrote a scientific description of the fish he was served by the Honourable William Forster, then the NSW Minister for Lands, in the proceedings of the Zoological Society of London.

to the success of this Institution because by their constant interference and insatiable desire to possess everything themselves they would have long ago disgusted a less stouter heart than mine'. In his autobiography he was even less kind, writing that his extensive collections of snakes staggered 'the slow-going bug and beetle-killers who thought that true science consisted in keeping a lot of these insects in a cabinet in apple pie order'.

In 1874 matters came to a head when the trustees accused Krefft of twelve offences, including drunkenness, misrepresenting museum visitor numbers, 'maliciously breaking up a fossil jaw', having furniture made for himself from museum materials, permitting indecent photographs to be taken and stealing seventy pounds worth of gold from display cabinets. Krefft denied all the charges. Meanwhile, a parliamentary committee into the museum's management found claims by Krefft that some of the trustees had abused their positions to be baseless. A series of meetings was called to review Krefft's position but he either called in sick or refused to show up, claiming the trustees were out to get him. When he failed to hand over the museum books and keys as requested, the trustees decided there was no alternative but to sack him.

Krefft was informed of the decision the next day and given until the end of the month to vacate the premises. Instead he locked the doors, barricading himself inside the building. Unable to obtain police assistance, the trustees hired two prize-fighters, who broke the doors down and found Krefft sitting in his living room in an ornate red leather chair. They picked him up, chair and all, and dumped him in William Street. He was never allowed back inside his beloved museum.

The next day a new curator – bird collector and former sugar plantation owner Edward Pierson Ramsay – was appointed (Krefft had called him 'an enemy of mine of long standing on account of my refusing to purchase the rubbish he used to offer'), and the following day the museum, which had been closed to the public for almost three months, reopened, ending a remarkable chapter of the institution's history.

As might be expected, Krefft didn't take the decision well. He wrote to Darwin, complaining 'had I been an Englishman by birth, had humbugged people, attended church and spread knowledge on the principle that the God of Moses and the Prophets made "little green apples" I would have gained the day, but a true believer in the theory of development (by natural selection) I am hunted down in this paradise of bushrangers, of rogues, cheats and vagabonds'. Darwin replied that while he was sympathetic to Krefft's plight, he could do little to help.

Krefft received similar answers from other men of public standing – Premier Henry Parkes wrote: 'I have great respect for your undoubted ability and am truly sorry that you should be involved in such a disagreeable difficulty ... but you must learn to keep a cool temper and a respectful bearing even to gentlemen who may be opposed to you.' Krefft fought for years for reinstatement and compensation, with some minor victories, but the saga broke him. He was declared bankrupt in 1880 and died a year later.

Krefft's reputation has been rehabilitated in recent years. His fateful armchair is now on display as a museum exhibit in its own right, and director and chief executive Kim McKay told *The Australian* newspaper in 2019 that it was her favourite artefact.

'Krefft was a character and a half,' she said. 'He was single-minded and a very difficult person to get along with, but he was incredibly smart, and he brought the formal study of science to the museum.'

The next major work on Australian snakes was produced by zoologist, painter, motorcyclist and flautist Edgar Ravenswood Waite. Disappointingly for us, Waite was by all accounts extremely diligent and not very eccentric, apart from his long list of hobbies, which also included maintaining his own private aquarium. (He would later sail with Douglas Mawson on his first subantarctic cruise in 1912 and became a world authority on the fishes of the Australasian-Antarctic region.) His entry in the *Australian Dictionary of Biography* describes him as 'bespectacled, with a domed forehead, symmetrical face, aquiline nose and an Edwardian beard'. In 1898 he was assistant curator in charge of vertebrates at the Australian Museum when he published *A Popular Account of Australian Snakes: With a Complete List of the Species and an Introduction to their Habits and Organisation*.

Where Krefft recorded forty-two venomous and twenty-one innocuous land snakes, Waite listed sixty-two and thirty-one (but reduced the number of sea snakes from fifteen to twelve). His work reflected advances in scientific knowledge, with Waite making the no doubt important observation that snakes 'cannot wink' and explaining the mystery of how they moved about:

> The movements of snakes are so rapid that no one unaccustomed to these reptiles can form any idea of their agility. You may be holding one in your hand when, almost before you are conscious of it, it has thrown two or three coils round your arm without you

being able to realise how the trick was done; or it may as suddenly uncoil, and, as the writer once experienced, have passed its tail up your coat sleeve, and be halfway down your back with equal speed and facility.

A special section at the start of Waite's book describes the latest advice on how to treat snakebite: 'the bitten part should be cut into numerous little cuts over and around the bites for about half an inch around, and sucked by the mouth freely and perseveringly; and this can be done without danger by any person'. In fact, the science of snake venom was taking giant leaps forward, although not without resistance. Prussian-born physician Augustus Mueller proposed injections of strychnine, a position championed by Queen Victoria, while at the University of Michigan Henry Sewall showed he could progressively inject pigeons with increasing amounts of pit viper venom without killing them. In 1894, thirteen years after Louis Pasteur immunised a sheep against anthrax, French physician Albert Calmette treated a cobra bite using the blood of a horse that had been injected with snake venom, an experiment that became the basis of all modern antivenoms. Horses, sheep and even rabbits have robust immune systems that can cope with small doses of venom much better than feeble humans can. Injected in small doses over time, they generate antibodies to fight the poison that can be extracted and treated for use in people. Calmette produced the world's first commercially available antivenom with the promise of treating all snakebites, but tests by the University of Sydney's Dr Charles Martin using a red-bellied black snake and a common tiger snake debunked the idea of a universal snake cure.

In 1901 Frank Tidswell, principal assistant medical officer for the New South Wales government, immunised a former ambulance horse by injecting it with ten grams of tiger snake venom over three years. Martin and Tidswell made several other important discoveries about the nature of Australian snake venom, but their antivenom never went into commercial production as Tidswell was diverted to other projects and Martin returned to England. The Australian antivenom project was finally completed in 1927 by the Walter and Eliza Hall Institute and the Commonwealth Serum Laboratories (which had been established in 1916), led by Neil Hamilton Fairley, who had just returned from several years in India, where snakes claimed thousands of victims annually. (In Australia, the documented number was more like twenty.) In late 1930 a tiger snake antivenom

COMMENCEMENT OF THE SNAKE SEASON.——THE FIRST VICTIMS, AT COLAC AND WHITTLESEA.

'Commencement of the snake season: the first victims'. Illustration by Richard Egan Lee for the *Police News*, 29 September 1877. (State Library of Victoria)

was released for commercial use. The institute's director, Charles Kellaway, became one of its first recipients after he was bitten by a tiger snake while trying to milk it.

Finally, the knowledge of how to produce an antivenom to Australian snakes was at hand. But this presented a new challenge. Making antivenom required venom, acquired by finding and milking deadly snakes – a process in which a handler grabs the snake by the back of the head and pushes its fangs through a rubber membrane stretched over a glass beaker. Squeezing the snake's venom glands forces drops of venom into the jar without the snake being able to turn and bite its handler – at least in theory (in practice, handlers are often bitten dozens of times during their careers). The quantity of venom obtained is so low that snakes have to be milked many times to obtain a useful amount; it took legendary American snake handler Bill Haast (who was bitten at least 173 times over his lifetime) three years and 69,000 milkings to produce one pint of coral snake venom. Milking requires concentration and skill, but finding the snakes in the first place called for a different set of attributes, chief among them bravery bordering on insanity. A surprising number of men put up their hands for this vital but potentially lethal task.

Fairley and Kellaway's chief supplier was Tom Eades, who moved to Australia from New Zealand at the age of sixteen to pursue his love of nature and, in particular, snakes. Eades performed shows in a different Sydney suburb each week and, sensing a commercial opportunity, took to dressing in Eastern clothes, painting his skin brown and calling himself Pambo, 'the great snake man'. Moving to Melbourne, he performed his politically incorrect snake show on Bourke Street and the St Kilda foreshore before he was appointed curator of reptiles at Melbourne Zoo in 1920 (at this point he presumably dropped the Indian costume, although the nickname stuck). He initially supplied Fairley and Kellaway with venom from the zoo's snakes but eventually became a full-time snake expert for the Commonwealth Serum Laboratories (CSL). In this role he milked thousands of snakes, including tigers, browns, copperheads and death adders, and was bitten so many times he reportedly developed a heightened immunity to tiger snake venom. A 1933 article in *The Argus* reported that 'Pambo' had again been admitted to hospital after being bitten on the finger while try-ing to put a tiger snake in a jar. 'This is the second time he has been bitten this year, but he has been bitten on many occasions previously,' the article noted. In the end, the bites weren't what did Eades in. Inhaling powdered snake venom caused a serious airway condition that eventually killed him in 1942.

* * *

Exotic pseudonyms clearly had commercial appeal at this time. Edward Royce Ramsamy was born in Lawrence, near Grafton in New South Wales, in 1921. His grandparents had migrated from India via Fiji, but he spoke only English, with a clear Australian accent. In the early 1940s he joined the carnival circuit, acting as spruiker in a show called 'The Carnival of Eastern Wonders' that included magic, a boxing kangaroo, 'the smallest horse in the world' and, after an unusual package was delivered in 1943, two large carpet pythons. Ramsamy was taken by the reptiles and saw them as the perfect attraction for US sailors on shore leave during the war in the Pacific. He added twenty black snakes and a frillneck lizard to his collection, built a 3.6-square-metre wooden enclosure that he called the 'pit of death', donned a turban and adopted the name Ram Chandra, taking his show on the road before eventually settling in Mackay, in northern Queensland. A poster declared:

AT THE SHOW, INDIA SPEAKS. Jungle Death Mystery. Jungle Death Uncanny. Jungle Death Weird. He is brilliantly educated. Fearless. Daring. Unnatural. Has handled the deadliest reptiles in the universe. Featuring RAM CHANDRA Indian Jungle Boy.

The advertising promised a lot (and hit all the search engine optimisation key terms) and Chandra aimed to deliver value for the ninepence entry fee, standing in the pit surrounded by fearsome reptiles. During one performance he was bitten by a tiger snake but refused to call an ambulance, administering his own first aid. He started to develop nausea, paralysis, breathing difficulties and blurred vision and was finally convinced to visit a hospital, where he was injected with antivenom. The next morning he talked hospital staff into releasing him early and he was back in the snake pit within hours, one arm in a sling. Just after eleven a.m. he was bitten again, and again administered his own first aid. This time he recovered, probably due to the lasting effects of antivenom applied the previous night. In 1956 he was bitten repeatedly by a taipan while conducting a snake demonstration for a group of senior ambulance officers in Mackay. His promotional material was updated to record the event.

Chandra wanted to educate people about snakes but, as his biographer and admirer Philip Jones noted, 'although he billed himself as a "snake expert", Ram was little interested in the scientific aspects of the species he used in his act.' He did, however, enthusiastically join the search for a cure for the almost always deadly taipan bite, coming up with one of the worst ideas ever: creating his own antivenom out of household substances. He drafted government medical officer Dr Ian Chenoweth into an experiment in which he would allow himself to be bitten by a taipan. The doctor would then inject him with his homemade concoction. The doctor's reaction to this proposal is unfortunately not recorded, but he only agreed to take part if the test subject was an animal and not a human being. Which is how Chandra, Dr Chenoweth (carrying his army pistol), a taipan and a kangaroo rat gathered in the doctor's surgery on a Saturday afternoon in March 1955. 'In the midst of the experiment a policeman arrived on postmortem business, and took a very dim view of the scene now being enacted – two metres of deadly taipan, a loaded pistol, a pale youth holding a kangaroo rat and clinical instruments much in evidence,' a newspaper reported. The experiment was allowed to continue. The kangaroo rat was injected with 'antivenom', then Chandra milked the taipan and injected its venom into the small marsupial. It died shortly afterwards.

Chandra survived the experiment (more than can be said for the poor kangaroo rat) and embarked on a statewide taipan survey, obtaining snakes that he milked for the CSL, but his lobbying for an official government position was unsuccessful. Finally, in 1972 he received a cheque in the mail for $2000 'in recognition of the work you have undertaken over many years when you were actively engaged in obtaining taipan venom for research in the development of an antivenene'. By this time Chandra had given up snake handling after he became partially paralysed from the waist down, possibly a result of the dozen or so snakebites he suffered during his career.

He received an Order of Australia medal in 1995 and died in 1998, aged seventy-seven, survived by his wife, Nolear, and eleven children.

She told ABC Radio a year after his death that her husband had loved snakes and would never let anyone kill one, but she wasn't sure why: 'I just don't know. Because when he was ... a young boy, he was really frightened of snakes, but then after travelling around the sideshow handling snakes, so I suppose that get into his bloodstream, and then thinking about doing the snakes.' An exhibition in Ram Chandra's honour at the Mackay Museum in 2009 included a stuffed snake that bit Chandra during one of his shows.

Chandra was one of a handful of 'snake men' operating in Australia at this time. Others included Frank Little, an expert bushman who reportedly collected 101 taipans between 1957 and 1980 and took catching the snakes so seriously he put sandshoes on – he was more often seen in bare feet, which may have contributed to him being bitten on the foot by a death adder in 1939. He recovered and lived until July 2000. George Cann and his sons George Junior and John made major contributions to snake research and education, with George Senior performing in Sydney snake shows as a teenager and keeping 200 tiger snakes in pits at his home while he was working as the curator of reptiles at Taronga Zoo. He was bitten on the nose by a brown snake at the 1924 Adelaide Show and once lost his sight for three days after being bitten by a tiger snake. His preferred method of treatment was numerous cups of tea; the first time he received antivenom was in 1961, after collapsing following a brown snake bite during a show. He had supplied brown snake venom to CSL and it may have saved his life. In 1965 he suffered a stroke, then disappeared from his hospital bed. He was found in nearby bushland looking for snakes. He died three years later at the age of sixty-eight.

Another snake man – or 'snakey', as they call themselves – Donald Thomson, collected more than 300 snakes while living with Wik-mungkan people in Cape York, where he learned the name 'taipan' for 'a giant copper-coloured snake ... which they stood in great dread' and introduced it into popular use. Meanwhile, the development of a brown snake antivenom can largely be credited to Roy Reynolds, who caught hundreds of them in the irrigation canals near Leeton in the New South Wales Riverina and sent them by train to Sydney Zoo on what became known as the 'brown-snake express'.

Another snakey, Charles Tanner, had a lifelong fascination for reptiles and collected hundreds, plus assorted mammals and frogs, for museums in Victoria and Queensland, mostly in his spare time. He was the first person to milk the inland taipan, also known as the fierce snake or small-scaled snake, often cited as the world's deadliest snake due to the extreme toxicity of its venom (one bite can kill 250,000 mice), although it is actually quite shy and is rarely encountered by humans. Only a handful of people have ever been bitten and all have survived after hospital treatment. Tanner wasn't one of them, but he was bitten a number of times by different snake species and developed an unfortunate allergy to antivenom, which colleagues attempted to treat by injecting him with tiger snake venom twenty-four times over thirteen months. Partway through the treatment he was bitten by a western brown snake and fell unconscious. Remarkably, he survived the ordeal, eventually dying in Cairns in 1996.

* * *

Not all snake handlers were that lucky. John Cann, son of George Cann Senior and author of the book *Snakes Alive!*, compiled a list of twenty-two snake handlers who died from bites between 1893 and 1977, including one who suffered a fatal attack during a 'snake bite demonstration' in Sydney. But few of the other twenty-one men on the list could match the heroism of Kevin Budden. The nature enthusiast had joined the Australian Reptile Club as a teenager in Sydney and constructed a snake pit in his backyard, a hobby his parents tolerated despite young Kevin being bitten numerous times. In April 1949 he travelled to north Queensland with two friends and amateur herpetologists, Neville Goddard and Roy Mackay, in the hope of catching a taipan for antivenom research; the snake had never been captured alive and there was no antivenom to the bite of the world's third-most toxic snake.[13]

The coastal taipan is especially dangerous because of its nervous disposition. If threatened, it will lash out, often after raising its forebody off the ground and flattening its head in the style of a cobra before striking with lethal efficiency. According to the Australian Museum, 'The muscular lightweight body of the taipan allows it to hurl itself forwards or sideways and reach high off the ground, and such is the speed of the attack that a person may be bitten several times before realising the snake is there.'[14] Before the 1950s a taipan bite was almost always fatal – there is just one recorded case of a victim surviving without antivenom and nurses reportedly found his blood had turned completely black. Helpful tip: avoid taipans.

---

13   Behind two other Australian species, the inland taipan and the eastern brown.
14   Holy shit.

It was advice Budden didn't take, although he, Goddard and Mackay returned from their Cape York expedition empty-handed. The next year Budden headed north alone and bagged twenty-seven snakes in four weeks in the Atherton Tablelands – mostly non-venomous pythons and tree snakes. In Cairns, he heard stories of giant brown snakes in residential areas on the outskirts of town, became convinced the locals were describing taipans, and set out to investigate. He found what he was looking for in a pile of rubbish at Edge Hill – a large taipan making a meal of a bush rat. According to a detailed account by snake expert David Williams,[15] Budden put his boot on the snake's neck, causing it to regurgitate the rat and lash out at its human captor. Budden carefully slipped his fingers behind the snake's head, keeping his boot in place until he was absolutely sure of his grip.

He carefully lifted the snake off the ground and walked to Edge Hill Road, where he hoped a passing driver would give him, and the deadly two-metre snake writhing in his hand, a lift to the home of a local snake catcher who could identify and bag the reptile. Remarkably, a truck pulled over. The driver, Jim Harris, later told the *Cairns Post* that Kevin was 'a game little bloke and as cool as they come'.

> I pulled up the truck and asked him what he had. He told me that
> he thought it was a taipan, and he asked me to drive him to Mr
> Stephens' home at Edge Hill as he was an authority on taipans and

---

15   The head of the Venom Research Unit at Melbourne University and chair of
      the World Health Organization's snakebite research group, Dr Williams has
      been bitten six times himself including by a deadly Papuan taipan during the
      filming of an episode of the ABC series *Foreign Correspondent* in 2007.

could identify it properly. I drove him to Mr Stephens' home and he sat next to me in the cab holding the snake in his hands all the way. He told me that he had trodden on it in rubble and had caught it, after it had struck at his boot.

By the time they arrived at their destination, Budden's hand was coated in saliva from the struggling and enraged snake. The improbably named Stephen Stephens confirmed it was indeed a taipan and his wife fetched a suitable bag. As Budden lowered the snake into the bag, his grip failed. 'It bit deeply into his left hand and then got away,' Harris said. 'He caught it again and held it out at arm's length by the tail and told Mr Stephens how to put a ligature on his arm. I wanted to kill the thing, but he would not let me. He kept saying that it was important for scientific research, and he had come to the far north specially to capture one.'

Budden was bundled back into Harris's truck, which sped towards town, meeting an ambulance halfway. As he was being loaded into the ambulance, Budden made Harris promise to look after the snake. True to his word, Harris kept it in the back of his truck until the next day. Meanwhile, efforts by doctors at Cairns Base Hospital, including injecting Budden with tiger snake antivenom, proved futile and Kevin died at 1.30 p.m. on 28 July 1950, twenty-seven hours after he was bitten. He was twenty years old. Truck driver Jim Harris was one of the pallbearers when Budden was laid to rest three days later in Cairns cemetery, a short walk from where he found the taipan that ended his life.

The snake's ordeal wasn't over yet. It was placed inside two sealed sugar bags and a box and flown to Brisbane and then to Melbourne.

At the Melbourne Museum, the box was opened by zoologist David Fleay, who quickly discovered the snake had escaped from the inner bag. It fell to the floor and reared in a striking pose. Fleay later described how he handled the situation: 'I hooked at the lashing flickering-tongued reptile with a snake stick and secured a lucky grip while its body twisted and writhed in furious protest.' He held on to the reptile like his life depended on it (it did) while an assistant offered a rubber-topped beaker that the taipan latched on to 'like a suddenly sprung rat trap': 'the abnormally large fangs dwarfing those of the biggest tiger snake were plainly visible through the glass as the snake continued its pressure'. Suffering from cramp in his hands from the tight grip, Fleay held the snake against the wall for a photo, then stuffed it into a specially made bag. 'It was a moment of great relief from the tension, a time for solemn handshakes all round. Dr Morgan, Roy Goodisson and I felt that in this healthy, freshly-caught reptile we had dealt with the most savage tempered, tough and resilient snake in our joint experience.'

The snake was milked six times before it died several weeks after its arrival in Melbourne. Four years later antivenom developed using venom from the Budden taipan saved the life of a ten-year-old Queensland boy named Bruce Stringer, who was bitten after he decided to climb into a hollow log during a game of hide-and-seek at a primary school near Cairns. It has saved many more lives since. The snake is now part of Melbourne Museum's collection. In 2014, samples of the original venom milked from the taipan sixty-four years earlier were found at the University of Melbourne. It was still toxic.

Fleay made a gigantic contribution to the understanding of Australia's native fauna – much more on him shortly – and all these men played a role in the development of life-saving taipan antivenom. That includes Ram Chandra, whose almost suicidal experiment had a positive spin-off: Dr Chenoweth suggested he milk the taipan regularly and he assisted in crystalising the venom and sending it to the CSL.

* * *

One more man provided huge quantities of taipan venom to the CSL, as well as a whole lot else. His name was Eric Worrell, the face of snakes and venom production to many Australians during a public career that lasted more than forty years.

Worrell was born in Granville, Sydney, in 1924 and developed an obsession with reptiles after his parents took him to watch George Cann Senior perform his renowned snake show at La Perouse, on the shores of Botany Bay. A young Worrell collected live lizards, frogs and fish and kept them in glass cases in his parents' shed alongside chickens, two rabbits and a tortoise named Phar Lap, charging neighbours a penny to view them. He added a snake to the menagerie after rescuing a diamond python from rock-hurling boys near Sydney's Central Railway Station.

As was common at the time, he left school at thirteen and took on a variety of jobs; by the age of seventeen his résumé included working in a plastics factory, as a timber hand, as a truck driver and as a construction worker, and he had travelled to New South Wales, Queensland and South Australia. In 1943 Worrell found himself in Darwin, where he joined the Civil Construction Corps as a black-smith. The city was in the midst of sustained bombing raids by Japanese aircraft and Worrell was hit by a piece of shrapnel during

Eric Worrell milking a tiger snake for its venom, 1968.
(National Archives of Australia)

one blast but not seriously injured. The job took him to Katherine, where he was able to expand his love for reptiles, and his reputation as an expert on the subject, by keeping a large number of venomous snakes in a box under his bed. Non-venomous creatures including tortoises and a three-metre python named Percy were stored in a tent nearby.

Worrell befriended a poet named Roland Robinson and the pair returned to the Northern Territory in a second-hand panel van after the war had ended. Basing themselves near hot springs at Mataranka, they caught snakes, lizards, turtles and fish by day, and freshwater crocodiles at night, using a canoe made of two truck-engine covers that Worrell welded together. Worrell captured wild buffaloes on film – narrowly escaping their charging horns on more than one occasion – and learnt from the local Jawoyn people. Kevin Markwell and Nancy Cushing, authors of the definitive biography of Worrell, say this is where he adopted the name Karliboodi, which means 'black snake' in the Jawoyn language, a name he used on some of his dozens of magazine articles. After several months in the outback Worrell and Robinson returned to New South Wales with four drums full of pythons and young crocodiles.

In 1949 Worrell bought a block of land at Ocean Beach to fulfil his lifelong dream of operating a reptile park where people could see and learn about his favourite animals:

> Everybody has a dream, a goal they set themselves and either modify to suit circumstances as years pass, or discard when they grow too old ... I wanted to live somewhere away from the city, on a large piece of land where I could keep all the strange reptiles I would bring back from my travels to all corners of Australia. I wanted to keep them in as near to natural conditions as possible so I could study their life stories, and so that people could look at them and learn that there was no reason to fear them.

The Ocean Beach Aquarium opened to the public in 1950, the second of its kind in Australia. (A snake park had opened in Adelaide in 1927, but the curator suffered a fatal tiger snake bite the following year and the park transformed into a koala farm.) Befitting the name, Worrell's aquarium displayed an array of interesting fish, but he stretched the definition somewhat with tanks containing venomous snakes and an outdoor snake pit full of black snakes, brown

snakes and copperheads. It was here that Worrell began his signa-
ture demonstrations of milking snakes for their venom, a practice
he would continue for decades. He supplied prodigious amounts of
venom to the CSL; in 1953 alone, he provided sixty-four grams of
dried venom, which may not sound like a lot until you realise it is
the product of more than 3000 milkings.

To keep the supply going he established a network of small-
time snake collectors and farmers who sent him live snakes (at least
one, believed to be a taipan, got lost in the post) and alerted him to
fruitful collecting areas. He was regularly on the road with friends
including George Cann and Ken Slater, walking twenty-five miles
a day and prodding wires into hollow logs; 'if there was any response
we hooked the snakes out with the wire or chopped open the logs.
Several logs contained two snakes while one I opened contained four
quite large tiger snakes.' On hot days the men would find relief by
wading thigh-deep in creeks, grabbing snakes out of the water and
from inside floating logs. Others were taken straight out of trees.
Their best day's catch was sixty-eight.

Worrell's first assignment for the CSL was to provide tiger snake
venom and he found more than 400 specimens around the Murray River with George Cann. The next part of the job didn't go so
well – the first snake Worrell tried to milk bit him. He recovered
after being raced to a doctor's surgery and injected with 3000 units
of tiger snake antivenom. He recalled another occasion when a
black snake 'sank its fangs into my biceps' and he recovered with
few symptoms apart from vomiting blood and feeling 'a little off
colour for a week'. In another 'amusing incident' – his words – he was
bitten by a tiger snake near the Murray River (the amusing part was

that his companion missed the exciting episode while he changed the film in his camera). Friends also found it hilarious when, after a bite near Tocumwal, Worrell had to be admitted to the maternity ward of the local hospital because there were no other vacant beds. 'Statistically I've worked out that I get bitten about every three thousandth snake that I milk – that is, about once a year,' he wrote in 1958. 'That's not a bad average.'

In 1952, two years after Budden's death, Worrell travelled to Queensland in search of taipan venom to help the CSL develop an antidote, joined by two entrepreneurs hoping to find a taipan to sell to Sydney's Taronga Zoo. The trio captured a 1.9-metre specimen in a cane field on their first day in Cairns. Three days later they cornered an even bigger taipan, and one of the men, John Dwyer, grabbed it by the tail, prompting the snake to lunge at his face. Dwyer's response was to dodge the attempted bite and swing the snake above his head like a lasso. 'Wal and I expected any moment that John would drop exhausted with the taipan on top, or that he would lose his grip and send it flying to wrap around our necks,' Worrell recalled. He eventually let go at an opportune moment to send the snake into the grass. It quickly and understandably slithered away but was found and captured later that evening. The taipan was smuggled on a train to Sydney and sold to Taronga Zoo.

Worrell returned from a second Queensland trip in 1955 with another taipan, forty other snakes, a crocodile and assorted lizards, turtles and fish that became part of the aquarium's collection. On his collecting trips he filled tanks, bathtubs and any dishes he could get his hands on with fish to be packed into sealed plastic bags, or occasionally plastic water bottles, for the journey home via air freight. He also collected about 200 black tiger snakes from tiny and unpopulated islands off the north-east coast of Tasmania.

By 1958 – the year Worrell published the partly autobiographical book *Song of the Snake* – his menagerie and vision had outgrown the aquarium, and work began on a 4.5-hectare park north of Gosford. The Australian Reptile Park opened in 1959, featuring two snake pits and a kiosk. In 1963 the park's most recognisable attraction, a 26.5-metre long, 50-tonne concrete dinosaur named Ploddy, was unveiled and over the next three decades the collection expanded to include alligators, tree kangaroos, cassowaries, Tasmanian devils and wombats, which for a time wandered free until a tendency to nip the ankles of visitors and bulldoze young children resulted in them being confined to enclosures.

The park boasted the first noctarium in the Southern Hemisphere, housing animals that prefer the dark, including possums, quolls, bandi-coots, potoroos and a number of grey-headed flying foxes, which were allowed to fly free inside the building. Deadly foreign snakes arrived, including a sidewinder, several species of rattlesnake, an anaconda and a coveted king cobra, the only one on display in Australia. One thing the park lacked was a saltwater crocodile, after its first saltie died just a few months after the park's opening. That issue was resolved when Worrell captured a wild male croc that was harassing female crocodiles at a Townsville zoo, earning itself the nickname Casanova.

Worrell's passion for his park and its animals was remarkable. However, a venture of that scale requires other skills. He was not a natural businessman and hated paperwork, which became an issue when government agencies, including the Australian Quar-antine Service, started cracking down on people keeping, catching and importing native and exotic animals. The National Parks and Wildlife Service also took the park to task for keeping more than 200 animals donated by members of the public instead of releasing them in the wild. The age of the self-taught amateur naturalist had been replaced by academic qualifications, forms and regulations, and Worrell was a relic of a bygone era.

The construction of a new four-lane freeway bypassing the central coast also hit the park hard and by the 1980s it was sinking into debt. In 1985 Worrell was bitten by a monocled cobra during a milking display. Within an hour he was blind and suffering from paralysis. He recovered thanks to the park's antivenom supplies, and the incident briefly increased gate takings, but the park was only saved when Worrell relinquished control as part of a divorce settlement with his second wife, Robyn.

After the divorce Worrell continued to live in the park and conduct occasional snake-handling and milking demonstrations until he suffered a fatal heart attack in 1987. He was sixty-two. Nine years later the park moved to more modern facilities at Somersby. The move required transferring more than 600 animals and the 50-tonne dinosaur, which received a ticker-tape parade through the streets of Gosford attended by 15,000 people. The Australian Reptile Park is still owned by Robyn (who deserves credit for keeping it afloat during Eric's troubled years) and her second husband, John Weigel, a self-described 'reptile nut' who started working at the park in 1981. Born in the USA, Weigel was expelled from his Colorado University dormitory after complaints about his growing snake collection. He was briefly paid to wrestle alligators in California before travelling to Australia to find Worrell, having dreamed of working at Worrell's reptile park since reading *Song of the Snake* as a teenager. In the four decades since, Weigel has milked an estimated 30,000 snakes without being bitten. The Australian Reptile Park continues to play a vital role providing venom to CSL and undertaking conservation efforts, including helping to save the Tasmanian devil. And Ploddy the dinosaur still overlooks the Pacific Highway near the Gosford exit.

As well as creating the park, Worrell published eleven books, more than seventy articles and several scientific papers, despite having no formal training. It's impossible to know how many lives were saved by his captivating mix of showmanship and science, milking thousands of deadly snakes in the reptile park snake pits. He also collected other deadly creatures for the CSL, including live Sydney funnel-web spiders, paralysis ticks, wasps, a frozen blue-ringed octopus and, in one unusual assignment, a collection of dried fleas. Not a single fatality has been recorded from a funnel-web bite since an antivenom was developed in 1981. Worrell's life was dedicated to collecting venom and changing perceptions of Australia's reptiles, a mission he resoundingly accomplished.

In the early twentieth century Australia's snakes were feared and hated; snake identification was taught in schools and the terrifying Mrs Snake was the villain of May Gibbs' iconic *Snugglepot and Cuddlepie*, first published in 1918. Today Australians take a strange national pride in the fact that our snakes top lists of the world's most deadly creatures. Worrell can't take sole credit for this change in attitude, but his pro-reptile message directly reached thousands of visitors to his park, and many more via a new medium for Australian naturalists: television.

That's a story for another chapter. But first there is a lot more to learn about David Fleay and his remarkable work with snakes and dozens of other Australian animals. His most outstanding achievements came with a much cuter critter that confounded naturalists for a century and a half. Oh, and it's also poisonous.

5

One of Nature's Nervous Mistakes

'I couldn't describe it. It seems made up of parts of two or three different sorts of creatures. None of us can account for it. It must have been an experiment, when all the rest of us were made; or else it was made up of the odds and ends of all the birds and the beasts that were left over after we were all finished.'

—The kangaroo explains a platypus to Dot in *Dot and the Kangaroo*, Ethel Pedley, 1899

A RUN-IN WITH A GRUMPY THYLACINE IS AN UNUSUAL place to start a story about the platypus and the men who unravelled one of the great mysteries of natural science. But a close encounter with a Tasmanian tiger in the 1930s was a rare event, especially when it was recorded in writing and on film. But, as David Fleay's wife Sigrid Fleay (pronounced 'flay') explained in a documentary made by Brisbane's BTQ Channel 7 in the 1980s, 'He's a most unusual man.' She continued:

> I think he's a genius. He's never had any help from the government, from any government at all. Everything he's done, he's done on his

own against tremendous odds. It shows the tremendous perseverance of the man, the determination and the sheer grit ... He's been absolutely devoted to the animals all these years and the animals have been his first consideration.

That devotion made life tough for Sigrid and their family. On his sister Mary's wedding day, Mary waited in her bridal gown while David skinned rabbits to feed his beloved pet owls and eagles before driving her to the church to give her away.

The thylacine incident occurred in 1933 when Fleay travelled from his home in Victoria to Tasmania to submit his application for the position of director of the Tasmanian Museum. He was unsuccessful (at twenty-six he was considered too young), but he took the opportunity to visit the city's zoo, where he was granted access to the enclosure of the zoo's – and, as it turned out, the world's – last captive thylacine, a creature he considered one of the animal wonders of the world. Fleay's cumbersome camera equipment required putting his head under a black cloth, a position that left him vulnerable to an animal that didn't appreciate its human visitor and delivered a sharp nip on the backside.

He managed to capture several photographs, in incredible sharpness and detail, and film footage of the thylacine yawning and pacing around its cage. If you have seen a video or photo of the last thylacine, chances are it was filmed by Fleay, who clearly didn't harbour any ill will over the injury. He wrote later in a passage that demonstrates the attractive prose, attention to detail and utter devotion to Australia's native fauna that were hallmarks of his entire life:

Still wearing the springer snare brand around the right hind leg, this long, lean, softly padding animal had an ethereal appearance. He regarded me incuriously, as ceaselessly on the move, he halted every now and then to indulge in the widest yawns I'd ever seen. The distinctive, darker cross-bands decorating mid-back to tail base stood out prominently against the olive-brown coat colour. How I longed to get this evidently hungry animal across Bass Strait for specialised housing and feeding. However in those far-off days a mere struggling teacher had no political pull, and the urgency of the species mattered to no one. At all events the animal's ambition for a change of diet caused him to bite my rump as I knelt while endeavouring to follow every movement in the focusing hood of a Graflex camera.

Fleay reluctantly returned home without the job or the thylacine, and he was devastated when he learned of its death in 1936. He was back in Tasmania nine years later in the hope of saving the species by capturing a breeding pair on an expedition backed by Sir Keith Murdoch, founder of the Australian newspaper empire. Fleay set off with four companions in November 1945 and headed into the 'the wilderness of the silent south-west, where the jagged mountains reared their bare, stony tops in awe-inspiring grandeur' without most of their equipment, which had failed to arrive on time.

During two months in the wild Fleay picked up a number of animals for his growing collection, including four black tiger snakes and a Tasmanian devil with four babies – but no thylacine. But he wasn't giving up yet. The next month he returned with his family and they set up camp beside the Collingwood River. Sigrid made the campsite comfortable, including creating a makeshift refrigerator in a butter box tied to a rock in the icy stream. This worked a treat until there was a flash flood that washed out the camp and, worse, as daughter Rosemary recalled: 'Surging brown foam-flecked waters, the colour of tea, were roaring past our camp, [and] sometime during that wild night our father's scant supply of beer, butter, meat and fishing lines headed seawards at a great rate, lost and gone forever.'

Fleay brought wire traps that unfolded to form a large cage that he placed out at night, with trails of bacon leading from the bush to a hinged trapdoor. The traps were successful in catching wallabies, Tasmanian devils and even domestic cats (quolls ate much of the bacon but were smart enough not to enter the cage), but the closest he came to snaring a thylacine was some tufts of fur on the trap. 'That was definitely the first time I ever heard him swear,' his daughter wrote. 'He had every intention of mounting a further expedition the following year hoping for better luck then, but to his everlasting sorrow this anticipated expedition was never to be undertaken.'

Out of time before winter arrived, the family packed up camp and boarded the retired troopship *Taroona* for the return journey across Bass Strait with a small menagerie including three wallabies, ten pademelons, three ringtail possums, eleven quolls, one bettong, one echidna, three owls, ten tiger snakes and eleven Tasmanian devils, stored in tea chests. Two of the devils escaped and were found in the ship's galley and under a lifeboat, respectively.

David Fleay's Tasmanian tiger tales are just a small chapter of a remarkable seventy-year career. His résumé includes a host of scientific discoveries and achievements, including determining that the

Tasmanian wedge-tailed eagle is a distinct species from its mainland cousin (it was named *Aquila audax fleayi* in his honour) and breeding the platypus in captivity for the first time – a feat that created worldwide headlines and would not be replicated for another fifty-five years. He also kept a pet boa constrictor named Boris under his house. (Boris was a gift from the director of the Taronga Park Zoo on Fleay's seventieth birthday.)

Fleay was unusually tall and angular and rarely seen without his business shirt, tie, braces, brown sports coat, narrow-brimmed Trilby hat and two pairs of woollen socks. He was quietly spoken but incredibly determined, inquisitive, with a firm handshake and an all-consuming dedication to the study and preservation of Australia's native fauna. Several people close to Fleay described him as having a unique ability to understand animals – to *think like a platypus* (among other creatures).

Fleay was born on 6 January 1907. His mother, Maude, was a gifted artist who loved painting the bush and studied under famed impressionist Frederick McCubbin. His father, Harry, was a chemist whose Ballarat shop sold concoctions such as 'Cobbs Corn Cure' and 'Fleay's Influenza Mixture', which was reportedly so potent it caused a drop in sales at a nearby pub. Fleay's love of animals was evidently deeply ingrained from the start – as soon as he could crawl, he collected centipedes and other insects. At eighteen months he was diagnosed with polio, an ailment he overcame after seven years of tender care from his mother.

David's wildlife collecting escalated as a teenager, filling the house and backyard with wild animals from the surrounding district, including a variety of reptiles, a powerful owl he named Ferox that he rescued from near-death, a feathertail glider named Erastus that arrived in the mail, posted in a cotton wool-lined matchbox by an uncle, a black swan that he hatched at home after saving an egg from rising floodwaters, and a particularly cantankerous wombat that knocked over most of the furniture and ate a wicker basket full of potatoes, basket and all. His father gave strict instructions to David not to bring snakes home, a rule the family believed he adhered to until they read an article he wrote years later disclosing there was a small colony in the roof.

Fleay was driven by an insatiable curiosity. 'As a boy wrapped in the delights of the bushland, I revelled in its untainted scented freshness, its mystery, vast extent and variety. I wondered long about the fascinating creatures that were its inhabitants,' he wrote in 1980. Visiting zoos and museums, he found information on the animals he saw – living or stuffed – to be almost non-existent, especially when it came to their internal motivations. This was a subject of endless fascination for him, although he knew that 'anyone who took a keen interest in the great outdoors (beyond money-making, of course) was considered more than a trifle round the bend'.

Fleay attended Ballarat Grammar, where he founded a field naturalists' club and established a sanctuary for birds, animals and insects, then moved to Melbourne in 1927, taking his menagerie with him, including Ferox, a mother and baby wombat, and a collection of tiger snakes fed with rats eagerly collected by fellow students at Melbourne University and Melbourne Teachers College, where a professor told him there was no future in studying native animals.

While dissecting a sheep's stomach, he met a New Zealand–born student named Mary Sigrid Collie, who reacted positively to an invitation to visit the basalt plains west of Melbourne to collect venomous snakes, a bold proposal as first dates go. The courtship was evidently successful; Fleay graduated with a science degree in 1931 and married Sigrid, as she was known, that December. The couple made their home in the Melbourne suburb of Hawthorn, with a large yard filled with cages and enclosures for a small private zoo comprising more than fifty different critters, including an assortment of possums, quolls, lizards, one tiger snake, several birds of prey (including Ferox), two dogs, one rabbit and an unspecified number of caterpillars.

Fleay worked briefly as a teacher at Toorak Central School, applying unsuccessfully for the Tasmanian Museum post but achieving a better result when he applied for the position of director of the new Australian section of the Melbourne Zoo. The zoo was battling financially and gave Fleay complete autonomy, allowing him to take a new direction with his exhibits. Popular attractions at the zoo in the 1920s included riding an elephant, throwing peanuts to the bears and watching Mollie the orangutan smoke a cigarette, but Fleay directed construction of enclosures that reflected the animals' natural habitats, including snake and lizard pits, a large aviary for wedge-tailed eagles and a penguin pool. His new platypusary received its first occupant in 1934, a male that Fleay named Binghi, and he was joined the next year by a young female.

One platypus can eat up to 1000 worms a day (plus assorted yabbies and grubs), an issue that was to dog Fleay on all his major undertakings over the next three decades. Feeding all his animals what they eat in the wild created a problem, at least in the mind of the zoo board, which considered it an unnecessary expense. Fleay's primary motivation was

David Fleay with a platypus in 1951. (Gordon F. De Lisle; Mitchell Library,
State Library of NSW)

always to keep the animals in a state as close as possible to how they
would live naturally while allowing them to be studied for scientific
research. His approach was evidently appreciated by zoo patrons:
attendance increased despite the Great Depression. But in what would
not be his last run-in with authorities, Fleay was forced to resign in 1937
after refusing bizarre directives, including feeding apples to Tasmanian
devils and horse meat to insect-eating tawny frogmouths.

Fortunately, another animal park was looking for a director.
Seventeen years earlier a flame-haired Melbourne doctor and philan-
thropist named Colin MacKenzie had been granted about thirty-two
hectares of bushland by the state government to conduct anatomical
research on native fauna. He fenced it off and built animal pens and

a house for a curator, and in 1934 the Sir Colin MacKenzie Sanctuary officially opened to the public. Three years later the sanctuary needed an enthusiastic and talented curator to oversee and enlarge its collection. David and Sigrid Fleay, their two young children and an extensive collection of native animals were moving to Healesville.

In fourteen years in Healesville, Fleay transformed the sanctuary into one of Australia's leading zoos, although a 1940 guidebook explained it was not intended as a tourist attraction: 'Primarily the aim is the preservation of all native animals quartered in the sanctuary and the breeding of others. With Mr Fleay the care and welfare of the animals and birds comes first. They are his personal friends.' He gained international renown and achieved many of his most notable achievements among the beautiful ferns and mountain ash forests east of Melbourne, many of them surrounding an animal with which he had a special affinity – the platypus. Fleay's collection instantly expanded the sanctuary, and the next year it expanded by one more after Fleay rescued a nine-inch-long baby platypus from a nearby road. The monotreme was christened Jill and she became the star of a daily platypus show that delighted thousands of visitors.

Fleay worked tirelessly seven days a week at the sanctuary, his only breaks coming on collecting trips in his Chevrolet, often to the Murray River region. On one occasion he returned to a boarding house where he was staying with his family with twenty-five tiger snakes, which then escaped during the night. Twelve were recovered. The Fleays were away on another expedition in 1939 when reports reached them of a ferocious bushfire tearing through the forest near the sanctuary, prompting an all-night dash across the state. The Black Friday fires razed more than 1.5 million hectares, killed seventy-one people, wiped out several towns including nearby Narbethong and Woods Point, and ash fell as far away as New Zealand – but Fleay's animals escaped the inferno. Inside the sanctuary gates, at least.

Fleay explored the surrounding country two days later to learn how the wild native animals had fared:

> Koalas and possum-gliders, of course, had no chance ... wallabies perished in numbers but many saved themselves in creeks only to have their feet hopelessly burned on hidden glowing embers ... Our sanctuary, by dint of hard days and nights of unceasing vigilance, had been spared the fire, so we gathered up these victims and liberated them among our own untouched forest. Some recovered – others did not.

One bright spot among the ashes was when Fleay's torch fell on a young male platypus swimming in an almost dried-up Badger Creek. Fleay picked the animal up by the tail and 'Jack' joined Jill in the sanctuary's platypusary. The pair had been at the sanctuary for five years when Jill began scooping up floating leaves in her bill, tucking them under her tail and carrying them to a long burrow she had excavated in a mound of earth. This captivated Fleay, who spent as much time as he could studying the nesting behaviour of an animal that remained a mystery in many respects – no one knew how long platypus eggs took to hatch or how quickly the young grew.

Fleay's curiosity got the better of him on 2 January 1944 and, as *The Argus* reported three days later, 'after a period of careful digging he received one of the most triumphant surprises of his life ... when he found a very fat bundle covered with short, satiny fur and with its eyes still closed'. The discovery of a plump nine-week-old platypus was indeed a pioneering moment – 'world history', as the paper declared – but Jill wasn't happy about it and she started destroying her nest in an effort to block out the sunlight. 'Alas,' Fleay wrote in his 1980 book *Paradoxical Platypus*, 'it seemed we had wrecked all chance of complete success by unwittingly breaking in too soon!'

Against Jill's objections, Fleay placed the baby back in the nest, inserted a hollow log to replace the section of collapsed tunnel, covered the burrow with earth and hoped for the best. After a couple of days Jill resumed her normal nesting duties and mother, father and their chubby and ridiculously cute daughter, Corrie – named for the old Coranderrk Aboriginal Reservation, which included the land where the sanctuary now stood[16] – were introduced to the public in March 1944. The event made global headlines, featuring on the front page of the *Illustrated London News*. As Fleay's daughter Rosemary recalled: 'the whole world had caught platypus fever.'

It was the height of World War II and the world needed a pick-me-up. After visiting the famous family, the US Ambassador to Australia, Nelson Trusler Johnson, wrote to Fleay: 'I wish there was some way in which I could communicate to Mrs Platypus our appreciation of the very fine exhibition which she gave us on our visit. She restored my confidence in the world.' London's *Daily Telegraph* took a different tack, clearly irked that the news was upstaging the

---

16 The reservation was the site of one of Australia's first land rights battles, led by Wurundjeri elder William Barak, known as the 'last king of the Yarra tribes', who led a march into Melbourne in the 1870s to oppose a plan to sell off the land for development. The protest, known as the Coranderrk rebellion, was successful, but the population declined as young residents were absorbed into European society, and the reserve closed in 1923.

heroic British men on the battlefield. The paper published a rhyme that concluded:

> *Shush, little mammal, you're not all that smart.*
> *This is no time to expect a star part,*
> *Sleep – and remove that smirk off your bill*
> *We are making more history than you ever will.*

The rhymester may have been right, but Jack and Jill still resonated fifty years later. In 1994 commemorative events were staged to mark the anniversary of the landmark event and Australia Post issued a special stamp. Despite repeated attempts by Fleay and others, platypuses weren't bred in captivity again until 1999.

The extreme difficulty in establishing and maintaining a captive breeding population explains why you won't find a platypus in a zoo anywhere outside Australia. Not that there haven't been attempts. The first platypus to reach a foreign shore alive was transported by animal dealer Ellis Joseph to New York's Bronx Zoo in 1922, a story described in Chapter 2. Joseph sailed from Australia with five platypuses, and four died en route. The survivor died forty-nine days later. When 'platypus fever' hit two decades later, the zoo decided to try again, asking Fleay to capture three platypuses and transport them to New York. Fleay threw himself into the task with characteristic dedication, catching nineteen platypuses in the creeks around Healesville, from which he selected the three best suited, in his expert judgement, to international travel: two females he christened Betty and Penelope, and a placid male named Cecil. Fleay planned the trip meticulously, packing 7000 frozen yabbies, 136,000 frozen worms, 22,000 live grubs, 23,000 live earthworms, forty-five live frogs and a supply of duck and hen eggs to make a 'platypus custard' on the *Pioneer Glen*. But he feared the worst when the ship sailed into a storm soon after leaving Brisbane and the animals refused to eat. 'It was a grave and anxious time,' Fleay wrote. 'The chances of getting the animals safely to New York seemed slight and receded with every hour. Should they die, following all the publicity, then only life as a refugee in Rio de Janeiro remained for me.'

Fortunately, everyone survived the storm and the platypuses were revived with fresh earthworms hoisted aboard in kerosene tins at Pitcairn Island, although Cecil gave more cause for concern when he reacted badly to higher temperatures as the ship crossed the equator and passed through the Panama Canal. Blocks of ice were placed in the platypusary and Fleay and his precious cargo sailed into Boston harbour after a month at sea. They were greeted with a limousine which ferried them to New York – Cecil, Betty and Penelope travelling in straw-lined boxes. The platypuses became instant celebrities, with their arrival reported in publications including the *New York Times*, the *Saturday Evening Post* and *Time* and *Life* magazines. Newsreels hailed the arrival of 'one of nature's nervous mistakes'.

After the platypuses' triumphant unveiling, David and Sigrid Fleay sailed home with exotic gifts including rattlesnakes, raccoons, six young alligators, a pair of ocelots and a skunk. It must have made for an interesting journey for the boat's other passengers: forty-seven US soldiers with their Australian war brides, forty refugees from Poland and Hungary, and the cast of the Broadway musical *Stardusters*. Sadly, Betty fell ill and died in 1948, but Cecil and Penelope adapted to their new home and provided years of entertainment to thousands of visitors. There were even hopes they might breed. But one day in 1957, a zookeeper reported that Penelope was missing. She had apparently slithered out from under her enclosure's roof and, despite a week-long search, was never found. Cecil died two months later.

The following spring, the zoo asked for three replacement platypuses, hoping to take advantage of advances in air travel. This was unquestionably faster, but the new route presented its own problems. Fleay built a miniature platypusary for the flight and strapped it to a rubber cushion in the cargo hold. The plane took off from Sydney in June 1958. Fleay checked on his charges during stops in Fiji and Canton Island and in between after being granted permission by the captain to visit the cargo hold mid-flight: 'They did warn me not to touch a certain lever. If I tripped it, they said the escape hatch would open and the contents of the hold, including me and the platypuses, would pop out of the pressurised plane like a cork from a champagne bottle.' He managed to avoid that disaster, but more drama awaited at the next stop, in Honolulu, where quarantine authorities wanted to remove and destroy the bedding and soil from the platypusary. After a string of frantic diplomatic cables, a compromise was reached – 10,000 Australian worms were airmailed to Hawaii and packed into fresh American soil before another flight to Los Angeles.

The original plan was to make the final leg of the journey from California to New York in a freight plane, but Fleay successfully pleaded with a United Airlines captain to allow him to transfer to a passenger airliner instead, with the Australian naturalist sitting in the rear of the cabin with a box containing Paul, the weakest of his three platypuses. When the plane landed, 'I still had three live duckbills but only by the skin of my teeth'. Recounting the episode in his 1960 book *Living with Animals*, Fleay wrote that 'Paul, I think, would have died if the trip had lasted two more hours'. Unfortunately, despite the careful attention of devoted keeper Jo Neglia, all three platypuses perished within the year. The USA did not have a platypus again for sixty-one years, until in 2019 a pair was donated to the San Diego Zoo by the Australian government. They are the only platypuses outside Australia.

Fleay was a key player in another international platypus trip that only came to light decades later. In early 1943, World War II raged across multiple theatres. Hitler's army had just suffered a historic defeat at Stalingrad, but U-boats still prowled the Atlantic and Britain's resources were stretched to the limit. So it must have come as a surprise to Australian prime minister John Curtin when a telegram arrived from Winston Churchill requesting six platypuses be sent to Britain forthwith. Conservationist Gerald Durrell described the scheme as 'magnificently idiotic'.

Academics have tried to place this episode in a broader context of empire and international geopolitics, but it seems Churchill just really wanted a platypus (or six of them, to be precise). He had collected exotic animals throughout his life, including black swans, a white kangaroo (a gift from the Livestock Owners Association of Australia), a budgie named Toby, who attended ministerial meetings, and a lion named Rota, which he sensibly kept at London Zoo.

There was one man for the job. In March 1943, government officials knocked on the door of David Fleay, who received 'the shock of a lifetime'. Fleay convinced the powers that be that getting six platypuses to England, and looking after them once they got there, was unrealistic at any time, let alone in the middle of a war. Instead, they agreed to transport one live monotreme – a healthy boy Fleay caught and named Winston. When Australia's foreign minister, Herbert 'Doc' Evatt, met Churchill and US president Franklin D. Roosevelt that May in Washington, he cabled the Commonwealth Director-General of Health: 'Churchill at Washington most anxious that platypus should leave immediately. What is present situation?'

Four months later, Winston boarded the heavily armed MV *Port Phillip*, where he was housed below deck in a wooden platypusary built by Fleay, who stocked the ship with 'enough earthworms, crayfish, mealworms and fresh water to have refuelled Winston on a complete round the world voyage' and delivered detailed instructions for the platypus's care on the long voyage ahead. The ship slipped out of Melbourne in September, crossed the Pacific and passed through the Panama Canal without incident, with Winston 'lively and ready for his food'. A telegram from Australia's Ministry of Information informed Churchill that the platypus was 'on its way to you accompanied by 50,000 specially chosen worms'. It added: 'Now that you have achieved your ambition to possess a platypus, you must decide where you are going to house the little creature. If you decide to keep it near you, you must send your cat Nelson into exile.' A press release was drafted announcing Winston's arrival and asking for worms to be sent from across Britain in jars 'packed in mould or moist tea leaves' to feed the prime minister's new pet.

Sadly, he never made it. Four days from Liverpool, the ship's sonar detected a German submarine, and the captain responded by detonating depth charges. The boat and its crew survived, but there was one extra Australian war casualty: little Winston. 'Tragically, the heavy concussion killed the platypus then and there,' Fleay wrote. 'After all, a small animal equipped with a nerve-packed, super-sensitive bill, able to detect even the delicate movements of a mosquito wriggler on stream bottoms in the dark of night, cannot hope to cope with man-made enormities such as violent explosions.'

News of Winston's demise reached Fleay in November but wasn't reported in the press and remained hidden in Churchill's personal files. The effort may have failed, but the international cooperation required helped repair an Australian–British relationship frayed by Churchill's reluctance to aid Australia's defence from the Japanese threat. Reports differ over what happened to the platypus. Churchill, noting the death was 'a great disappointment to me', wrote to 'Doc' Evatt informing him he had sent the platypus to the Royal College of Surgeons to have it stuffed. Several accounts, including Fleay's, say it was returned to Churchill and became a permanent fixture on his desk. Winston is notably absent from other wartime reports and published photographs but wouldn't have been totally out of place – Churchill's desk at Chartwell featured an assortment of strange items, including a bust of Napoleon and a bronze cast of his mother's hand. This story appears to have been confirmed by Field-Marshal Sir Alan Brooke, wartime chief of the Imperial General Staff, who visited Healesville in 1945 and cuddled two-year-old Corrie. It was his first encounter with a live platypus. His only previous experience with the animal, he told Fleay, was the mounted specimen he had seen on Churchill's desk.

Returning to Healesville from the US after four months' leave in 1947, having delivered the three platypuses to New York and given talks about Australian fauna at zoos across America, Fleay was greeted with acclaim from politicians and the public. The sanctuary board, however, took issue with his newly acquired US animal collection and sacked him without warning, citing the removal of two echidnas without the committee's permission and dubious allegations about the tidiness of the sanctuary. They advertised for a new director, prioritising administrative skills, and asked Fleay how much it would cost to buy his wildlife collection. He wouldn't part with the thirty-five animals, which he considered members of his family. It was a smart decision; within twelve months, five koalas in the sanctuary had died, along with famed platypus mum Jill. Her partner Jack was deemed too difficult to manage and was released into the wild.

This state of affairs prompted a government inquiry and Fleay was reinstated in 1949 as a 'natural history consultant'. He was able to locate and recapture Jack, but his connection to the institution to which he had shown so much devotion had been broken. In January 1952 – two years after he became the first man to milk a taipan in a dramatic confrontation recounted in the previous chapter – he left the sanctuary and started afresh in Queensland, moving north with Sigrid, their two youngest children and an assortment of animals, including a platypus named Teddy. Fleay had found a parcel of land on the southern tip of the Gold Coast, where he could keep and display his animals without interference. Fleay's Fauna Reserve, Australia's largest private animal collection, opened without fanfare on Easter Sunday 1952.

The Fleays operated on a shoestring budget in their early years in Queensland – money was so tight the park could support only one platypus, although Fleay's expertise was called on to rescue several wild platypuses that were washed out to sea in a cyclone. Gradually the park found its feet and Fleay was kept busy running the park, breeding snakes and other animals, travelling, and writing a weekly nature column for Brisbane's *Courier Mail*. During their 1954 Australian tour, Queen Elizabeth II and Prince Phillip spent a day in Brisbane at Government House with the Fleay family and a selection of Australian animals. Teddy the platypus was displayed in the Government House bathtub and a wombat named Winkie chased the young queen around the lawn. Sigrid wrote the next day that Elizabeth 'laughed and laughed at the antics of the playful little wombat and turned her lovely smile on each of us in turn'.

In 1983, aged seventy-six, Fleay wanted to secure the future of his nature reserve and handed it over to the Queensland government. After four years of negotiations and renovations the park reopened in 1987. Sigrid died that year and Fleay passed away at home in 1993, aged eighty-six. He left an enormous legacy, including eight books (four more were published posthumously) and dozens of magazine articles. He founded the Queensland Wildlife Preservation Society, set up two successful wildlife parks, unravelled the mysteries of the koala's diet and bred more than thirty species in captivity for the first time, including platypuses, taipans, koalas and emus. Add to all that his life-saving work on taipan antivenom, which his daughter Rosemary considered her father's 'gift to the nation'. Unlike some other passionate naturalists, Fleay easily navigated the transition from the era dominated by amateur enthusiasts to modern-day professionals, for a simple reason – he was decades ahead of his time. His animals-first approach is now the model for all modern zoos.

The paradox of the platypus begins with its name. For starters, it isn't actually called a platypus, at least in scientific nomenclature. Early colonists used names including duck mole, water mole and duck bill. The first platypus described by Europeans was speared by an Aboriginal man in the Hawkesbury River in 1797, an event witnessed by Governor John Hunter, who drew an illustration titled 'an amphibious animal of the mole kind' in the second edition of David Collins' *An Account of the English Colony of New South Wales*. Collins wrote: 'the most extraordinary circumstance observed in its structure was its having, instead of the mouth of an animal, the upper and lower mandibles of a duck.' When English naturalist George

THE DUCK-BILLED PLATYPUS.
(ORNITHORHYNCHUS ANATINUS.)

The platypus, illustrated in *The Mammals of Australia* by Helena Forde and Harriet Scott, 1869. (Dixson Library, State Library of NSW)

Shaw examined the animal – or at least the dried skin of one – in 1799, he named it *Platypus anatinus*, which means 'flat-footed' and 'bird-like'. But the name 'platypus' was taken – it had been used on a wood-eating weevil five years earlier. As it happened, a German anatomist, Johann Blumenbach, was given a specimen by Joseph Banks and named the curious Australian creature *Ornithorhynchus paradoxus*, which means 'puzzling bird-billed animal'. A compromise, *Ornithorhynchus anatinus* – 'duck-like bird-snout' – was adopted.

Shaw had reason to examine the platypus especially closely, and not just because it was an unknown species from the other side of the world. He didn't want to be embarrassed by a zoological hoax. 'It naturally excites the idea of some deceptive preparation by artificial means,' he wrote. It wasn't an unrealistic concern. Asian traders made a tidy profit selling fakes created by sewing together body parts from different animals to gullible European sailors. The best known today is the Fiji mermaid, a part-monkey, part-fish creature allegedly caught in the Pacific that went on display in London in 1822 and was later exhibited by P.T. Barnum in New York. After 'the most minute and rigid examination' (he reportedly took a pair of scissors to the dried skin to check for stitches), Shaw was convinced the platypus was a real animal. But the question of what kind of animal it was remained an open question.

Organising animals into their correct categories – applying order to nature – was a preoccupation of nineteenth-century zoologists. The platypus presented a major challenge. Shaw classified it as a mammal, but rivals noted that the platypus's genitalia were more like a bird's. Blumenbach believed it was a transitionary creature between mammals and birds, like a bat. Others pointed out its fish-like qualities. French biologist Étienne Geoffroy Saint-Hilaire – founding president of the Paris Acclimatisation Society, whom we encountered several chapters ago – believed it was a new class of vertebrates, creating a cross-channel scientific rivalry with British scientists led by brilliant zoologist Richard Owen. In 1832 Owen published results of his research that showed platypuses produced milk – confirming that they fit somewhere in the mammal family. Saint-Hilaire countered that the milky liquid didn't come out of teats, as it did in all other known mammals, but was excreted through the animal's fur and might be something else. And there was another problem: mammals were supposed to produce live young. Finding out whether platypuses did or not was the mission of one of Australia's most prominent early naturalists.

George Bennett was born in 1804 in Plymouth, England. The son of an organist, he studied medicine and befriended a young Owen, who was then working as an anatomy lecturer, and showed a yearning for adventure from a young age. He embarked on his first international voyage at age fifteen and in 1829 joined a scientific expedition to the Pacific in the role of surgeon-naturalist, returning with a large collection of specimens, including a gibbon from Sumatra and a live pearly nautilus. He also brought with him a six-year-old girl named Elau from Erromanga Island in the New Hebrides (now Vanuatu), whom he claimed to have rescued from cannibalism.[17] Of the trio, the nautilus seems to have generated the most excitement; it was

17   This may have been accurate, since cannibalism was practised on the island
      until well into the twentieth century. The first two Christian missionaries
      dispatched there were promptly killed and eaten. Today, the Tourism
      Vanuatu website includes the helpful information that 'the standard cooking
      time for a human is three to five hours'. Elau lasted a little longer in England,
      dying in 1834.

the only one to rate a mention in his obituary in the *Sydney Evening News* when he passed away, at age ninety, in 1893.

Bennett set sail again in 1832, bound for Sydney, and became one of Australia's most prominent early scientists. His influence is evident from his appearance in multiple chapters in this book – he served as the first secretary and curator of the Australian Museum, was a key supporter of acclimatisation, and acted as an agent for John Gould.[18] Bennett shot a large number of platypuses and also captured some alive, letting one out for a swim with string tied to its leg and keeping a pair in his Sydney home for five weeks, feeding them bread and chopped meat and allowing them to roam free in his bedroom. They didn't live long enough to fulfil Bennett's dream of sending them to England alive, but he sent their preserved bodies, and dozens more, to Owen for examination, although he drew the line at Owen's request to shoot one female platypus every week during the breeding season, fearing the species would become extinct. Another hurdle was finding platypuses at this time – between June and October – which Bennett had attempted for years without success.

He was beaten to it by young Scottish naturalist William Hay Caldwell, who sailed to Australia in 1883 with the mission of solving the 85-year-old riddle of whether the platypus lays eggs (Aboriginal people had told Bennett they did, but he didn't believe them). He headed to north Queensland and set up camp on the banks of the Burnett River near Bundaberg, where he noticed echidnas and platypuses were common, as well as a large Aboriginal community,

---

18   His expert opinion guided Gould, who stated confidently that platypuses don't lay eggs, the biggest mistake in his works on Australian animals.

of which Caldwell later wrote: 'I afterwards found that without the services of these people I should have had little chance of success.'

Inspired by Caldwell's offer of £10 to 'anyone who would show me Ceratodus (lungfish) spawn', local Indigenous men waded through the creek and dug up burrows. They delivered several echidnas to Caldwell, including one with a freshly laid egg in its pouch. Then he hit the jackpot – Caldwell called it 'lucky chance'. A female platypus was shot while laying twin eggs – one had just been laid and one was still inside her body. Even Bennett couldn't argue with that. On 29 August Caldwell rode to a nearby station and wrote a short but historic telegram: 'monotremes oviparous, ovum meroblastic' (rough translation: monotremes lay eggs that are soft like reptile eggs) to Professor Archibald Liversidge at the University of Sydney, who sent it on to the British Association for the Advancement of Science, which, in a stroke of good timing, was meeting in Montreal, Canada. The news 'took the delegates by storm'. Historian and environmental scientist Libby Robin describes it as 'Australia's most significant contribution to Darwinian biology for the century'.

It was appropriate, since the platypus had played a vital but largely underreported role in the works of Darwin himself. During the *Beagle*'s voyage it stopped over in Sydney in 1836, and Darwin ventured west to the Blue Mountains, where he was struck by Australia's peculiar wildlife and took particular interest in the platypus after spotting several in a creek on an evening stroll from the homestead where he was staying on the western side of the mountains. His host, a local superintendent named Andrew Browne, helpfully shot one so Darwin could examine it more closely. Decades before he openly questioned divine creation, the young naturalist was struck by the similarity of the platypus's behaviour to that of water rats in his native England, posing an obvious question: why would an omnipotent God create two different species to fill the same biological niche on two different continents? 'A Disbeliever in everything beyond his own reason might exclaim, "Surely two distinct creators must have been [at] work; their object however has been the same and certainly in each case the end is complete",' Darwin wrote in his diary. 'Would any two workmen ever hit on so beautiful, so simple and yet so artificial a contrivance?' In his seminal works Darwin answered the question: all animals – including humans – were descended from the same evolutionary line and had adapted to their local conditions. He cited the platypus as an example of a species on the evolutionary tree somewhere between reptiles and mammals. Some historians have argued that his visit to the Blue Mountains – and his first encounter with a monotreme – was as significant in the formulation of his theory as his more celebrated visit to the Galapagos Islands a year earlier.

It was another thirty-five years after the publication of *On the Origin of Species* before Caldwell solved the monotreme mystery. Remarkably, it was solved again only days later when German naturalist Dr William Haacke, unaware of Caldwell's landmark discovery, displayed an egg he found in an echidna's pouch at a meeting of the Royal Society of South Australia. Caldwell won the race and international scientific acclaim, but he seemed more concerned with his continuing search for the lungfish (he finally found its eggs a month later).

Caldwell returned to England in 1887 with an extraordinary 1300 pickled echidnas, which he passed on to others to investigate their anatomy.[19] He turned his attention to churning out patents for inventions ranging from improved photographic film to the fuel supply for internal combustion engines and something called 'Torbet Lactic Oats'. Bennett wrote several books, including the voluminous *Gatherings of a Naturalist in Australasia*, ran a thriving medical practice, and was awarded a memorial medal by the Royal Society of New South Wales in 1890 for his contribution to science. He died in Sydney three years later. Four species are named after him, including Bennett's tree kangaroo and Bennett's wallaby.

More than 130 years later, our knowledge of platypuses and their reproduction is almost complete – they live for up to twenty years and females breed almost every year of their lives, laying between one and three eggs at the end of a nesting burrow up to thirty metres long. The eggs hatch after about ten days but the mother stays in the burrow to suckle their young until they emerge, covered in thick fur and ready to swim in the freshwater streams that platypuses call home, from tropical Queensland to Tasmania's icy highlands. Males can travel up to eleven kilometres a night in search of food but the animals spend about seventeen hours a day in their underground burrow – so sightings in the wild are rare, and memorable. The platypus and echidna are definitely members of the mammal family, in their own special category of monotremes. But the word 'almost' is still required because, more than 200 years after Shaw's initial description, no human has actually seen a platypus lay an egg.

---

19   This was still in the age of large-scale slaughter in the name of scientific research. In three months Aboriginal hunters in his employ killed seventy female platypuses in a single pond, so his historic find wasn't entirely down to luck.

* * *

Many of the gaps in our understanding were filled by the original 'platypus man', Henry Burrell. He published the first major work on the platypus – titled *The Platypus* – in 1927 after a lifetime of study, was the first person to keep and observe platypuses in captivity, speculated that the platypus had some kind of 'sixth sense' (electroreception, a platypus talent common in sharks but unique among mammals, was confirmed by scientists in the 1980s) and built the first artificial platypusary, which he used to transport the first platypuses to reach a foreign shore alive. Like David Fleay, he also crossed paths with the thylacine, taking a photograph that is still controversial today. All impressive achievements for a man the 1958 *Australian Encyclopedia* described as a 'comedian-turned-naturalist'.

Burrell was born in 1873 at Rushcutters Bay, in Sydney. Unfortunately, details of his early life are hard to find apart from tantalising lines like this in the *Australian Dictionary of Biography*: 'After slight schooling he led a wandering, knock-about life which included some years as a comedian on the vaudeville stage.' Everyone agrees he was a cheerful, insightful and funny character who settled as a grazier at Manilla, on the Namoi River in northern New South Wales, in 1901. He immediately established a small private zoo, where he kept a collection of marsupials and birds. While collecting water plants for his ducks, Burrell saw his first platypus, and would later confess to having fallen in love at first sight. From this meeting, the idea of establishing a platypus among my pets never left my mind.' Burrell wrote to the Sydney Zoo asking for advice on keeping a platypus in captivity and was told that it couldn't be done. Subsequent events justify adding 'indefatigable' to the list of Burrell's commendable character traits.

In January 1910 he trapped a female platypus in a river and transplanted it into an enclosure he had constructed out of bricks and wire netting, with a concrete pond. He added four more platypuses in short time and made detailed observations about their behaviour and eating habits, running into the same surprising problem that would later bedevil Fleay. He described spending six hours a day looking for food for his new pets, collecting piles of worms, shrimps, beetles and pond snails, 'and this, apparently, was not enough'. A typical platypus weighs between 1 and 1.5 kilograms and can eat more than half its bodyweight in a day. Burrell later described one devouring 300 prawns in one night. Sadly, one by one Burrell's platypuses died until only the original female was left. It escaped by tearing its way through the enclosure's wire netting.

Burrell's response was to improve the enclosure. He created what the zoo director called 'the most amazing contraption that we have ever seen in use in animal transportation' – the world's first portable platypus habitat. It was divided into two parts: a large water tank, connected by a sheet-metal tunnel to a labyrinth of sloping fake burrows. The platypusary allowed Burrell to exhibit a platypus at Taronga Zoo for three months in 1910 (after that its food ran out and it was released into Centennial Park), a landmark achievement that proved the doubters wrong. It also paved the way for the first platypus to land on foreign shores – yes, another delivery to the Bronx Zoo.

The mastermind of the project was animal trader Ellis Joseph, whom we met in Chapter 2. His first attempt, in 1916, failed after a platypus sourced by Burrell died one week after leaving Australian shores. Joseph wouldn't let the idea go and spent the next three years trying to keep a platypus alive in captivity, with numerous animals sacrificed in the trial-and-error process. In 1922 he set sail on the steamer USS *West Henshaw* with five male platypuses in Burrell's platypusary (and an assortment of birds, mammals and reptiles), bound for San Francisco.

One didn't make it past the first stop, at Newcastle. Once at sea, the ship ran into a huge swell, with waves washing over the deck and smashing into the platypus tank, and two more monotremes succumbed days later. A fourth platypus died while the ship was anchored off Honolulu. The last platypus somehow survived the rest of the sea voyage and a train ride across the continent to New York, arriving on 14 July after a journey of 1600 kilometres, in Burrell's words 'both man and animal completely tired out'. The zoo director was more effusive: 'The spell of 10,000 years has been broken. The most wonderful of all living mammals has been carried alive from its insular confines of its too-far-distant native land, and introduced abroad.' The platypus was put on display for one hour a day and survived for forty-nine days, at the time a significant achievement.

Despite his accomplishments, which also included a number of articles detailing his platypus observations, Burrell appears to have been frustrated with a lack of recognition and support in official circles; he complained in his landmark 1927 book about 'the impossibility of obtaining official sanction to work as a private collector' that 'had brought my fieldwork practically to a standstill'. His quest for approval may have landed him in hot water sixty years after his death, when a University of Tasmania researcher named Carol Freeman published an article alleging Burrell had faked a widely used photo of a thylacine with a chicken in its mouth that first appeared in the *Australian Museum Magazine* in 1921.

The background in the image was obviously staged, using hessian, rocks and broken branches to make it look like the thylacine was in the wild when it was in fact in a concrete enclosure, and the photograph was cropped and touched up before publication. But Freeman's conclusion that the animal itself was a stuffed model has been challenged by other experts, who think the photo is of a living thylacine in Hobart's Beaumaris Zoo. Regardless of the life status of the photo subject, the chicken in its mouth was definitely deceased – and may have contributed to the perception of the thylacine as a poultry killer, given the photo's widespread publication. Freeman believes the photo might have been a 'prank' by the former comedian and doesn't think he meant any harm. 'We're immersed in our own little worlds and what interests us and how we see things, not the bigger picture of what might happen. I think Tasmanian farmers and even naturalists bore much more ill intent with the thylacine than Harry Burrell,' she told *Australian Geographic*.

In 1985 researchers confirmed Burrell's 'sixth sense' theory using experiments in which a large perspex screen was suspended in the water attached to a live battery, and the platypus, which keeps its eyes, ears and nasal cavities closed underwater, easily swam around it. Further research revealed an array of 40,000 electroreceptors in the animal's bill that are powerful enough to detect food even if it's buried in the mud on the bottom of a creek (a freshwater shrimp, the platypus's favourite food, generates an electric field by flipping its tail that can be detected by a platypus ten centimetres away), enough, in the words of one researcher, to provide the platypus with 'a three-dimensional view of its electric world'.

The discovery was another showstopping headline for biology generated by the humble platypus. Darwin celebrated the platypus as an evolutionary signpost, a biological leftover from a time when reptiles evolved into mammals more than 200 million years ago. In a letter to eminent geologist Charles Lyell defending his theory, he argued the unknown progenitor of all current mammals was 'more probably more closely related to *Ornithorhynchus* than to any other known form'. Genetic sequencing in 2008 showed that Darwin was right: monotremes were the earliest offshoot of the mammalian family tree; their genes are an amalgam of reptile-like and mammal-like features, making them a vital clue to the evolution of modern mammals. Among other unusual attributes, platypuses have ten sex chromosomes, more than any other mammal (humans make do with two); they don't have stomachs (their gullet leads directly to their intestines); and males have venom genes similar to those found in snakes as well as poisonous spurs, which they use to fight each other during mating season; these induce in any human unlucky enough to be stabbed by one 'a long lasting and excruciating pain that cannot be relieved with conventional painkillers'. Scientists discovered in 2020 that the animal's fur is biofluorescent, giving off a blue-green glow when illuminated by ultraviolet light. Why? No one knows.

But their story is even more impressive, with electrolocation evidence that the platypus has continued to adapt to its specialised environment. Monash University professor Uwe Proske described an animal widely regarded as primitive as instead 'a highly evolved mammal': 'We believe it left the mainstream of mammalian evolution a long time ago, long enough to have evolved a completely new sensory system.'

If you type the word 'platypus' into Google, one of the helpful suggestions under the heading 'people also ask' is 'What even is a platypus?' Australia's leading monotreme authority, Mervyn Griffiths, has a simple answer. The platypus, he declared, is 'the animal of all time'.

6

Tasmanians

TASMANIA IS DIFFERENT.

Separated from the Australian mainland for 12,000 years, its animals and plants have evolved in almost total isolation – which gives us Tasmanian devils, twelve types of birds found nowhere else on Earth (including the green rosella and the scrubtit) and the pandani plant, a primeval-looking heath that grows up to twelve metres tall.

Tasmanians are different, too. The state produced its own unique brand of naturalist who had more in common with America's famed mountain men than the amateur scientists and wildlife pioneers across Bass Strait. In the US, Daniel Boon, Davy Crockett and John 'Grizzly' Adams are folk heroes. Australia has a similar cast of fascinating, wild-bearded but largely unknown characters who deserve their share of the spotlight. They had a wide range of motivations, spanning the spectrum from idealism to self-preservation, and provide a crucial insight into the transformation in Australians' attitudes to our native wildlife. Even if it was often by accident.

The first European arrivals in Tasmania killed large numbers of native animals for food. The Tasmanian emu was hunted to extinction around 1865 and the forester kangaroo, a subspecies of the eastern grey kangaroo, almost followed it into oblivion. In the early years of the colony – then known as Van Diemen's Land – most settlers gathered around Hobart and Launceston and the fertile plains in between, but eventually they were tempted into the wilder parts of the state. Thousands of men ventured beyond their farm gates in the hope of striking it rich; gold, silver, tin, lead, nickel and copper were all found on the island in varying quantities. (This spirit was still alive in the 1950s, when an overzealous state premier offered £1000 for the discovery of uranium; the reward remains unclaimed.)

Many of the prospectors had already tried their luck in gold rushes in Victoria, New South Wales and New Zealand and headed bush during an economic depression in the 1880s, committing themselves to weeks of isolation; 'eking out his food and dragging a wet swag through uncharted forest and buttongrass plains,' a man might 'yet have nothing at all to show for it, or worse, find a promising deposit only to have someone else take the credit for it', as C.J. Binks sums it up in his book *Pioneers of Tasmania's West Coast*.

Other challenges included mine shafts collapsing, creeks flood-
ing, or getting lost in the bush. Miners were in constant danger of
being hit by falling objects or crushed by trolleys full of rocks, or
contracting miner's lung, a grim sickness caused by constantly inhaling mine dust and tiny, sharp fragments of grit. The improvised use
of dynamite presented obvious hazards, and one prospector was
blinded after a sharp twig pierced his eyeball. It was hard work.

When native wildlife appears in prospectors' diaries it is almost
always in the context of a hot meal, but some pioneers saw more
value in the plants and animals they encountered.

Tasmanian bushwalkers huddled around camp stoves still talk in
reverential tones about the 'Prince of Rasselas', a legendary bushman
renowned in the 1940s and '50s for his generosity, imposing stature and
hearty laugh. In one version of the tale he was an illegitimate member
of the British royal family who was paid to live in solitude at the end
of the world. The truth is less exotic but scarcely less remarkable.

Ernie Bond was born in Hobart in 1891, the son of businessman
and politician Frank Bond and his wife, Sarah Emma Cowburn.
Ernie followed the rush of miners to the remote south-west after
osmiridium was discovered in creeks in the Adams Valley in 1924. The
naturally occurring alloy was prized as a key ingredient in fountain-
pen nibs and electric-light filaments; it was also used by police to
record fingerprints and by the military to create poisonous gases.
In the mid-1920s it was worth £30 per ounce – about seven times
the value of gold. Miners called it 'osie' or, less imaginatively, 'metal'.

The town of Adamsfield was hastily established and at its
height had a population of more than 1000, three grocery stores, a
bakery, butcher, bush hospital, police station, pub/billiards hall and

a 'gumboot smith's emporium' (a boot repairer and general trader). Getting there involved a 35-kilometre hike from the township of Fitzgerald (near present-day Maydena), with an overnight stop at the Florentine River. Supplies could be transported by pack teams for fourpence per pound and enterprising locals carried huge loads on their backs for one shilling per pound (about twenty cents per kilogram). Bushman and part-time policeman Arthur Fleming once reportedly carried a 200-pound (90-kilogram) pack from the Florentine Crossing to Adamsfield without a break for an unspecified wager.

Ernie Bond followed the Sawback Track to Adamsfield in 1927, fell in love with the magnificent wild scenery and decided to build a home in the nearby glacial valley known as the Vale of Rasselas at

Ernie Bond on the Rasselas Track. (Libraries Tasmania)

the foot of the snow-capped Denison Range. A three-room residence he called Gordon Vale was erected in two months using wood split mostly from one huge swamp gum. He established an extensive fruit and vegetable garden, baked his own bread and washed it down with potent home-made honey mead. Bond ran a successful business, employing up to six staff, bottling raspberries, strawberries, gooseberries and blackcurrants and carrying them over a ridge to the town.

Bond became an expert on the local birds and animals, including kangaroos, thylacines, quolls, platypuses and Tasmanian devils. He recorded their habits and supplied specimens to the Tasmanian Museum in Hobart for study. He wrote in his diary that he had been enlisted to 'catch and preserve devils, tiger cats, tigers and other animals of interest for scientific research work', storing specimens in a 44-gallon drum.

Adamsfield was all but abandoned after the onset of World War II. Bond's employees left, and for the next eighteen years his only company was his dog and visiting trappers and bushwalkers. Intrepid Tasmanian walker Keith Lancaster recorded a visit to 'the hermit of Gordon Vale' in 1947 after a two-day trek:

> Any doubts as to the outcome of my intrusion were soon dispelled as this hefty, bearded six-footer welcomed me inside and poured forth his unstinted hospitality. Imagine my delight at being pressed to the table for the evening meal in company with his other guests, and how I responded to the tasty mutton and vegetables he packed before me. But this excellent first course paled into insignificance when the strawberries and cream were produced and each allotted

a huge dinner-plate full! And then came the custard and jellies, a magnificent repast, the like of which one can only dream about whilst out on mountain excursions. Sensing my delight and amazement at the excellence of the fare, Ern Bond's grey eyes twinkled and his face wreathed under the pointed beard as he remarked, 'Yes, we do ourselves fairly well here.'

In 1953, an article in *Wild Life* magazine reported that Bond's visitors 'came at first from the Hobart Walking Club and then later, as his fame spread, from all over the Commonwealth'.

By the early 1950s, however, the bridge over the Florentine had burnt down, making Adamsfield even more remote, and Bond's health was failing. He returned to Hobart in 1952, leaving Gordon Vale to the Hobart and Launceston bushwalking clubs. He sold fruit at roadside stalls for several years and died in 1962, aged seventy.

There was another bizarre chapter in the Gordon Vale story. During the Cold War, a reclusive Utah millionaire named Martin Polin identified Tasmania as the best spot on the planet to survive the apparently inevitable nuclear holocaust. He bought twenty-three properties in remote parts of the state, including Gordon Vale and a site on the central plateau, where he built a concrete bunker and stacked it with supplies. After Polin's death in 2007, Gordon Vale was put on the open market and purchased by the Tasmanian Land Conservancy. It is classified by the Tasmanian government as a historical archaeological site and in 2013 was included in the Tasmanian Wilderness World Heritage Area. Ernie Bond's huts have been almost completely reclaimed by nature, with some fence posts and oddly out-of-place European plants the only evidence this was once home to a prince.

* * *

Other prospectors developed an affinity for the wildlife they lived with beyond the frontier. Bob Warne, who struck gold at Reward Creek, about 50 kilometres south of Queenstown, in 1935, wrote fourteen years later about quitting the goldfield and burning his hut to the ground so it wouldn't be used by snarers: 'those animals in there are my friends ... perhaps in the years to come an old Black Jay may eye the spot wistfully, and remember a man who lived there and fed him bread and honey.'

Precious metals also lured the legendary Deny King into the wild south-west in the 1930s, but there is much more to the story of Tasmania's greatest bushman and self-taught naturalist. Charles Denison King was born in 1909 at Huonville in the south-east of the island. When King was seven the family moved to an isolated property in the Weld Valley, where his mother, Olive, fostered her children's sense of wonder and Deny developed a love for nature and bushcraft that would define his life. He showed a passion for birds from an early age, collecting grubs to feed the local currawongs and constructing wings in failed attempts to join them in flight. He was enlisted as a collector for the Tasmanian Museum and embarked on long trips into the bush, regularly staying out overnight with no tent, sleeping bag or compass – but he always found his way home. He visited Lake Pedder, a stunningly beautiful and remote lake ringed on its eastern shore by a white quartzite beach, collecting plants and insects. His specimens became even more important when the lake was flooded in 1972 as part of a gigantic and unnecessary hydro-electric development.

As a teenager, Deny accompanied his father on prospecting trips and in 1934 they moved to Cox Bight, near Port Davey in Tasmania's south-west, where they mined for tin using picks, shovels and occasionally gelignite. It was one of the most isolated outposts in the world, only accessible by boat or a week-long walk, and it became Deny King's home for more than fifty years. He had a five-year break during World War II, when he served in the Middle East and New Guinea, building roads, bridges and airstrips – skills that would prove useful on his return. In New Guinea, King recorded every new species he came across, including crocodiles, turtles and giant tropical butterflies.

On his return to Australia in 1945, Deny broke his leg during a bridge-building demonstration. It proved a life-changing moment: at Toowoomba Army Hospital he met a young, dark-haired Red Cross officer who became the love of his life. Margaret Cadell didn't immediately reciprocate Deny's affection, but three years of long-distance courtship won her over. At one point Margaret agreed to visit Tasmania for a holiday and Deny was so determined to be in Hobart to meet her that he walked eighty kilometres in thirty hours, swimming across New River Lagoon and crossing the forbidding Ironbound Range with his suit in his backpack and a billy can around his neck. They made the return journey by boat; Margaret was horribly seasick, but on arriving at Port Davey there was a hot bath waiting for her. King's biographer Christobel Mattingley writes that: 'on retiring to her sleeping bag, Margaret discovered more obvious evidence of Deny's thoughtfulness. He had warmed it with a hot brick carefully wrapped in newspaper.'

King had built his home on the banks of Moth Creek and fitted it out with homemade furniture. He grew potatoes, cabbages, carrots and beans, plus a selection of fruit trees and a flourishing rhubarb patch. Birds were welcomed into the house, where they fed on their own block of cheese. Pygmy possums slept in the knife drawer, and wombats, wallabies and pademelons were regular visitors to the garden (spotted-tail quolls were less welcome, due to their habit of stealing Deny's socks). The scenery was incredible – a harbour backed by craggy mountains. How could Margaret say no? In 1949 the couple were married in St David's Cathedral in Hobart. They sailed to Port Davey that evening.

King was quietly spoken, immensely strong and renowned for his humour and remarkable work ethic. Twice a year he sailed to Hobart, a 23-hour trip along one of the most treacherous stretches of coastline in the world, and returned with supplies for the mine and the family home. In 1955 he created a gravel airstrip – a colossal task for one man – and the first plane landed two years later.[20] He built two huts to accommodate tourists and bushwalkers and ferried visitors to the start of Tasmania's iconic walking trails – often sending them off with a hot loaf of freshly baked bread.

Scientists were also regular visitors and King became an important source of knowledge of south-west Tasmania's unique plants and animals. He found a previously undescribed species of freshwater crayfish in his mine in 1954 and a type of sandfly never previously recorded in Tasmania; he collected moths, snails, limpets and barnacles

---

20 The strip is still used for scenic flights, and the writer can attest that it is home to possibly the most pungent toilet in Tasmania.

for museums in Tasmania and Victoria. In a channel he spotted deep-sea whiptails, an intensely ugly fish that experts said could only survive at least one kilometre below the surface; it turns out the high tannin content at Port Davey drastically cuts light levels, allowing deep-sea species to survive in shallow water.

King also conducted rigorous fieldwork, observing birds, marsupials and invertebrates and contributing substantially to scientific understanding of bush rats, pygmy possums and the other creatures that shared his house. He made an even more significant contribution to the field of botany. He accompanied visiting specialists on collecting trips and discovered several species new to science.

King supplied daily information to the Bureau of Meteorology and was appointed fire warden for the far south-west. The Kings were foundation members of the South-West Committee, which pushed for a national park to protect the south-west corner of the state. A renowned animal lover, King hated having to snare animals for food and would even stop to move worms out the way when ploughing potatoes. He once brought a sick possum inside and placed it on warm bricks to recover.

But birds remained his favourite. King could identify the calls of dozens of birds, knew how many of each species lived at Port Davey, where they nested, what they ate (not just cheese) and when they migrated. His meticulous diary entries recorded the plight of the critically endangered orange-bellied parrot, a small, strikingly coloured bird that winters in coastal Victoria and South Australia and flies to Tasmania each summer to breed. It is considered one of the world's most endangered species; in 2016 there were just seventeen living in the wild, five years later seventy were counted at Port Davey thanks to conservation efforts that King started.

When Margaret died of cancer in 1967, a little owl kept King company, sleeping on a post beside him all day in the garden. (King wrote in his diary: 'I feel as though half the world has fallen away.')

In 1980, renowned photographer and film-maker Lord Snowdon visited to take photos for his book *Tasmania Essay*. According to the book:

> Snowdon thought the whole trip was worthwhile to meet Deny King. The photographer was greatly moved by this man who lived in the rugged south, in an environment of self-sufficiency which could hardly be imagined in a city. Living there in isolation, Deny King has a certain regal dignity about him, moving, sitting, standing in his formidable kingdom.

King was appointed to the Order of Australia in 1975 and in 1990 became the first person to receive the Governor's Commendation for his 'outstanding efforts over many years in preserving and sharing the unique environment of Port Davey with all Tasmanians and those who appreciate nature's treasures'. He retired from tin mining in 1985 and died of a heart attack in Hobart in 1991. His ashes were scattered at Port Davey.

* * *

Tasmania's furry inhabitants powered one of colonial Australia's booming industries. Wallabies and pademelons were slaughtered in their thousands to make shoes; possums were turned into rugs and clothing; wombat fur was prized for rugs used in carriages that trundled down London streets. Koala skins from the mainland lined coats and hats. Other animal skins were tanned and turned into pouches and gloves. Quolls, Tasmanian devils and even platypuses didn't escape the hunters' traps.

By the 1850s Tasmanian skins had a reputation as the best in Australia. Over the course of the nineteenth century, the global market exploded, as an emerging middle class suddenly had the means to dress like the wealthy. An advertisement for a public fur auction in St Louis, Missouri, in 1919 listed 26,000 wallaby skins, 6200 wombats, 50,000 ringtail possums and 500,000 Australian rabbit skins (other interesting furs for sale included 300 mountain lions, 44,000 house cats and twenty-nine polar bears).

The hunters who supplied these skins mostly lived on farms or in small towns bordering Tasmania's central plateau and headed into the bush to collect furs during the hunting season, which lasted for three or four months each winter. They built huts deep in the bush with whatever materials were on hand, leaving their wives to keep the farms running and raise children. Tasmanian winters bring biting frosts, storms and heavy snowfalls; some hunters fashioned snowshoes by nailing planks of wood to their boots. *The Mercury* reported on a hunting party stranded in the bush for a full hunting season: 'They endured great hardships … and they lived like savages in the hope of making a good return.' It was hardly an isolated case. But hunting could be very lucrative: a good season could deliver the equivalent of two years' normal wages.

In 1928 a large area of Tasmania's north-west, stretching from Cradle Mountain to Lake St Clair, was declared a reserve under the *Animals and Birds Protection Act*, making hunting illegal at any time of year. The market for skins collapsed in the 1950s with the availability of cheaper fabrics, and trapping and snaring animals was eventually banned across Tasmania in 1984. One can only guess how many animals died before this; in the decade after World War I, more than five million skins were sold in Tasmania, and the 1931 hunting season alone was worth an estimated £250,000 to the state economy.

This wholesale destruction wasn't restricted to Tasmania. In Queensland, a bounty system resulted in the deaths of more than 27 million animals between 1877 and 1930 (the legislation establishing it was called, appropriately, the Marsupial Destruction Act). One MP told the Legislative Assembly in November 1876 that 'the marsupial pest has become an evil of such magnitude, in several districts of the colony, as to demand the immediate and earnest attention of the government'. Bounties were paid for kangaroos, wallabies, bandicoots and kangaroo rats, as well as for dingoes and foxes. In New South Wales, bounties were paid for 21 million kangaroos and three million smaller marsupials over twenty years.

Meanwhile, according to the Australian Koala Foundation, more than eight million koalas were killed for the fur trade between 1888 and 1927, with pelts shipped to London, the US and Canada. There are about 40,000 wild koalas in Australia today. Along the coast and on offshore islands, seals were killed in their tens of thousands for skins and oil. In 1804, at the peak of the plunder, 107,591 seals were killed in and around Bass Strait, valued at a reported £303,046, making them Australia's first export commodity. Agricultural exports would not reach the same value for another twenty years.

One surprising result of this destructive industry was that skills gained from snaring the local wildlife were, it turns out, well suited to another enterprise that would also have a great impact on Tasmania's wild areas – tourism. As interest in visiting the wilderness for recreation grew (the Hobart Walking Club was founded in 1929), there was an increasing demand for men with knowledge of the bush to guide walking parties.

Paddy Hartnett was one of them, a brilliant hunter and incurable alcoholic who sought solitude hunting in the bush, sometimes for months at a time. He designed and built Du Cane Hut, the oldest standing shelter in the Cradle Mountain–Lake St Clair National Park, and is memorialised in Hartnett Falls and a striking pile of rocks known as Paddy's Nut.

One of fourteen children, Hartnett was born in 1876 at Quamby Brook, near Deloraine in northern Tasmania. As a young man he was comfortable wandering in the bush and tried his hand at wood-chopping, prospecting and hunting. In 1910, while visiting the wild Du Cane Range on a prospecting trip, the tourism potential of the area occurred to him. Within months he had identified a site at the foot of Falling Mountain and started building Du Cane Hut. He was soon supplementing his hunting income by working as a bush guide, leading parties of visitors on packhorses to experience the area's wild splendour. Highlights included Lake Windermere, Mount Ossa (Tasmania's highest peak) and Barn Bluff.

Hartnett became renowned for his bushcraft and his odd habits. One freezing night he built a big fire, then lay down on the coals, put a bag over his head and went to sleep. He was an amateur scientist, acquiring a passable knowledge of geology and sending small marsupials and frogs to the United States in kerosene tins. Between bushwalks he continued hunting and occasionally prospecting, while his wife, Lucy, ran the business side of the operation. She joined him in the wild for two years from 1923, bringing their seven-year-old son with her and making an 80-kilometre journey by foot to three of Paddy's four camps (Pelion East, Du Cane and Kia Ora – names familiar to Overland Track hikers).

Sadly, Hartnett turned more and more to alcohol. He was eventually admitted to the Royal Derwent Mental Diseases Hospital, where his doctors noted that he spoke to '"angels" … for hours on end' and thought that birds were telling him to go to New Zealand. He was discharged in 1930 but continued to struggle, although records show he still made prospecting trips to the west. He died of cancer in 1944. Despite the sad end to his life, Hartnett left a significant legacy. He was a pioneer of nature tourism in Tasmania and was the first to build visitor accommodation in the Cradle Mountain area. The section of the Overland Track from Pelion Plain to Lake St Clair follows the tracks he made in his hunting and guiding career.

* * *

Tasmania's best-known pioneer of nature tourism was born at Spittal an der Drau, a small town in the Austrian Alps, in 1874. Gustav Weindorfer held several jobs in Vienna, including clerk at his uncle's brewery, before telling his parents in 1900 that he had decided to migrate to Australia. In Melbourne, while working in the office of a steamship company, he made weekly visits to the Botanic Gardens and started a beetle collection. In 1901 he joined the recently formed

Field Naturalists Club of Victoria and soon gained a reputation as an enthusiastic and knowledgeable botanist.

Another member of the club would have a huge impact on Gustav's life. Kate Cowle was the daughter of a Tasmanian pastoralist, highly intelligent and ten years Weindorfer's senior. They bonded over a shared love of nature and music – she would play the piano while he sang Austrian folk songs. They were married in 1906 and embarked on a five-week honeymoon in north-east Tasmania, trekking, sleeping in a leaky tent and collecting botanical specimens. From the top of Mount Roland, the Weindorfers saw the jagged profile of Cradle Mountain for the first time.

Gustav visited Cradle Mountain three years later and immediately fell in love with the wild scenery, which reminded him of his native Austria. He returned the following year with Kate, who became the first known woman to climb the mountain, and certainly the first to do it in an ankle-length skirt and bone-collar blouse. When Gustav reached the summit he stood with arms outstretched and declared: 'This must be a national park for the people for all time.' Determined to attract visitors to the mountain and to encourage the creation of a national park, Weindorfer selected a site on a sheltered rocky rise and constructed a house he called Waldheim, or 'forest home'. When it opened for business in 1912 it featured wooden bunks, mattresses stuffed with sphagnum moss and a huge fireplace. A sign on the wall read: 'This is Waldheim, where there is no time and nothing matters.'

Visitors to the hut praised his home-brewed coffee, wombat stew and hospitality. He led walking tours through the surrounding wilderness and in the evenings regaled visitors with tales from his youth in Vienna. When not entertaining guests, Weindorfer ventured into the mountains around Cradle Valley, cutting tracks and collecting botanical specimens. He kept detailed weather records and maintained regular correspondence with scientists.

In 1916, Kate fell ill and died. Weindorfer's parents and brother also died within the year. Adding to his misery, rumours circulated that Weindorfer was a German spy. The anti-German sentiment was so strong that Weindorfer's mail was censored and his home raided. He went for months at a time without seeing another human, but his loneliness was eased by his bond with the local wildlife.In winter he would build a fire and open the door, and 'one by one, in they would come, without their usual fear of man ... and share

Gustav Weindorfer and his dog at Lake Lilla in 1922. (Stephen Spurling;
National Library of Australia)

with me in stillness the grateful warmth'. In 1919 he read a paper on
the animals of Tasmania at the Victorian Field Naturalists' Club,
detailing his observations of the native inhabitants of Cradle Valley.
Weindorfer tested wombats' swimming abilities by dropping one
into a river:

> Nearly ten seconds elapsed before it came to the surface, when the
> spitting, spluttering animal, swimming much after the fashion of
> a dog ... made for the nearest shore. It was again seized, and the
> performance was repeated twice, each time with the same result.
> Finally ... it relieved its dusky-coloured pelt of the adhering water
> by a vigorous shake, and, by slowly waddling along, left the scene
> of the experiment.

Weindorfer was unquestionably a nature lover, but he was also a
man of his time. He continued hunting for most of his life but was
increasingly concerned about animal extinction. He campaigned
tirelessly to see the Cradle Mountain area preserved, touring Tasmania in 1921 to give lectures in Launceston and Melbourne and
enthusiastic interviews to the local press. The next year the area
stretching from Cradle Mountain to Lake St Clair was declared a
'scenic reserve and wildlife sanctuary'. Weindorfer continued to
entertain guests at Waldheim until his death in 1932.

* * *

Some bushmen saw the commercial possibilities of the state's native
wildlife – and no animal was more prized than the thylacine. By
the 1920s thylacine numbers had declined drastically and seeing

one was a rare event. Self-taught naturalist James Harrison became Tasmania's top procurer and supplier of thylacines and other native creatures. *The Examiner* noted: 'Harrison's knowledge and experience are extensive, so much so that the directors of mainland zoos have placed large orders for Tasmanian animals in his hands.' In 1922, he departed for Melbourne Zoo with twelve kangaroos, six wallabies, six Tasmanian devils, two possums, two kangaroo rats and two bandicoots. He advertised in the press for live thylacines, offering £25 for fully grown animals and a 'lesser price' for young tigers with 'good teeth'. These animals were mostly bought from bushmen who had trapped them either deliberately or by accident, but Harrison also caught three tigers of his own. One suffered bad cuts around its neck but after several weeks the wound healed and Harrison reportedly sold it to a Melbourne doctor as a pet.

Australasian Animals Series.   No. 3.—TASMANIAN DEVIL.

A Tasmanian devil pictured on a postcard in 1905. (State Library of Victoria)

In 1928, on obtaining a Tasmanian tiger that had suffered a broken leg in a rabbit trap, he asked a local doctor to set the bones. The thylacine was put on public display, and Harrison's grandson, Neil McCulloch, recalled decades later that the leg healed well: 'I remember having been within one metre of the thylacine, but never touched or pat him as he was very timid.' This thylacine, one of the last caught alive, was sold to the Hobart Zoo. The Thylacine Museum estimates that Harrison sold twenty-five Tasmanian tigers to zoos in Hobart and the mainland after keeping them in cages on his Wynyard property. He likely supplied the two female thylacines sent to London Zoo in January 1926, one of which died after industrial action on the docks delayed the ship's landing. Harrison kept a range of native wildlife at his own property, including wombats, quolls, Tasmanian devils, eagles, platypuses and cockatoos. He also maintained a small private museum in his house, displaying preserved Tasmanian animals including fifteen thylacine skins and four mounted specimens.

A 1935 report in the *Burnie Advocate* described a chance encounter with Harrison on a train:

Mr Harrison is a veritable walking museum – from one pocket he produced the formidable curved spur of the male platypus and a fossil shark's tooth with the enamel still intact, from the tertiary beds at Marrawah. From another pocket came a small two-headed snake in a glass tube, from Parrawe, and in another tube was a fine specimen of the red-backed spider from Queensland, the bite of which is considered very deadly.

Details of Harrison's extraordinary life – he was also booked by local fairs and swimming carnivals as a 'human cork' to demonstrate his uncanny floating ability – can only be pieced together from newspaper reports. It seems that he was born in India in 1873; his parents, Thomas and Ann, were on their way from England to Tasmania. The family settled on the state's north-west coast and lived there for thirty-four years before James relocated to Wynyard, about fifteen kilometres inland, where he worked as a real-estate agent, married a Miss Sarah Reeve and had five daughters. He was highly regarded in the community and in 1927 made a generous donation to the Burnie Museum, including a mounted eagle, an emu egg, three sperm-whale teeth, a stuffed platypus, a death adder, a Queensland locust, a boomerang and the 'shin bone of a Tasmanian native (500 years old)'.

In 1928 he took six platypuses to Kangaroo Island, where they were released into the wild by conservationists (the island's current platypus population is descended from these animals and from another group introduced by David Fleay in 1940). Even more ambitious was Harrison's scheme to transport Tasmanian owls to Lord Howe Island to control a growing rat problem, in contravention of local wildlife laws. When five of the protected owls were found on his property packed and ready for shipping, they were released by police and 'both Harrison and those from whom he had bought the owls ... warned against further taking of wholly protected birds'.

While Harrison supplied most of the thylacines sent to zoos around the world, the claim of capturing the last captive thylacine went to famed tiger hunter Elias Churchill.

Details of Churchill's life are even murkier than Harrison's. Churchill was publican of the Duke of York Hotel in Hobart and spent years in the bush snaring wild animals – including, he claimed, at least eight thylacines. Decades later he recounted catching the last known living Tasmanian tiger. 'I could see he was a nice specimen, so decided to get him to the zoo,' Churchill told nature writer Michael Sharland. Churchill said he wrapped a snare around the thylacine's snout, tied its legs together with another snare, slung it around his neck and carried it to the hut he had built beside the Adamsfield track in the Upper Florentine Valley. After being chained at the hut for several days, the tiger was transported on the back of a packhorse and then by train, 'and arrived in good condition at the Hobart Zoo'.

* * *

The Hobart Zoo was the legacy of a remarkable woman.

While hardy men were hacking their way into Tasmania's wildest country, digging for tiny traces of metal and killing the state's native wildlife in astonishing numbers, Mary Grant Roberts was conducting some of the earliest scientific work on those same animals, forging a reputation as a brilliant zookeeper and a champion of social causes. She was born in 1841 and, if her *Australian Dictionary of Biography* entry is to be believed, didn't do anything interesting until she married Henry Llewelyn Roberts in 1863. After the wedding, Mr Roberts went about establishing a successful agricultural business and his wife assembled a collection of birds and animals in the gardens of their property, Beaumaris, at Battery Point.

By 1895 the collection was extensive enough to open to the public. The native animals on display included echidnas, wallabies, wombats, bandicoots, quolls and possums, plus exotic species such as foxes and meerkats and a large array of Australian and exotic birds. Roberts wrote in her diary of a visiting family from Minneapolis who 'thoroughly enjoyed the birds and animals', even though a monkey stole the father's hat. ('He said the pleasure of the afternoon was worth a new hat.')

She obtained Tasmanian tigers that had been trapped in snares, paying up to £20 each and rehabilitating them before showing them to the public. She also sent thylacines to Sydney, New York and London, along with large numbers of other Australian animals. In 1908 a shipment arrived at the London Zoo containing 700 Tasmanian animals, including lizards and birds. She tried repeatedly to breed thylacines, without success. She was not alone on that front – there is only one recorded example of a thylacine being born in captivity, at Melbourne Zoo.

But Roberts' real love was Tasmanian devils. A devil with three joeys in its pouch was donated to her zoo after it was found with its foot caught in a trap. The mother did not survive but Roberts raised the young animals almost as pets; two of them became the first devils known to breed in captivity. She described the historic moment in a paper published in the Zoological Society of London's *Proceedings*, ending with a passionate defence of the species, which had been referred to as the 'satanic meat lover', the 'diabolical bear' and 'Beelzebub's pup':

I have derived much pleasure from studying the habits and disposition of the Tasmanian devils, and have found that they respond to kindness, and certainly show affection and pleasure when I approach them. Others who do not understand them may think of them as they like, but I, who love them ... will always regard them as first favourites, my little black playmates.

Roberts ran the zoo almost entirely on her own, welcoming visitors and tending to the animals with the help of only a few colleagues, including Professor Theodore Thomson Flynn, an eminent marine biologist and the father of film star Errol Flynn, who deserves a brief detour.

After leaving school at fifteen, Theodore won a scholarship to Sydney University, then answered a newspaper advertisement to become Tasmania's first biology professor. He found a fossil whale in cliffs near Wynyard, conducted vital work on marsupial

THE TASMANIAN TIGER.
(THYLACINUS CYNOCEPHALUS.)

The Tasmanian tiger, illustrated in *The Mammals of Australia* by Helena Forde and Harriet Scott, 1869. (State Library of NSW)

embryology, joined Douglas Mawson on an Antarctic expedition, and was one of the earliest voices for preservation of the thylacine. He published papers on monotreme eggs, Tasmanian devils, sea spiders and the freshwater sponge, among other topics. Flynn was an active early member of the Tasmanian Field Naturalists Club, leading field trips to collect marine specimens on the Freycinet Peninsula and arguing for its preservation. A well-groomed man rarely seen without his bowler hat, he was reportedly an engaging speaker and occasional practical joker who once produced a marsupial from his pocket at a staff dance. He spent time in Northern Ireland as chair of zoology at Queen's University, Belfast, eventually retiring to Surrey, England, in 1948. Flynn's Tarn, near the summit of Cradle Mountain, is named after him.

Back to Mrs Roberts. She was a strong advocate for the welfare of native animals, founding the Game Preservation Society and the Anti-Plumage League, which campaigned against feathers in ladies' hats. Somehow she also found time to establish the Tasmanian branch of the Girl Guides, sit on committees for the Art Society, Mothers' Union and Young Women's Christian Association, act as a delegate to the Tasmanian National Council of Women and join the Royal Society of Tasmania, Victoria League, Hobart District Nursing Association, RSPCA, Overseas Club, Tasmanian Field Naturalists Club, Linnean Society, Liberal League, the Orpheus Club and the Queen Mary Bridge Club. Roberts met state ministers in Sydney and Melbourne to push for animal rights and her letters were regularly featured in *The Mercury*, passionately advocating for creatures that couldn't speak for themselves. In 1919 she wrote in defence of Tasmania's vanishing ringtail possums:

The ruthless slaughter now going on will soon exterminate them altogether. Many a night have I watched their gambols as they hung suspended in the peppermint bough in the light of the campfire, carrying on their pretty chatterings. They are quite little bush companions and I would like to see them rigidly protected.

Even in her seventies she would tend to her animal and bird collection early in the morning, then receive visitors and go into town in the afternoon on business, including making arrangements with shipping agents to send animals overseas and going aboard to pay the ship's butcher to feed them. On the way home she would make half a dozen social calls, then write letters and maybe attend a meeting. A profile in the *Australian Women's Weekly* described her as a 'human dynamo'.

Mary died in 1921, aged eighty-one, two years after her husband. *The Mercury* described her passing as 'a clear loss to the community':

Beginning without scientific training or any special knowledge, and taking the thing up as a hobby, she very soon gave to this collection of birds and animals a special and personal character ... the question now, which is of public importance, is whether this work will die with Mrs Roberts ... [it] is too big and important to be allowed to go by the board for lack of public interest.

Her daughter Ida donated Mary's collection of 200 birds, marsupials, mammals and reptiles to the Hobart council, which shifted the zoo to a site on the Queens Domain. More animals arrived from around Tasmania, the mainland and overseas, including a pair of lions, two polar bears, a Bengal tiger, a porcupine, six prairie dogs and a leopard named Mike.

Over the next decade the zoo obtained more than twenty thylacines, two of which it sent to London Zoo in exchange for an elephant. In 1937, beset by financial problems and with rising public opposition to capturing wild animals (particularly thylacines), the zoo closed its doors.

All that remains of the Hobart Zoo today are the ruins of a handful of enclosures in an overgrown paddock. On 9 September 2000 – International Threatened Species Day – a gate was installed, telling the story of the zoo and the last captive Tasmanian tiger, which died after being accidentally locked out of its sheltered sleeping enclosure on a freezing September night in 1936. After its death, the thylacine's body was sent to the Tasmanian Museum. What happened to it is a mystery. No sign of it was ever seen again.

7
Marsupials in the Media

'This country is home to some pretty unique fauna,
not to mention animals.'
— **Russell Coight**

NYONE WHO DOUBTS THE IMPACT OF AUSTRALIAN naturalists should look no further than a nine-year-old Victorian schoolgirl who was bitten by a tiger snake in her backyard in November 2020. The snake is one of Australia's deadliest, and the girl's mother immediately called an ambulance and tried to calm her daughter until help arrived. 'I asked Grace to stay calm and not move, but she told me: "It's okay, Mum, I know what to do because Russell Coight taught me",' she said in a radio interview.

The advice worked, but Coight is perhaps not the first wildlife expert you would want your children to turn to in an emergency. In his TV series *All Aussie Adventures*, Coight ran over an echidna, electrocuted a kangaroo, stomped on a bandicoot and demolished a wedge-tailed eagle's nest. There's also the consideration that he is a fictional character, the brainchild of comedians Tom Gleisner, and Glenn Robbins, who dreamed up Coight as a parodic celebration of a special kind of Australian naturalist.

'We were particularly amused by the sort of people who described the outback as an extremely dangerous place, and the only way to survive was to follow their advice,' Gleisner told me. 'Now they are all on YouTube telling you how to make a fire with a stick and a piece of moss, but back then it was TV where these people lived.' These TV naturalists were usually self-trained and had a certain rough Australian edge that set them apart from their international counterparts like David Attenborough, Jane Goodall and Jacques Cousteau. By bringing native animals into the living rooms of everyday Australians, they helped to transform the way Australians think about wildlife.

* * *

Before the arrival of television, nature lovers used earlier forms of media to get the message out, starting with quills and paintbrushes. Some incredible women were the first to take up the cause, including Fanny Elizabeth de Mole, Louisa Atkinson (who documented her Blue Mountains wanderings in a series of newspaper columns and a novel, *Gertrude the Emigrant*, the first to be published by an Australian-born woman) and Louisa Anne Meredith.

Meredith helped to 'invent the travel book', in the words of Peter Macinnis, author of *Curious Minds: Discoveries of Australian Naturalists*. After arriving from England in 1839, she wrote popular accounts of colonial life and the plants and animals she encountered. She discovered new species of seaweed, illustrated papers for the Royal Society of Tasmania and lobbied her husband – a member of the Tasmanian parliament – to pass laws conserving wildlife and natural areas, including a bill to protect the black swan.

A snake with bottlebrush orchid (*Coelandria smillieae*) in Mackay, Queensland, illustrated by Ellis Rowan in 1887. (National Library of Australia)

Another early naturalist, Marian Ellis Rowan, travelled around Australia with her husband, former British naval officer Frederic Charles Rowan, after he went into business in the exciting new field of electricity. Marian, known as Ellis Rowan, packed her watercolours, gouache and paintbrushes, and reportedly made an arresting sight in remote mining towns, forests and gullies, dressed in floor-length skirts, high-necked blouses, gloves and hat, an umbrella crooked over her arm. She visited remote corners of Western Australia and Queensland and, following the death of her husband in 1892, England (where she had an audience with Queen Victoria), Europe, India, Cuba, the West Indies and the United States, where she lived for seven years. In 1916 she visited the colonies of Papua and New

Guinea (still separate at the time), where she contracted malaria and, with the help of local guides, painted forty-seven species of birds of paradise from life – a monumental achievement when you consider she was aged seventy at the time.

While beautiful plants were her main focus, Rowan took the opportunity to sketch other interesting subjects when she came across them, including numerous butterflies and beetles. She once found a snake in a trap and, 'fearful lest it would be lost or injured before I could get its brilliant colouring ... gripped it behind the head with one hand and painted it with the other'. When she showed the sketch to a visiting collector for the British Museum:

> He exclaimed in surprise that it was new to science: 'I suppose, womanlike, you destroyed the original?'
>
> 'Womanlike, I kept it,' I replied, and produced it preserved in spirit. He took it off with him, and the next time I saw it was in the museum.

* * *

Australia's first celebrity nature writer was Donald Macdonald, whose beloved newspaper columns and books helped Australians to see their country in a new light. An effusive obituary in *The Australasian* described him as a national treasure: 'Donald Macdonald was a writer whose influence upon the youth of Australia, so far as the love of birds and animals is concerned, was more profound and enduring than that of any man in his or any other generation.' Acclaimed author Gideon Haigh described Macdonald as 'a veritable newspaper in his own right'.

Macdonald was 'probably' (according to the *Australian Dictionary of Biography*) born in 1859 in Fitzroy, then a working-class suburb of Melbourne. He embarked on a journalism career in the Riverina at the *Corowa Free Press*, where he honed his entertaining writing style. In 1881 he joined *The Argus* and marked himself for greatness when he was assigned to cover an intercolonial cricket match between Victoria and New South Wales. At the time the accepted reporting method was to record a chronological account of the day's events, detailing the comings and goings of every batsman. Macdonald's entertaining report stood in stark contrast and quickly won him a following; his byline became synonymous with accurate and entertaining sports writing. For the rest of his career at *The Argus* he attended every important cricket match in Melbourne, and most interstate tests, and travelled overseas with the Australian team for forty years.

In the 1890s Macdonald wrote a series of reports on the week-end manoeuvrings of Victoria's small military force, and by default became the newspaper's defence correspondent. That made him the obvious choice to send to South Africa when tensions boiled over between the British and two independent Boer states. He was at sea when the Boer War broke out in October 1899. After landing he rushed to the front and found himself in the town of Ladysmith just in time to be part of a disastrous 118-day siege. Macdonald wrote detailed reports of the siege but, like everything else in the town, his letters couldn't get out. They eventually made it back to Australia on the same ship that took Macdonald home. They were published in *The Argus* and compiled in a popular book, *How We Kept the Flag Flying*, which described life in the besieged town in Macdonald's characteristic absorbing style.

Macdonald had been attracted to the outdoors since his childhood, and after returning home he wrote an article for *The Argus*, titled 'Where the pelican builds its nest'. It generated such an overwhelming response from readers that it inspired a weekly column, 'Nature Notes and Queries', that ran for almost thirty years and over 1400 instalments. Macdonald answered questions from curious readers on topics ranging from beekeeping to dingo trapping, mushroom picking, map reading, goannas, penguins, 'some interesting trees', Indigenous placenames, how to find water, and the nesting and breeding habits of many, many types of birds.

When Macdonald didn't know the answer to a reader's question he was happy to defer to other experts and nature lovers. One of these was the Victorian bushman and ornithologist Charles McLennan, whose contributions – published under the heading 'Mallee Bird Notes' – documented one of the world's rarest and most mysterious birds.

The night parrot is small, chubby, nocturnal and ground-dwelling – it lives in clumps of spinifex during the day and comes out to forage at night – and was presumed extinct for almost eighty years. After being named by (who else) John Gould in 1861, the bird was last sighted alive in 1912 (when a rare live specimen was promptly shot dead). In 1990 a team of researchers made a chance discovery of a dead night parrot on the side of the road. In 2013, self-taught naturalist John Young produced a series of photographs and a few seconds of video of the elusive bird. Two years later ornithologists Steve Murphy and Rachel Barr captured a live night parrot in western Queensland (they named him Pedro) and attached a tiny radio transmitter to its leg. The editor of *Birdlife* magazine described the find as 'the birdwatching equivalent of finding Elvis flipping burgers in an outback roadhouse'.

Bizarrely, Young's reputation in the bird world was shredded after he handed in more evidence of night parrots several years later. Closer inspection revealed some major issues; of the four night-parrot eggs Young claimed to have photographed, two were from other parrots, and two were probably made of plaster or clay. 'You'd have to ask the individual in question as to why he did that,' Australian Wildlife Conservancy CEO Tim Allard told the ABC after the organisation quietly removed Young's research from its website.

The parrot's range is believed to extend into the desert areas of Victoria, although there have been no confirmed sightings. But McLennan (via Macdonald) published three detailed accounts of a bird in 1908 and 1913, which he said lived in the 'tall dense spinifex grass' in the north-west corner of the state. His descriptions of the bird all point to direct encounters with the night parrot.

In Macdonald's final years, although his health deteriorated and he had to stop travelling to cricket matches, he kept writing about birds and the natural world. He submitted his last 'Nature Notes' column just days before he died of emphysema in November 1932. It was published two days later. The Donald Macdonald Reserve in Beaumaris, Melbourne, features trails through native bushland – and a cricket oval.

Macdonald inspired a new generation of Australian nature writers, including Alec Chisholm, whom we met in Chapter 3. Chisholm was a journalist, historian, editor, literary critic, naturalist and conservationist. In a seventy-year career he edited three newspapers and the ten-volume *Australian Encyclopedia*, a job that took him ten years and won him the Order of the British Empire. His enthusiasm for nature also conveyed a subtler message about Australia, which officially became a nation when Chisholm was only ten years old. In a 1948 letter, Chisholm wrote that 'patriotism can be regarded as essentially sound only when it is based upon, or at least stimulated by, knowledge and appreciation of one's own country'.

Chisholm was born in 1890 in Maryborough, in central Victoria. The seventh of eight children, he left school at age twelve but combined his love of birds and writing from an early age, penning articles as a teenager for *The Emu* and writing letters to the local newspaper protesting the killing of egrets for feathers to use in ladies' hats. They must have been good letters – in 1911 the newspaper hired him as a journalist. Over the next several years Chisholm worked for the Brisbane *Daily Mail* and Sydney's *Daily Telegraph*, and by 1933 he was writing about nature and sport for *The Argus* and *The Australasian* in Melbourne. In the late 1930s he travelled to Europe to research *Strange New World: The Adventures of John Gilbert and Ludwig Leichardt*, uncovering the explosive diary we encountered in Chapter 3.

Throughout his busy writing career, Chisholm found time to promote legislation protecting birds and their habitats. He participated in the first live broadcast of a lyrebird call (on Sydney radio in 1931), advised the Queensland government on natural history, was active in many conservation organisations and took visiting foreign dignitaries on birdwatching expeditions. He was passionate about protecting and raising awareness of the wilderness over the back fence – gum trees and the birds that made their nests in them. He was particularly captivated by bird songs and was convinced of the importance of bird names; as chair of the Ornithologists' Union Vernacular Committee, he helped to replace disparaging names like 'wart-faced' and 'thickhead' with more complimentary titles such as 'regent' and 'whistler'.

Chisholm died in 1977, aged eighty-seven. He didn't entirely see eye to eye with the emerging environmental movement of the 1970s, but he remained committed to the notion that a love of Australia had to include a devotion to its bushland inhabitants. He was an advocate for 'a new loyalty to the land' –

> based on the interest and value of both fauna and flora, and so setting its combined face against, in particular, the destruction of birds by pesticides, the wholesale slaughter of marsupials by bullets, and the reckless devastation of scenic beauty. If and when such an attitude develops – in defiance of the lure of dollars – Australia may indeed be described as the Lucky Country.

* * *

Chisholm's successor as author of the 'Nature Notes' column also lived a remarkable life dedicated to advancing environmental awareness. Crosbie Morrison was born in Melbourne in 1900 and showed an early interest in nature. He recalled that after the arrival of twin brothers when he was six, 'I had to amuse myself to a greater extent. This took the form of watching grasshoppers. They have very interesting faces ... before long I could tell the difference between the types.'

Morrison studied zoology at the University of Melbourne and spent six months on the Great Barrier Reef inspecting plankton.

His photographs of the reef were published in *The Times* and the *Illustrated London News*, and in 1926 he was offered a three-year cadetship with *The Argus*. He quickly graduated to the role of general reporter and in 1937 took over the 'Nature Notes' column when Chisholm became editor of the paper. A year later Morrison was poached by Sir Keith Murdoch to edit a new monthly magazine, *Wild Life*, a lavishly illustrated natural history publication featuring contributors including David Fleay. To promote the magazine, Murdoch arranged for Morrison to appear on radio station 3DB-3LK during the neglected Sunday night shift. To everyone's surprise, including Morrison's, his broadcasts – which opened with a laughing kookaburra and a lyrebird call – were a gigantic hit. In fact, it's hard to overstate just how popular they were. A 1943 survey found that 74 per cent of Victorian radios turned on at the time were tuned into Morrison's show.

Morrison had no experience in radio but he was a natural: his warm voice, breadth of knowledge and informal style made him a hit. The program's run was quickly extended and lasted for more than twenty years, eventually being syndicated across Australia, New Zealand and South Africa. Morrison was recognised in the street and his public lectures attracted large crowds. Decades later, conservationist Vincent Serventy recalled:

> People have forgotten the influence Crosbie Morrison had, but I'll never forget the time he came to speak at a wildlife show organised by the Western Australian Naturalists' Club. No one knew he was coming yet the announcer only had to say that our special guest was 'The Voice' for the whole crowd to go wild … He was really admired all over the country.

After World War II, Morrison led a campaign for the creation of a new authority to manage all of Victoria's national parks. It took a decade, but in 1956 the state government announced the creation of a national parks authority to oversee Victoria's thirteen national parks, covering 188,900 hectares, and appointed Morrison as director. Meanwhile, Morrison continued his radio broadcasts and *Wild Life* magazine. His desk in the Herald and Weekly Times building on Flinders Street became legendary: members of the public sent him all manner of natural curiosities, including living and dead bugs, spiders and lizards. The morning mail delivery must have been hair-raising.

Morrison also made some of the first forays into another new medium that would reach a new generation of Australians and create a new genre of naturalist – motion pictures. Footage shot during a birdwatching camp-out in Alice Springs in 1952, using a camera given to him by a friend, Prime Minister Sir Robert Menzies, was used in the documentary *Beyond the Alice*. Morrison was working on a new film about marine life when he collapsed and died of a brain haemorrhage in 1958. Letters from Menzies and British prime minister Harold Macmillan were among the condolences sent to his family.

By this time Morrison wasn't the only naturalist spreading his message on the big and small screen. In its first week of broadcasting in 1956, the ABC featured reptile expert Eric Worrell, whom we met in Chapter 5, milking a tiger snake. The next year, Worrell appeared on TV milking and handling taipans, and he made several short films for the ABC. Wearing a tan safari suit, he was a regular guest on a program called *Animal Life and People's Pets* for a decade, pulling all manner of creatures from sacks, bags and cages. The host, a young vet named Pam Tinsley, later recalled:

He brought a dingo in once, [named] Diana, and she escaped and we couldn't find her, so they broadcast it on the ABC radio and she was found happily ensconced in a pub in Surry Hills and so Eric picked her up and we got her on the program then ...

Whenever a snake or reptile expert was required on TV or radio, Worrell was more than happy to answer the call. He supplied animals for television shows like *Skippy* and movies such as *Jedda*, notable as the first Australian film to be shot in colour and the first to feature Indigenous actors in the two lead roles, and starred in a cornflakes commercial.

The ABC featured animals from its earliest broadcasts. It screened David Attenborough's pioneering series *Zoo Quest* from 1954–64 and from 1970 aired the popular program *Bush Quest*, featuring painter Robin Hill sketching Victorian wildlife. But the honour of Australia's first environmental television program is usually bestowed on *Nature Walkabout*, which was created in 1965 by Vincent Serventy. The show ran for twenty-six episodes (twice the number originally commissioned), filmed over six months. Serventy, his wife, Carol, and their three young children travelled around the country in a four-wheel drive and caravan. 'I had a great time,' Serventy recalled years later, 'but, with three young children, Carol hated it. She has hated caravans ever since.'

Serventy also wrote or co-wrote more than seventy books and was a passionate fighter for the environment. He joined campaigns to save Lake Pedder, Fraser Island, Lake Eyre and the Franklin River. He fought for koalas, wombats and sharks, and helped stop a plan by Queensland premier Sir Joh Bjelke-Petersen to issue oil drilling leases in the Great Barrier Reef.

Serventy met another famous name in Australian natural history through the West Australian Naturalists' Club, although he didn't know it at the time; Harry Butler was an enthusiastic schoolboy when Serventy took his class on a nature walk in 1940. Butler was born in 1930 at a railroad construction camp in Western Australia, where his father worked. He rode his pushbike 30 kilometres to school each day and explored the bush with his Aboriginal friends. After leaving school at age fifteen he became an active member of the naturalists' club, helping Serventy organise wildlife shows and travelling with him to procure specimens for museums. Butler made guest appearances on *Nature Walkabout*, designed tourist resorts, and pitched the idea of his own nature program to the ABC. The result was *In the Wild*, which screened over twenty-six episodes between 1976 and 1981 and made Butler a household name.

Butler pioneered a new style of nature documentary in which the host was very much the star of the production. He also established the quintessential look for an Australian TV naturalist: khaki shirt with sleeves rolled up above the elbow, several buttons undone and ingrained with dust, and shorts, weather-beaten hat, boots and a scruffy beard. Accepting his Australian of the Year Award in 1979, he said: 'I suppose my voice, the grotty clothes, and the beat-up fingernails characterise the sort of man Australians imagine as the typical Australian.' The bullets in his hatband were real – he had carried a rifle since his teenage years, when he cashed in feral goats and rabbits for a threepenny bounty, and as a TV star he continued this practice for the show.

Butler's rough edges and hands-on approach were a hit with viewers. The series established many of the tropes that would be followed by later TV naturalists. Butler waded waist-deep into tropical creeks, drove his battered four-wheel drive across flooded rivers and kicked over dead trees before reaching inside a hollow branch to extract a goanna or other startled animal.

Butler insisted that his uncanny ability to unearth hidden native animals wasn't staged. In 2006 he said:

> I mean, there's no script, I've not the slightest idea of what we're going to be saying next ... you say to the cameraman, the soundman and director, look ... if I pull off that piece of bark there's going to be an animal under it. I'm not quite sure what sort of animal ... but it'll be an animal. There will be one there, I can tell that, so we'll just have to suck it and see ... And therefore I can't tell you what I'm going to say because I don't know what it is.

Butler was an ardent believer that nature and commercial development could co-exist: 'I'm a little different to most conservationists', he conceded. This stance drew criticism, especially when he supported the hugely controversial (and ultimately abandoned) Franklin Dam project, as well as plans for uranium mining in Kakadu National Park. It was a position he held from the early 1960s, when he worked as a conservation consultant for West Australian Petroleum on Barrow Island, off the Pilbara Coast near Exmouth. The island, which is roughly 25 kilometres long and 10 kilometres wide, was a Class-A nature reserve, a breeding ground for turtles and a vital habitat for native mammals, reptiles, birds, insects and plants, including twenty-four found only on the island. It also has a lot of oil. When West Australian Petroleum discovered that fact, it hired Butler to advise the company on how to extract it with minimal impact to the native inhabitants.

That effort is hailed today as a huge success, at least from the oil industry's point of view. The first well was drilled in 1964 and there are now 900 of them on the island, plus an airstrip, more than a thousand kilometres of roads, and accommodation infrastructure to support up to 4000 workers, who fly in and fly out on two-week shifts. Since 1967, the Barrow Island oilfield has yielded more than 335 million barrels of oil worth more than $1 billion. It is now also the heart of a gigantic natural-gas project – which Butler also backed, despite a negative report from WA's Environmental Protection Authority. For his part, Butler kept introduced species

Harry Butler rescues a king brown snake from drowning during 'Operation Ord Noah', a wildlife rescue mission following the damming of the Ord River and the creation of Lake Argyle near Kununurra, Western Australia, c. 1971. (Kununurra Historical Society)

off the island, fined workers who harmed animals, and replaced damaged vegetation and topsoil.

In the early 1980s Butler turned his back on TV to focus on consultancy work. He was hired by the Tasmanian government as the front man for a plan to dam the Franklin River, a proposal that became a flashpoint in Australian environmental history. The Tasmanian Hydro Electric Commission wanted to drown thirty-three kilometres of the Franklin River and the surrounding rainforest for the dam, but environmentalists – who had honed their skills on the failed campaign to save Lake Pedder from a similar fate in the 1970s – were ready. Thousands descended on the river and about 1500 (including future Australian Greens leader Bob Brown) were arrested. Still, the Tasmanian government pushed ahead with the idea until the river was saved by intervention from the newly elected federal Labor government in 1983.

One rallying point for the anti-dam movement was the discovery of a cave beside the river in 1977 that was quickly recognised as one of Australia's richest archeological sites, housing evidence of human habitation during the last ice age. Butler's proclamation that the cave could be excavated and any important Aboriginal artefacts removed before it ended up hundreds of metres underwater drew a sharp rebuke on the front page of *The Mercury*, denting his already strained credibility. He incurred the wrath of the environmental movement again in 1987, when he was hired as an adviser to the Northern Territory government and opposed expanding the Kakadu National Park World Heritage Area, likening degraded sections of the park to 'a clapped-out Holden'. Coincidentally, the area under discussion was home to rich deposits of gold, platinum, palladium and uranium.

(Kakadu National Park, including the areas mocked by Butler, was eventually nominated by the federal government for World Heritage Listing, over the Northern Territory government's objection.)

Butler defended his approach his entire life, once commenting: 'I've achieved more by working with mining companies and other developers than I ever would have lying down in front of bulldozers.' In a 2006 radio interview, he said that 'greenies' had hijacked environmentalism and missed the 'big picture', which in his mind was managing human use of the natural environment.

Despite the controversies, Butler was a passionate nature lover. In one episode of *In the Wild* he explained his approach to conservation:

> It's all part of the delicate fabric of life: plants and animals interwoven in a glorious net that has taken centuries to happen; and we can destroy it so easily. My job is to keep it, so that your kids can see it all in all times to come … and enjoy it … We need this, not just for their own sake, but because all this has to be here for everybody, forever. There is no single, simple solution to the problems of continued existence for anything. Any answers are as complicated as life itself. Only one thing is certain: if we are to preserve our environment and save the priceless wildlife, we need much, much more knowledge.

In 2012, Butler was named a National Living Treasure and an Officer of the Order of Australia. After his death in 2015, the Western Australian Museum opened a $16 million Harry Butler Research Centre, including new storage facilities for eight million items.

His son Trevor told the ABC: 'He'd think it was thirty years too late, speaking honestly. You know, "Why didn't you do this before? ... Just bloody get on with it!"' Trevor told *The Australian* that his father 'showed how big business and conservation are all part of the same pie, that you can't have one without the other'. Several species are named 'butleri' in his honour, including six reptiles, a marsupial mouse, two fish, a flea and a parasitic worm.

* * *

Butler eventually lost public support but Australians' appetite for adventurers with an individualistic streak in this era appears almost insatiable; in one week of 1977 the film *World Safari* grossed more than *Star Wars*. The star was a Dutch immigrant named Albertus Zwier 'Alby' Mangels, who filmed *World Safari* over six years with a 16-millimetre camera. The documentary included encounters with wildlife in Australia and overseas, and bizarre stunts including Mangels and his friend John Fields driving across Africa in a two-cylinder car they bought from a Nairobi bicycle shop, crossing the Sahara Desert and fields of live landmines. A sequel, *World Safari 2*, was even more popular (and dangerous – Mangels' jeep collided with a bus in Brazil), but a third instalment bombed and Mangels disappeared from public view after a cameraman claimed he staged many of his stunts, including some involving 'wild' animals. In 2017 he said he had no regrets: 'I'm glad that I went broke because the lessons I learned and what I got out of that was worth it ... Most people don't even live life. They exist, and they're always living somewhere else in their mind. Living now is important to me. Sit under a tree and just be there ... that's where I'm at now.'

* * *

Two brothers, Mike and Mal Leyland, became household names via the small screen. Born in England in the 1940s, the brothers moved to Australia with their parents as young boys. In 1956 Mike won tickets to the Melbourne Olympics and his father bought him a film camera to take with him. He recorded footage of the games and family trips, including an excursion to Uluru – then known to non-Indigenous Australians as Ayers Rock – in 1961. (Mal said years later: 'We actually tried to drive up the side of the rock, with Mike at the wheel and me and a friend of ours sitting on the hood. We didn't get very far before we realised it wasn't going to happen.') After showing their movie of the trip to producers at Channel 3 in Newcastle, he was hired as the station's first news cameraman. Mal, meanwhile, got a job as a cadet photographer at the city's daily newspaper.

Bitten by the exploration bug, they took some time off in 1963 and became the first people to sail the 2300-kilometre length of the Darling River, documenting the adventure in the film *Down the Darling*, which they sold to the Nine Network. The brothers then upped the ante by driving across Australia from west to east, crossing the Simpson Desert and filming waterfalls cascading off Uluru after heavy rain for the first time – footage that made them famous.

The success of that film and a third, documenting their trip in an open boat from Darwin to Sydney, led to the iconic TV series *Ask the Leyland Brothers*. The show invited viewers to write in and suggest topics – 'if it's interesting, we'd like to hear from you', Mike explained in the first episode. Channel Nine executives were sceptical about the interactive format, but letters poured in and the Leylands headed off to all corners of the country, and New Zealand. They visited national parks and natural and historic landmarks from shipwrecks to Indigenous rock art to outback mines.

They also introduced audiences to wildlife, including koalas, Tasmanian devils, quolls, echidnas, emus, fur seals, snakes and great white sharks. The brothers presented a sympathetic view of often-maligned creatures and promoted conservation, although they were a product of their time (in one episode, they marvelled at a baby koala clinging to a dog like an adorable but terrified jockey). They also visited a Tasmanian bushman who claimed to have seen a live thylacine: 'Definitely [it was a thylacine]. All the stripes and everything.'

Their wives Laraine (Mal) and Margie (Mike), and the couples' young children became regulars on the show, and viewers embraced the laid-back, amateurish style of the filmmaking – Mal later said it was stipulated in the contract that 'the shows should not be too polished'. A total of 156 episodes aired between 1976 and 1984, when the brothers made the disastrous decision to branch out into tourism. The result, after six years of construction, was Leyland Brothers World, which opened in 1990 on the mid-north coast of New South Wales. The theme park featured rides, a playground, student camp, museum and a movie studio; the centrepiece was a 1/40th scale fibreglass replica of Uluru (about 235 metres long and nine metres high – still pretty big). It may not have been the smartest investment in any era, but it was catastrophic during an economic recession. Interest rates of 27 per cent exploded the project's budget, Mal lost his house to the bank, and the brothers endured a bitter split as receivers stepped in and took over the theme park. 'In hindsight Leyland Brothers World was a huge mistake, the biggest mistake we ever made,' Mal told the ABC's *Australian Story* in 2015, adding that the brothers were 'ready to rip each others' throats out'. Leyland Brothers World was sold at auction and the Uluru replica became the Rock Roadhouse, which remained popular with locals and tourists until it burned down in 2018. The camp, now known as the Great Aussie Bush Camp, survives and is used by 45,000 children every year. 'Their place in television history, the Leyland Brothers, it's there forever,' entrepreneur and environmentalist Dick Smith told the ABC. 'Historically, the films are incredibly important, especially because of ... the fact they are not overly professional, they are not the magnificent Attenborough-type BBC production.'

The 1970s and '80s were a good time to be a naturalist on Australian TV. Malcolm Douglas was a crocodile hunter turned conservation crusader whose film *Across the Top* smashed ratings records when it aired in 1976. It was the result of a four-year trip Douglas undertook with mate David Oldmeadow in 1964 from Darwin to Cape York with a 16-millimetre Bolex camera. 'We didn't have a clue what we were doing,' Douglas said in 1994, going on to describe his approach to nature TV: 'It's professional but a little bit different, probably a little rough around the edges, a little bit wild like me, and that's what appeals to people. What you see on the screen is what you get.'

What you saw – in *Across the Top*, about fifty subsequent documentaries and the popular series *In the Bush with Malcolm Douglas* – was Douglas using his bush skills to explore remote parts of the country never visited by most Australians, including the Kimberley and Arnhem Land. He caught and cooked fish and other animals, often using techniques he learned from First Nations people, whom Douglas portrayed in a positive and sensitive way that stands out for the

time; the Gugadja people of the Great Sandy Desert named him
'white fella bush man' after he excelled in a spear-throwing contest.
Melbourne TV critic Jim Schembri dubbed him 'the Obi-Wan of
the outback' and emphasised his conservation work: 'We have to
remember that he was so committed to conservation. His love of
animals was second to none, he lived with animals – he had them
jumping around his house.'

Schembri was speaking from personal experience – after Schembri
wrote a scathing review of one of Douglas's early documentaries,
Douglas sent him a postcard, inviting him to visit his Broome animal park. Schembri took him up on his offer and found that 'his
house was full of kangaroos and critters scuttling along the ground'.
Douglas showed his visitor a baby crocodile and Schembri asked
if he could pat the surprisingly cute reptile on the head. 'You can,'
Douglas replied, 'but it will cost you.'

Two hunters posing with a dead crocodile near Rockhampton, Queensland, c. 1872.
(State Library of Queensland)

'What will it cost me, Malcolm?'

'A finger.'

In 1983 Douglas had opened a crocodile park outside Broome that was hugely popular with tourists and produced meat and skins in commercial quantities – at one stage Douglas claimed to have 4000 crocodiles, more than half the total West Australian population. Most of those had hatched at the park but the big crocs on display were rescued or relocated from areas where they had threatened humans. 'I was a professional crocodile hunter when I travelled around Australia, but I was one of the first people to think, "This is not right."' Douglas said. 'In a perfect world I wouldn't have any crocodiles here; they should all be out there in the Kimberley swimming around, but people and crocodiles don't mix.'

A drunken visitor to the park proved the point when he decided to scale a fence and sit on a five-metre croc named Fatso; the man was lucky to escape with his life. Douglas later expanded his operations to include the Malcolm Douglas Wilderness Wildlife Park, which housed more native animals, including cassowaries, snakes, kangaroos and his new love, dingoes, and conducted breeding programs for animals including bilbies, which once lived in the Great Sandy Desert.

Artist and desert survivalist Jack Absalom was another khaki-clad outback bushman who enjoyed television success via a series of ABC documentaries. Born in 1927, Absalom spent most of his childhood on the Nullarbor Plain. It was a tough upbringing, especially after his father broke his back in an accident and it was left to eight-year-old Jack to support the family. He trapped rabbits and dingoes and collected and sold a rare desert parrot; one writer described the striking Naretha bluebonnet as 'a small parrot that looks like it has sneezed into a palette of blue eye shadow'. 'It's the only place in the world you could get them – so they were a prize,' Absalom said in a 1981 interview:

> I would pick out probably twenty nests ... and I could easily have 120 birds. That would be a year's wages if I could rear them all. And the guards and the engine drivers and the porters on the trains used to do all the business for me. I'd get letters [addressed to] 'the bird boy at Naretha'.

In the 1950s he left Naretha for the big smoke, heading for Sydney. He got as far as Broken Hill, where he met local girl Mary Wills. The couple got married, had five children together and the Sydney leg of the trip was permanently shelved. Absalom worked as a kangaroo shooter, in the local mines and for the Silverton Tramway Company, and enjoyed success as a boxer, in between trips into the outback with Mary. In 1972 he acted as a guide for artists Eric Minchin and Roy Gundry on a painting trip to the Flinders Ranges. 'He watched them for a couple of days and eventually he just went up to Eric and said, "Give me one of those canvas things, I want to see what I can do",' his friend and fellow artist John Pickup recalled decades later. 'He painted something, went home, and told his family: "I'm a professional artist".' Absalom admitted he knew 'nothing about art'. 'I've never had a lesson in my life,' he said. 'But I believe when you do something you've gotta give it your all. Like I always say – boots and all – I don't fiddle around.'

By the next year he had added a gallery to his house and started collaborating with four other Broken Hill artists – Pickup, Pro Hart,

Minchin and Hugh Schulz. The group, dubbed the 'brushmen of the bush', toured around Australia and to Paris, Rome and New York, changing perceptions of the Australian outback and raising millions of dollars for charity.

Media appearances by the group brought Absalom to the attention of the ABC, which saw potential in a series hosted by an outback painter and survival expert. Absalom had written a best-selling book, *Safe Outback Travel*, in 1976 after coming across a family stranded in the desert trying to take a short cut to Lake Eyre. The scene was re-enacted at the start of one of his documentaries, *The Road to Survival*, and in many of his programs he seems in a state of near constant despair at people – usually tourists from the city – doing stupid things in the outback. In one episode of *Absalom's Outback* in 1988 he advised viewers how to repair a leaking petrol tank with a bar of soap and a handful of dirt. Other helpful tips included how to make a magnet out of a piece of wire and how to use a can of beer as a fire extinguisher if your cigarette butt ignites the car upholstery.

Absalom also passed on his knowledge of desert wildlife and his admiration for the stockmen who made a living in the harsh frontier. He published two cookbooks featuring bush recipes, including one for camel stew that he said was given to him by the owner of an outback cattle station. The ingredients include 'three medium-sized camels', 500 bushels of potatoes and a ton of salt. Preparation involves simmering the camel meat for four weeks in '1000 gallons of brown gravy'. The stew serves 3800 people; 'if more are expected,' the recipe suggests, 'add two rabbits.' Absalom added a personal note: 'I haven't tried [this recipe] as I have had trouble getting the three medium-sized camels.'

He continued travelling and painting up to his death, aged ninety-one, in Broken Hill in 2019.

* * *

Bush survival tips were the bread and butter of another ABC presenter who followed Absalom. Former army major Les Hiddins appeared as a guest on the ABC program *A Big Country* in the late 1980s discussing using Indigenous knowledge to survive in the wild. Viewer response was so strong that the ABC offered Hiddins his own series – *Bush Tucker Man* ran over three seasons and twenty-three episodes between 1988 and 1990.

Hiddins had first taken an interest in bush survival while visiting Arnhem Land after returning from active service in the Vietnam War. He started asking the Yolŋu people what 'bush tucker' was available and used the knowledge in his role as the main author of the Australian Army's military survival manual. As well as several series of his popular TV show, Hiddins wrote twelve books, including four for young children. Some of his gear, including his Akubra hat, is now on display in the National Museum in Canberra. 'They wanted to put me in there too, but I objected to that,' he joked in a 2019 interview.

Two more early TV naturalists made an enormous contribution to conservation and the promotion of one of Australia's most maligned creatures. Back in the 1960s, when Vincent Serventy was driving around the country with his caravan filming *Nature Walkabout*, a remarkable couple were starting decades of groundbreaking work under the water. Valerie Heighes was born in Sydney in 1935. After a tough childhood that included nine weeks partially paralysed with polio, she borrowed her brother's spear gun to try some spear-fishing outside her family's waterfront home. She was spotted by a member of St George's Spearfishing Club and invited to help lift the club's female representation. She quickly showed her talent by winning women's competitions, and met the club's dashing male champion – Ron Taylor, who was a year older and had been spear-fishing since the early 1950s.

Ron had recently borrowed a Bell & Howell 16-millimetre camera and built a housing for it that allowed him to film underwater. 'He asked me if I would swim in front of the camera for him and pat fish and pick up eels,' Valerie said decades later.

> I had long blonde hair to my waist and wetsuits hadn't been invented then so I was still doing it in a bikini. We found that Movietone News would buy Ron's 16mm film and blow it up to 35mm and put it on the news theatres in the city. They only wanted sharks, manta rays and dangerous things, so every weekend we went out looking for sharks to film.

Movietone showed the films around the world and paid £24 per newsreel, more than double Valerie's wage at her day job, which was illustrating *Bugsey Bear* and *Foxy Fagan* comic books. She had another boyfriend at the time, but a shared love of the ocean won out. 'I knew I wouldn't have much of a life with the other guy. He was a musician – he was brilliant. He was a wonderful man but I'm not musical at all,' Valerie said. 'I was a pretty good diver and one day I said to Ron, "I think you should marry me". And he did.'

It was the start of a lifelong love affair – with each other and with the wildlife of the ocean. The couple enjoyed filming all kinds of marine creatures, but they quickly realised 'sharks sell – and we had to make a living. Also, they're exciting. And you get a feeling of great satisfaction after spending time with a group of sharks and getting to know them, and having them actually get to know you, because they're not stupid. They have a very small brain but they use all of it.' Of more than 1000 shark species, Valerie explains, 'only about seven are potentially dangerous. The rest are all sweethearts.' Even in the rare cases when sharks do attack humans, she says, they aren't trying to eat them. They're curious: 'they don't have hands so they feel with their teeth'. Very comforting.

'I've never come close at all to being eaten by a shark,' she told the ABC, although there have been a number of close encounters – where 'close' means 300 stitches in her leg. That came after she was luring blue and mako sharks to Ron's lens off the coast of San Diego. 'I was in the water … we had two underwater cameramen – one was my husband – and we had two shark wranglers. We were hoping for about five sharks, or six.' She estimates twenty-six showed up. 'It was just too many … I felt a gentle bump on my leg, looked down, leg's in the shark's mouth, I thought, "Oh damn." I grabbed its nose and started punching it in the gills, I knew better than to pull away.'

The shark let go and Taylor kicked hard. She feared she would bleed to death, but always had one thing on her mind.

> I surfaced and I called out to the above-water crew that I'd been bitten, they better get the cameras on, they better get the sound on, then I waited to be rescued. My first thought was to get rid of the shark, then get to the surface, then, "Are the cameras rolling?" It's useless getting bitten by a shark if nobody's going to film it.

The closest Ron came to death was when a shark knocked out his mouthpiece while filming a thrilling – and reckless – sequence for the 1971 documentary *Blue Water, White Death* with a throng of oceanic whitetip sharks feeding on a whale carcass. Thankfully, he managed to grab onto a shark cage before losing consciousness.

Pioneers of underwater cinematography, the Taylors were the first to film great white sharks in the wild, the first to film them without the protection of a cage, and the first to film sharks at night. They invented a new kind of chainmail suit to protect divers from shark bite. *Blue Water, White Death* established their reputation as the world's pre-eminent shark filming team and they were approached in 1974 by Hollywood producers Richard Zanuck and David Brown, who asked them to read a novel by freelance writer Peter Benchley about a shark terrorising a small resort town. 'They asked, "Do you think you could get a great white shark to do this?"' Valerie recalled. 'We said it would take a while but yes, we could film that, so they bought the rights.' The result was *Jaws*, the first film to earn $100 million at the box office.

'Every time you see a whole great white shark in *Jaws* it's an Australian shark, shot by Ron,' Valerie explained. Director Steven Spielberg used three mechanical sharks in the production but the Taylors' footage, shot off South Australia, included one of the movie's most dramatic scenes, when a shark attacks a cage containing oceanographer Matt Hooper (played by Richard Dreyfuss). To make the size of the real sharks on screen match Spielberg's gigantic mechanical version, the cage was constructed on a smaller scale and a short-statured stuntman was hired to play Hooper. But the terrifying sequence that was included in the final film was an accident. 'If the [stunt] double had been in the cage he would have been killed,' Valerie recalled. 'He saw the great white shark and he said, "I'm not getting in there".'

It proved a smart decision. 'The shark went crazy, it got tangled in the cage and broke the winch off the side of the boat. Ron saw the whole lot come tumbling down and he kept filming.' The footage was incredible, but in the script, Hooper was supposed to be inside the cage. In Ron's footage, it was empty. Spielberg's solution was to rewrite the scene to show Hooper battling a (mechanical) shark inside the cage before escaping to the ocean floor while it was demolished by the real shark. As for the stunt double, 'he never went near the water or the boat again'.

The Taylors were surprised and horrified by the reaction to the film, with the public turning on sharks. 'It was a fictitious story with a fictitious shark. We didn't understand why people took it so seriously,' Valerie said, noting New Yorkers didn't become terrified of being attacked by a gorilla after watching *King Kong*. While they kept working on major Hollywood productions, including *Blue Lagoon* and *The Island of Doctor Moreau*, the couple turned their attention to promoting and preserving underwater species. Ron had experienced an epiphany during a competitive spear-diving event in the late 1960s – 'I just thought: "What am I doing down here killing these poor, defenceless marine creatures?" he told the ABC in 2005. 'So I just packed up, went home – didn't even weigh my fish in – and never went back to another spearfishing competition' – but their full conversion to conservation came during the filming of *Blue Water, White Death*, when they filmed the death of a female whale calf. 'They cry,' Valerie said.

In 1971 the Taylors discovered a site now known as Cod Hole near Lizard Island, 240 kilometres north of Cairns. They made the boat captain promise to keep the location secret, but it wasn't long before word got out that you could hang out there with a group of more than thirty potato cod – a gigantic grouper that lives for decades and grows to up to two metres in length and 100 kilograms in weight. The fish are known as the dogs of the sea due to their friendliness, an attribute that made them an easy target for sports fishermen. It also made for captivating underwater footage, shot by the Taylors, that became key to a campaign that resulted in Cormorant Pass, including Cod Hole, becoming one of the first sections of the Great Barrier Reef to earn protected status. Sadly, the potato cod might be too friendly for its own good – four decades of being handfed by humans may be contributing to a decline in numbers in recent years.

The couple used their profile and platform to advocate for a range of conservation efforts. In every case, the Taylors used the lesson learned from those early Movietone films: compelling visuals make the news. They helped to make the grey nurse shark the first shark species in the world to be protected by law; fought to save Australian sea lions from being killed by fishermen; successfully campaigned to stop the Coral Sea Islands being mined for guano and Western Australia's Ningaloo Reef being drilled for oil; and advocated for protection of the waters of the Great Australian Bight, where southern right whales migrate from Antarctica each year to mate, give birth and nurse their young.[21]

---

21   There were an estimated 55,000 to 70,000 whales in Australian waters in the
      1700s. By the twentieth century, whaling had reduced numbers to as few as
      300. They are now recovering – slowly.

Another of their documentaries led to protection of the wreck of the SS *Yongala*, a passenger ship that sank in a cyclone off the Queensland coast in 1911, with the loss of 122 people and a racehorse named Moonshine. The wreck was discovered almost completely intact on the sea floor in the 1950s, by which time it had become an artificial reef and home to marine life including turtles, sea snakes, barracuda, bull sharks, eagle rays and the guitarfish. The Taylors' first conservation effort was affixing a brass plaque to the wreck declaring that fishing was banned, even though there was no actual law to that effect. But their documentary resulted in one.

Almost fifty years of fighting for the protection of marine species and ecosystems was recognised when a chain of offshore islands in South Australia was renamed the Neptune Islands Group (Ron and Valerie Taylor) Marine Park in 2012. The park is an internationally significant habitat for great white sharks – more than 1400 of them inhabit the area.

The partnership came to an end when Ron died of leukemia in 2012. At the time of publication Valerie was well into her eighties, still diving and still fighting to protect marine life.

There are fewer fish in the ocean today, and the water is a lot dirtier. That makes Valerie sad, but she doesn't despair. 'Nature doesn't make mistakes. She's very good at balancing everything, be it plant or animal, including us, and we've just got out of control. I'm waiting to see what she's going to do to bring us under control – and it might not be very nice,' she said in an ABC interview.

> I don't know, I've had my day. I've had the greatest life of anybody I know. I've had incredible adventures, I've met wonderful people.

I've been handed, as a gift, the entire world, my husband and I ...
and all I can say to people who say, 'How do you get to do this?',
when there's the opportunity, grab it and run. Don't say, 'Oh gosh,
I've got to go to the dentist.' Go for the adventure.

The Taylors helped transform sharks from mysterious killers to
wild animals that deserve respect, admiration and protection. Even
victims rarely blame sharks anymore for acting on their natural
instincts in their own environment. A father of two who had to
be revived by paramedics after he was attacked by a bull shark in
Perth's Swan River in 2021 said he opposed any form of shark cull:
'You can't blame a shark for being a shark.'

On land, figures like Malcolm Douglas, Harry Butler and Donald Macdonald used the power of film and popular media to raise
awareness and shift attitudes about native animals. The outback was
suddenly not a far-off forbidding place, and the bush – epitomised
by the intrepid khaki-clad naturalist – became a familiar part of the
national psyche, even if most of us will never encounter a feathertail
glider or frillneck lizard.

Ron and Valerie Taylor were also at the forefront of concrete
conservation efforts to ensure the animals and places they loved
didn't survive only as the stars of nature documentaries. And that
battle is just beginning.

Epilogue: Not the End

I N JUDBARRA/GREGORY NATIONAL PARK, 359 KILOMETRES south-west of Darwin, Dr Michael Hammer – curator of fishes at the Northern Territory Museum – wades through a gorge in a rubber suit carrying a pack that puts 400 volts into the water, stunning fish so he can collect them. 'This is the purple spotted gudgeon,' he says. 'There's only meant to be one species up in the Northern Territory, but there are at least twelve, so we're trying to work it out.' Elsewhere in the park enthusiastic experts are using tools including a cheese knife and an ice-cream scoop to uncover new varieties of spiders. 'This little patch here probably has the second-highest density of tarantulas I've ever seen, and I don't really know why,' says the Queensland Museum's Dr Robert Raven. Other finds include butterflies and a variety of other previously undocumented creatures, including seven types of gecko and an unusual-looking amphibian. 'We're calling it the fat-arse brown frog,' Gaye Bourke, of the Australian National University, tells writer Ken Eastwood, who is documenting the expedition for *RM Williams Outback* magazine.

The researchers were part of Bush Blitz, a $12-million partnership between the federal government, citizen science organisation Earthwatch and BHP Billiton. Bush Blitzes visit remote areas that are difficult to access and haven't been well researched, especially when it comes to insects, spiders, fish and reptiles. Since the program began in 2010, Bush Blitz has added more than 1700 new species to the scientific record, including 500 new spiders. A trip to Little Desert National Park in Victoria uncovered new moths, lichens and leaf bugs as well as seven types of tiny jumping spider, two of which had only previously been found in Western Australia and one of which hadn't been found anywhere. An expedition to the heart of the Gibson Desert found a previously unknown species of native snail – more beautiful and much smaller than their introduced cousins. 'They mostly eat native leaf litter or algae,' the Western Australian Museum's Corey Whisson said. 'They can also be incredibly small, so when the area we are surveying is 42,000 square kilometres, finding a tiny snail is like finding a needle in a haystack the size of Belgium.'

And they have barely scratched the surface. In April 2020 scientists used an underwater robot to reach depths of up to 4.5 kilometres in the Indian Ocean off the coast of Western Australia. They found thirty new species, including a mesmerising giant siphonophore – a deep sea relative of the jellyfish that is really a floating colony of tiny cloned organisms covered in stinging tentacles that form a long string, coordinating to move, lure and devour prey in ways scientists are still trying to understand. One in the Ningaloo Canyons was forty-five metres long, making it the longest animal ever recorded. 'The word soon spread and people came pouring into the control room to share the excitement,' senior research scientist Nerida Wilson told *The Guardian*. 'It was just amazing to see this huge organism spread out like a spiral UFO, hovering in the water column. We couldn't believe what we were seeing.' And who knows what else lurks in the ocean depths. Less than 10 per cent of Australia's marine waters have been comprehensively surveyed by scientists. On land the figure is just over 50 per cent. According to the federal government, Australia has 147,579 'accepted described species' – about one-quarter of the estimated total of Australian mammals, birds, reptiles, fish and insects. (Estimates of the total number of living species on the planet range from 3 million to over 100 million. If that upper estimate is right, humans have documented less than 2 per cent of them.)

Many of the unfound specimens can only be seen under a microscope, but sometimes scientists make a startling discovery. In the jungles of Indonesia, Dr Kevin Rowe and a team from Museums Victoria identified an entirely new species of rodent in 2015. Measuring forty-five centimetres from nose to tail, it has large ears, sharp teeth and unusually long pubic hair. 'We think [the hair] may serve some function in helping animals be successful in mating, but we really have no idea,' Dr Rowe said. The creature has been named the hog-nosed rat for its pig-like snout. 'I am still amazed that we can walk into a forest and find a new species of mammal that is so obviously different from any species, or even genus, that has ever been documented by science,' Dr Rowe said in a radio interview.

But for each new species discovered, more are lost. Five of the species described in John Gould's *Birds of Australia* are now extinct:

the Norfolk Island kaka (a large, colourful parrot that was tragically easy to catch; the last known specimen died in a cage in London in 1851), the paradise parrot (discovered by John Gilbert in 1844 and last seen in 1927), the robust white-eye (which was native to Lord Howe Island, where they gathered in large flocks before being feasted on by black rats), the grey-headed blackbird (last recorded in 1975) and the vinous-tinted thrush, another species once endemic to Lord Howe Island and now found only in museum cabinets in Washington, Berlin, New York, the Netherlands, the United Kingdom and Sydney.

Both of these Lord Howe Island species were victims of a shipwreck. On 15 June 1918, the SS *Makambo* ran aground on rocks off Neds Beach, allowing a few black rats to escape onto the island; there are now estimated to be more than 150,000 of them. The vinous-tinted thrush, which nested on the ground, was easy prey. Six years after the shipwreck, the species was extinct. Within a decade, all the robust white-eyes were gone.

As of 2012, when birdwatcher Sue Taylor wrote *John Gould's Extinct and Endangered Birds of Australia*, two more of Gould's subjects were considered possibly extinct. A further eight were classified as critically endangered, twenty-five as endangered and nineteen as vulnerable. Zoologist Fred Ford found that of the animals featured in Gould's *The Mammals of Australia*, forty-six species are either threatened or extinct. Among those to have disappeared are the pig-footed bandicoot, desert rat-kangaroo, broad-faced potoroo (last seen by John Gilbert in the 1870s), and the eastern hare wallaby, which Gould described after a remarkable personal encounter:

While out on the plains in South Australia I startled a hare kangaroo before two fleet dogs; after running to the distance of a quarter mile, it suddenly doubled and came back upon me, the dogs following close at its heels; I stood perfectly still until the animal had arrived within 20 feet before it observed me, when to my astonishment, instead of branching off to the right or to the left, it bounded clear over my head.

A comprehensive 2019 study documented 100 uniquely Australian species that had become extinct since the arrival of Europeans, including thirty-four mammals, nine birds, four frogs and the Lake Pedder earthworm. Researchers estimated the real figure would be ten times higher, including animals that died out before they were noticed by Europeans. And those numbers are growing.

A truckload of koala skins in the Clermont area, Queensland, c. 1927.
(State Library of Queensland)

According to the International Union for the Conservation of Nature, Australia has eighty-six species that are listed as critically endangered, including the mountain pygmy possum, the Leadbeater's possum (Victoria's animal emblem), the swift parrot, the hawksbill turtle, the Lord Howe Island stick insect and Gilbert's potoroo, the world's rarest marsupial. Described by John Gilbert 'in immense numbers' throughout Western Australia, there are now about 100 clinging to survival in pockets of bushland near Albany.

The yellow-footed rock wallaby, collected by Frederick Strange, has all but disappeared in Queensland and New South Wales and numbers are falling dramatically in their last refuge, South Australia's rugged Flinders Ranges. The platypus, beloved by David Fleay and Henry Burrell (and Winston Churchill), is being considered for threatened status after losing one-fifth of its habitat in the past thirty years. More than 130 species of fish and sharks found in Australian waters are listed as endangered, as are several snake species. In February 2022, koalas were officially listed as an endangered species in Queensland, New South Wales and the Australian Capital Territory in response to dramatically declining numbers brought on by land clearing, bushfires, disease and other threats.

Summon, if you will, the imaginative powers to transport yourself back 200 years, when there was an abundance of native mammals, birds, reptiles, fish and insects almost impossible to comprehend today. In 1866, Samuel Mossman wrote in *Our Australian Colonies*: 'There is no other region on the globe where the trees and shrubs are so prolific in indigenous animals.' Explorer Phillip Parker King noted that the feathertail glider 'is exceedingly numerous in the vicinity of Port Jackson', while black swans were recorded in 'astonishing numbers' in Tasmania's Derwent River. In central Australia, early observers reported 'countless swarms' of the now-threatened black-footed rock wallaby, while further north a collector in the late nineteenth century noted of the pale field-rat (now classed as 'vulnerable'):

> I have travelled through square miles of country where the ground was literally undermined by these rodents to such an extent that the hoofs of my horses and nearly every step would break through and sink deep down in the burrows.

Meanwhile, offshore, 'immense shoals' of whales were reported off the New South Wales coast, and in 1804 Reverend Robert Knopwood noted after sailing into Hobart that 'we passed so many whales that it was dangerous for the boat to go up the river'.

As late as 1902, an article in *Town and Country Journal* described the following scene in New South Wales:

> the water was teeming with aquatic birds, with swans, ducks, teal, shags, divers and pelicans ... the white-headed eagle and the osprey with many hundreds of cranes, some of them snow white, were also often to be seen quietly perched in the neighbouring trees ... the water itself was literally swarming with all kinds of fish ... I must also speak of the countless flocks of beautiful parrots ... large flocks of pigeons in dense vine-draped bush, and at night ... the sparkle of innumerable fireflies, while the voice of the More-pork, the scream of the curlew, and the screech of the possums, the howl of the dingoes, and the croaking of frogs in chorus.

Even seemingly abundant animals are suffering dangerous population declines. The grey-headed flying fox, Australia's largest bat, is familiar to residents of East Gippsland and golfers at Yarra Bend in Melbourne's leafy inner suburbs, and a 2015 count put the national population at over 600,000. But that is a far cry from the early 1800s, when individual colonies were said to contain more than a million bats. The numbat once populated much of southern semi-arid and arid Australia, from Western Australia to north-west Victoria and western New South Wales. By the 1970s, numbats had disappeared from 99 per cent of their range. Today there are fewer than 1000 mature individuals left. The burrowing bettong, once widespread on the mainland, is now confined to a small number of islands off the coast of Western Australia.

The failure to notice such huge changes over a long period of time has been labelled 'shifting baselines syndrome'. First coined in 1995 by a fisheries scientist named Daniel Pauly, the term describes the way each generation inherits a new baseline (for example, how many fish they catch, or how many bats they are used to seeing) and a 'new normal'. No single generation observes the decline from abundance to extinction, and every species that goes extinct is eventually, before disappearing completely, rare – and, as a result, often not missed. Worryingly, the timeframes for each generation appear to be shrinking; humans seem able to adjust even to cataclysmic events like rising temperatures or a global pandemic, forgetting what 'normal' looked like years, months or even weeks ago.

Internationally, the tale is no better. In the 1930s an estimated 10 million elephants roamed Africa. Today there are fewer than 450,000, a decline mainly attributed to decades of poaching and conflict. In 1873 Charles Hagenbeck's agents filled the yard of the Hotel de la Paix in Singapore with tapirs, orangutans, a panther and a bear; Hagenbeck's had two local hunters scouring the Malaysian Peninsula to fill orders for rhinoceros, tigers and panthers. Today there are fewer than 400 Sumatran tigers in the wild. Panthers have been eradicated from 93 per cent of their former habitat, and the Javan rhino is one of the world's most endangered species, with fewer than seventy surviving. Bornean orangutans are listed as endangered and Sumatran orangutans as critically endangered. The Tapanuli orangutan is the rarest of the great apes, with fewer than 800 remaining in the jungles of northern Sumatra.

'World's most lovable animals, koala bears, to be seen only in Australia': 1930s tourism poster. (National Library of Australia)

According to the United Nations, one million plants and animals globally are at risk of extinction, many within decades. Humans will be victims too, even as the global population surges towards eight billion people. 'The health of ecosystems on which we and all other species depend is deteriorating more rapidly than ever. We are eroding the very foundations of our economies, livelihoods, food security, health and quality of life worldwide,' Sir Robert Watson, chair of the Intergovernmental Science-Policy Platform on Biodiversity and Ecosystem Services, said in 2019. 'It is not too late to make a difference, but only if we start now at every level, from local to global.'

Australia punches well above its weight in terms of its share of the world's animal species – the island continent is in the top handful of nations when it comes to mammals and birds, and is home to more types of reptiles than any other country on Earth. The vast majority of those species – four out of five mammals, nine out of ten freshwater fish and almost half our birds – are not found anywhere else. Australia also leads the world in animal extinctions; since 1788, Australia saw as many mammal species go extinct (thirty-four) as were lost in the rest of the world combined. North America lost just one species during the same period (the sea mink).

An estimated 90 per cent of Australian mammal extinctions are linked to feral foxes and cats; pet and feral cats kill 1.7 billion native mammals, birds and reptiles every year. Native species often have small ranges and slow breeding cycles that put them at a severe disadvantage when competing with introduced species. Tree rats native to tall forests in northern Australia have one or two young a year, while introduced black rats can have litters of up to twelve young six times a year. The breeding abilities of introduced rabbits and cane toads are the stuff of legend, while Indian mynas can have eighteen chicks in a year, compared to five for a rosella. Mynas also have the destructive habit of booting native species from tree hollows and stealing their nests, a serious problem for the evictees, considering it takes up to 120 years for a mature tree to form a hollow – and fewer trees are reaching that age due to ever encroaching human activity.

One effect of having fewer native creatures in the bush is a build-up on the forest floor of leaf litter and other debris – perfect fire fuel – that would otherwise be eaten, broken down by insects or used to make burrows or nests. Bushfires over the summer of 2019–20, supercharged by climate change and months of drought and record temperatures, tore through 12 million hectares of forest in south-eastern Australia, razed hundreds of properties and claimed the lives of thirty-three people and an estimated 1.25 billion animals. In total, scientists say almost 2.5 billion animals were killed, injured or lost their homes in one of the worst wildlife disasters in recorded history. About 10,000 koalas perished and the beloved marsupial became the international face of the natural tragedy.

Millions of hectares of native forests had already been deliberately plundered by humans – an area the size of Tasmania in the past twenty years alone – and a large chunk of what's left after the fires and two centuries of exploitation is designated for logging, including endangered animal habitat. The World Wildlife Fund has criticised the relaxation of Australia's environmental laws, pointing out that the greater glider – rarely spotted but easily recognised thanks to its oversized fluffy ears – lost 52 per cent of its habitat after it was officially listed as 'vulnerable' under the *Environment Protection and*

Biodiversity Conservation Act. The fires pushed the species closer to the brink of extinction by scorching a third of its remaining habitat. Australia's unique plant species are also in danger; thirty-eight have already been declared extinct, including the fringed spider orchid and Daintree river banana; 191 are critically endangered and more than 1300 are classified as threatened. One of the rarest is the delicate and beautiful dwarf spider orchid – there are just two left in the wild.

But amid the devastation, there are stories that provide reason for hope. The striking and multicoloured Gouldian finch – named by John Gould after his wife, Elizabeth – had all but disappeared in Queensland but has recently been sighted in large flocks for the first time in decades. Scientists attribute the revival to better land management practices, including lighter grazing of inland savannas. For other species, humans are playing a more hands-on role. In September 2020, twenty-eight captive-bred eastern quolls were released into a 400-hectare reserve in the Barrington Tops area of New South Wales, fenced off to prevent the invasion of introduced pests. The 'insurance population' for the endangered species now tops more than 100 quolls.

The last, best hope for their equally endangered relative, the northern quoll, rests in human hands – a chance to make amends after pushing the quoll to the brink of extinction through one of history's most misguided initiatives. The quoll's population dropped by more than 95 per cent in Queensland after 2400 cane toads, native to South America, were released in 1935 to control beetles that were munching on sugarcane (itself an introduced species). The plan didn't work (the beetles live high on the upper stalks of the sugar cane and toads live on the ground), but the toads thrived. Their population exploded to an estimated 200 million and is expanding westward by about fifty kilometres every year. A toad looks like a delicious lunch to a quoll, but it is a deadly one thanks to the toxic venom the toad excretes when threatened. The poison has already wiped out most of the quolls in the Northern Territory, and in 2009 cane toads crossed the Western Australian border, closing on the quolls' last stronghold in the Kimberley. Dr Jonathan Webb from the University of Sydney hit on an ingenious solution:

> I was reading a modern version of *Little Red Riding Hood* to my kids, and in that story Grandma sews raw onions into the wolf's stomach, so when the wolf wakes up he feels sick and refuses to eat another grandma again. It dawned on me that if we could teach northern quolls to associate sickness with cane toads, we might have a way of conserving them.

The problem for a predator such as the quoll is that eating a toad usually kills them, rather than putting them off eating more toads. So researchers took a group of sixty-two young quolls from a captive breeding program and taught half – the 'toad-smart' group – to associate eating a cane toad with feeling sick by feeding them small toads (too small to be deadly) laced with a nausea-inducing drug. Those quolls were then found to be less likely to attack a small living toad and lasted five times longer once released into the wild then their companions.

In 2019 a select group of fifty-four quolls was released on a small island near Darwin, with the help of Kenbi Traditional Owners, to monitor how they interact with the local toad population. Early results are mixed. 'This is one of the hazards of having your laboratory out in nature,' says University of Melbourne PhD candidate Ella Kelly, one of the leaders of the project. 'It is disappointing that when we went back we didn't catch as many quolls as we thought we might, but it is really exciting that there are young quolls on the island living with cane toads. It is now a matter of biting our nails while we wait another year to see if the population can grow and thrive with the cane toads.'

If the offspring of the 'toad-smart' quolls inherit their mothers' instinct to avoid eating toads, it points to the enticing prospect of what scientists call targeted gene flow – animals passing on learned behaviour genetically. If this is what is happening, breeding programs could be used to produce enough quolls with 'toad-smart' genes, which could be released in the Kimberley before the cane toad's inevitable arrival. The bigger picture could be far more significant, potentially helping species from Tasmanian devils to corals on the Great Barrier Reef. 'It is one of the first projects to look at the idea of actually using targeted gene flow for conservation purposes by moving adapted individuals into areas where populations are at risk of threats like new diseases, invasive species or climate change,' Kelly says. 'If it works, then in the right circumstances it could become a new tool for saving threatened species.'

Go quolls.

There is also hope for Gilbert's potoroo after three of the furry marsupials were transported to Bald Island, 1.5 kilometres off the coast of Albany. The island's potoroo population now outnumbers that of the mainland colony. And at the tip of South Australia's Yorke Peninsula, tammar wallabies are establishing a foothold a century after the species became extinct in mainland South Australia due to a loss of habitat and fox predation. In a fortuitous and somewhat ironic twist on a misguided chapter of Australian natural history, the wallabies survived in an unlikely location – Kawau Island, New Zealand, where they were introduced by Governor Sir George Grey, whom we met back in Chapter 1. Eighty-five of the wallabies were removed from Kawau Island in 2003 and used to start a breeding program that has given the marsupials a chance at survival in their original habitat.[22]

Governments could be playing a much more active role in helping these efforts along. Researchers estimate it would cost $1.6 billion to return all of Australia's threatened species to healthy status (by restoration of habitat and restrictions on landclearing, among other methods). That sounds a lot – it is a lot – but the annual federal budget is just over $500 billion and Australians spend $12 billion a year on their pets. Federal government spending on threatened species, meanwhile, dropped from $86.9 million in 2017–18 to $49.6 million in 2018–19. It received a boost after the 2020 bushfires, but is still well short of the budget in other comparable countries. With an almost identical number of threatened species (about 1700), United States governments spend about $2.1 billion a year on wildlife conservation.

---

22 The tammar wallaby was the first Australian animal described by a European. While shipwrecked on the Abrolhos Islands, 80 kilometres off the Western Australian coast, in 1629 following the wreck of the *Batavia*, Dutchman Francisco Pelsaert observed 'a large number of cats, which are creatures of a miraculous form, as big as a hare; the head is similar to a civet cat, the fore-paws are very short, about a finger long ... the tail is very long, the same as a meerkat; if they are going to eat, they sit on the hind legs and take the food with the fore-paws, and eat exactly the same as the squirrels and apes do.'

Research continues on the approaching catastrophe for our native animals, but most of the reasons for their disappearance are well understood – destruction of habitat, invasion of feral pests, overdevelopment and a warming planet. We have the solutions to tackle most of these problems. Do we have the will?

* * *

To the first Europeans who arrived on Australian shores, the animals they encountered were curiosities at best and useless at worst. Edward Wilson believed he was doing God's work when he tried to import creatures from around the globe to set loose in the new colony, and his enthusiastic partners in the acclimatisation movement saw little value in the local wildlife except to enliven dinner menus. Meanwhile, from the early years of the colony Australian animals were loaded onto ships and sent back to the mother country, where they became attractions in travelling menageries or private collections. The business of finding, capturing and transporting animals around the globe made a small number of men very rich, and slowly helped turn the wheel towards more ethical treatment of animals, including the advent of the modern zoo.

Australia's native animals were hunted and killed in immense numbers. By the time the impact was realised, it was too late to save some species, such as the thylacine, which remains a national tragedy. But the era also gave rise to a thriving nature-based tourism industry and some of Australia's first environmentalists, who advanced knowledge of the country's native fauna, albeit in occasionally unconventional ways. Their work added to the knowledge of Australian wildlife and made native animals a more respectable subject of scientific and community interest. Foreign-born naturalists like John Gould, John Gilbert, John Lewin, Allan Cunningham, Gustav Weindorfer, Gerard Krefft and Amalie Dietrich were succeeded by local-born enthusiasts like comedian-turned-naturalist Henry Burrell, reptile ambassador Eric Worrell and naturalist extraordinaire David Fleay who propelled the field of Australian nature study into the twentieth century and the age of modern media.

Australians gained a new understanding and love of their natural environment through the writing of Donald Macdonald, the wildly popular radio broadcasts of Crosbie Morrison, and the TV exploits of the many described in the previous chapter. Each made their contribution, big or small, to Australians learning more about their native wildlife. The koalas painted by John Lewin, the birds collected by John Gould, the platypus carried in a box on the lap of David Fleay, on a commercial flight to New York, the snakes milked by Tom 'Pambo' Eades and the sharks filmed by Ron and Valerie Taylor have all become part of Australia's national identity, featured on coins, stamps and licence plates, in songs, as Olympic mascots and in advertisements. They are part of how we see ourselves as Australians.

That important – vital – work continues thanks to enthusiastic naturalists like Peggy Rismiller, also known as the 'echidna lady'. Rismiller first saw an echidna in Frankfurt Zoo and moved from the United States to South Australia's Kangaroo Island in 1988 to study them in the wild. It turns out echidnas are surprisingly difficult to research – 'they are very elusive, secretive, cryptic and not attracted to anything – so basically finding them is being in the right place at the right time,' Rismiller told *Australian Geographic* magazine in 2020. Her decades of dedicated research have unlocked secrets of echidnas' mating habits – eggs are laid not in burrows like the platypus, but in a 'pseudo-pouch' (a fold of skin formed by a female's abdominal muscles). A newly hatched echidna is about the size of a five-cent coin and weighs about half a gram. They live in the pseudo-pouch for about fifty days before being moved to a nursery burrow when they start to develop spines – an understand-able move by the mother. But many questions remain unanswered, including why echidnas from Queensland to Tasmania hibernate for several months a year, how long they live, why they occasionally like to go for a swim in the ocean (possibly just because they enjoy it), and why their numbers – like those of so many other beloved Australian animals – appear to be in decline.

The loss of any species is a tragedy, and the possibility of mass extinctions within our lifetimes is real. After millions of years of evolution on a mostly isolated island, each of these animals deserves the chance to survive in its own right. But if we need another reason to take a stand for Australia's native animals, it is to protect the legacy of the unusual and exceptional people who have dedicated their lives to finding and understanding our native wildlife.

References

Introduction

Heather J. Aslin and David H. Bennett, 'Wildlife and World Views: Australian Attitudes Toward Wildlife', *Human Dimensions of Wildlife: An International Journal*, vol. 5, no. 2, 200, pp. 15–35.

William Dampier, *A New Voyage Around the World*, Argonaut Press, London, 1927, via Project Gutenberg: https://gutenberg.net.au/ebooks05/0500461h.html.

'Editorial: Last gasp of an icon', *The Mercury*, 7 September 2016.

Ann Moyal, *Platypus: The Extraordinary Story of How a Curious Creature Baffled the World*, Allen and Unwin, Crows Nest, 2001.

Penny Olsen, *Upside Down World: Early European Impressions of Australia's Curious Animals*, National Library of Australia, 2010.

Penny Olsen and Lynette Russell, *Australia's First Naturalists: Indigenous Peoples' Contribution to Early Zoology*, National Library of Australia, Canberra, 2019.

Robert Paddle, *The Last Tasmanian Tiger: The History and Extinction of the Thylacine*, Cambridge University Press, New York, 2000.

Bernard Smith, *European Vision and the South Pacific*, Yale University Press, New Haven, 1985.

Chapter 1

'Acclimatisation society's dinner, held at Scott's Hotel, Collins Street West on Wednesday, July 6 1884', *The Yeoman*, https://nla.gov.au/nla.obj-15075180/view.

Acclimatisation Societies of New Zealand, '10,000 Birds', 23 July 2014, http://www.10000birds.com/acclimatisation-societies-of-new-zealand.htm.

'A Moose Loose Aboot the Hoose', *Stuff.co.nz*, 25 July 2012.

Dr George Bennett, *Acclimatisation: Its Eminent Adaption to Australia: A Lecture Delivered in Sydney*, republished by the Acclimatisation Society of Victoria, WM Goodhugh and Co. Printers, Melbourne, 1864.

Rhianna Boyle, 'Elephants in the Top End, Kangaroos in the Top Paddock: The Colourful History of Introduced Species', *The Lifted Brow*, 22 January 2015.

Dr F. Buckland, *Acclimatisation of Animals: A Paper Read Before the Society of Arts*, London, republished by the Acclimatisation Society of Victoria, Melbourne 1861.

George C. Bonpas, ed., *Life of Frank Buckland*, Eleventh Edition, Smith, Elder and Co, London 1886.

Catherine de Courcy, *Evolution of a Zoo: A History of the Melbourne Zoological Gardens 1857–1900*, Quiddlers Press, Melbourne, 2003.

Craig Donofrio, 'The Father and Son Who Ate Every Animal Possible', *Atlas Obscura*, 19 January 2017, http://www.atlasobscura.com/articles/the-father-and-son-who-ate-every-animal-possible.

Thomas R. Dunlap, 'Remaking the Land: The Acclimatization Movement and the Anglo Ideas of Nature', *Journal of World History,* vol. 8, no. 2, 1997.

Linden Rae Gillbank, 'The Acclimatisation of Victoria', *Victorian Historical Journal*, vol. 51, no. 4, 1980.

Michael Green, 'Little Fox, Big Problem', *The Age*, 3 May 2014.

J. Cecil Le Souef, 'Acclimatisation in Victoria', *Victorian Historical Magazine*, vol. 36, no. 139, 1965.

Michael A. Osborne, 'Acclimatizing the World: A History of the Paradigmatic Colonial Science', *Nature and Empire: Science and the Colonial Enterprise*, vol. 15, 2000, pp. 135–151.

Peter Osborne, 'The Queensland Acclimatisation Society: Challenging the Stereotype', *Royal Historical Society of Queensland Journal*, vol. 20, no. 8, November 2008.

Eric Rolls, *They All Ran Wild: The Story of Pests on the Land in Australia*, Angus and Robertson, London, 1977.

Helen Tiffin, ed., *Five Emus to the King of Siam: Environment and Empire*, Brill, Leiden, 2007.

Caroline Wazer, 'The Exotic Animal Traffickers of Ancient Rome', *The Atlantic*, 30 March 2016.

'William Buckland', Oxford Museum of Natural History, http://www.oum.ox.ac.uk/learning/pdfs/buckland.pdf.

E. Wilson, *Answers Furnished by the Acclimatisation Society of Victoria to the Enquiries Addressed to It by His Excellency the Governor of Victoria at the Instance of The Right Hon. The Secretary of State for the Colonies*, Wilson and Mackinnon, Melbourne, 1864.

'Edward Wilson: Public Benefactor, a Life Sketch' (from *The Argus*), Wilson and Mackinnon, Melbourne, 1928.

Chapter 2

'Arrival of the Dingo', National Museum of Australia, https://www.nma.gov.au/
   defining-moments/resources/arrival-of-the-dingo.

Francis Buckland, *Curiosities of Natural History (fourth series)*, Macmillan and Co,
   New York, 1868.

Berry Carter, *Lama Down Under: Alpaca, Llama, Guanaco, Vicuna*, Agmedia,
   Melbourne, 1996.

Leigh Dayton, 'How Did the Dingo Get to Australia?', Science.org, 4 April 2016.

Ed Glinert, *The London Compendium: A Street-by-Street Exploration of the Hidden
   Metropolis*, Penguin Books, London, 2004.

'Good Words' Commissioner, 'Jamrach's', *Dictionary of Victorian London*, 1879,
   https://www.victorianlondon.org/shops/jamrachs.htm.

The Granville Guardian (published by Granville Historical Society), vol. 22, no. 7,
   September 2015, www.granvillehistorical.org.au.

Carl Hagenbeck, *Beasts and Men, Being Carl Hagenbeck's Experiences for Half a
   Century among Wild Animals*, abridged, trans. Hugh S.R. Elliot and A.G.
   Thacker, Longmans, Green and Co, London, 1912.

Elizabeth Hanson, *Animal Attractions: Nature on Display in American Zoos*,
   Princeton University Press, 2004.

Ilmar Leetberg, 'The Savage Art of the Human Zoo', *The Australian*, 19 February
   2012.

Jack Loney, 'Australian Sea Stories', *Marine History*, List Publishing, Geelong, 1985.

'Mr Charles Ledger and His Alpaca Contract with New South Wales', *Sydney
   Morning Herald*, 27 December 1859, p.5.

Penny Olsen, *Upside Down World: Early European Impressions of Australia's Curious
   Animals*, National Library of Australia, Canberra, 2010

Wesley Page, ed., *Bird Notes: The Journal of the Foreign Bird Club for the Study of
   All Species of Birds in Freedom and Captivity*, volume VII, W.T. Moulton,
   Brighton, 1908.

Christopher Plumb, *The Georgian Menagerie: Exotic Animals in Eighteenth-Century
   London*, I.B. Tauris and Co, London, 2015.

Nigel Rothfels, *Savages and Beasts: The Birth of the Modern Zoo*, John Hopkins
   University Press, Baltimore, 2008.

Naomi Russo, 'On This Day: The World First Sees a Live Platypus', *Australian
   Geographic*, 8 July 2015.

John Simons, 'The Scramble for Elephants: Exotic Animals and the Imperial
   Economy', in Melissa J. Boyde, ed., *Captured: The Animal within Culture*,
   Palgrave Macmillan, London, 2014.

John Simons, *The Tiger That Swallowed the Boy: Exotic Animals in Victorian England*,
   Libri Publishing, Faringdon, 2001.

John Simons, *Rossetti's Wombat: Pre-Raphaelites and Australian Animals in Victorian
   London*, Middlesex University Press, London, 2008.

Bernard Smith, 'European Vision and the South Pacific,' *Journal of the Warburg and Courtauld Institutes,* vol. 13, no. 1/2, 1950, pp. 65–100.

'The First Elephants in Australasia', *Australian Zoo and Circus Animals Historical Journals,* 13 November 2012.

Madeleine Thompson, 'Thylacines in the Bronx', *Lost Species Today,* 1 October 2016.

'The Thylacine Museum', naturalworlds.org, http://www.naturalworlds.org/thylacine/.

Angus Trumble, 'Rosetti's Wombat: A Pre-Raphaelite Obsession in Victorian England', Lecture delivered at National Library of Australia, 16 April 2003.

Chapter 3

Australian Mammalogy: Journal of the Australian Mammal Society, vol. 7, nos. 3–4, June–December 1984.

Mark Barrow, *A Passion for Birds: American Ornithology after Audobon,* Princeton University Press, 2000.

George Baitsch, 'Ludwig Leichhardt – the Life and the Legend', Paper presented in Munich Germany, 2006, www.fig.net.

William Beard, *Journey Triumphant: The Story of Leichhardt's Famous Expedition from the Darling Downs to Port Essington,* W.E. Baxter, Sussex, 1955.

Alec Chisholm, *Strange New World: The Adventures of John Gilbert and Ludwig Leichhardt,* Angus and Robertson, Sydney, 1941.

Alec Chisholm, 'The Diaries of S. W. Jackson', *Emu – Austral Ornithology,* vol. 58, no. 2, 1958, pp. 101–123.

Phillip A. Clarke, *Aboriginal Plant Collectors: Botanists and Australian Aboriginal People in the Nineteenth Century,* Rosenberg Publishing, Sydney, 2008.

Pat Comben, 'The Emergence of Frederick Strange, Naturalist', *The Proceedings of the Royal Society of Queensland,* vol. 122, December 2017, pp. 67–77.

Millais Culpin and Alfred Jefferis Turner, *Brisbane, Butterflies and Beetles: The World of Amalie Dietrich,* Brisbane History Group, 1989.

Paul Daley, 'The Bone Collectors: A Brutal Chapter in Australia's Past', *The Guardian,* 14 June 2014.

Ken Eastwood, 'Cold Case: Leichhardt's Disappearance', *Australian Geographic,* 3 August 2010.

Matt Fishburn, 'Phillip Parker King's Stowaway', *Journal of the Royal Australian Historical Society,* vol. 103, June 2017.

C.T. Fisher, 'Scientific Report: From John Gilbert to John Gould: Two Previously Unpublished Letters with the Correct Version of a Third', *Australian Zoologist,* http://publications.rzsnsw.org.au/doi/pdf/10.7882/AZ.1985.002?code=rzsw-site.

Jordan Goodman, 'Losing It in New Guinea: The Voyage of HMS *Rattlesnake*', *Endeavour,* vol. 29, no. 2, June 2019.

Jordan Goodman, *The Rattlesnake: A Voyage of Discovery to the Coral Sea*, Faber and
Faber, London, 2005.

'Human Remains Found in Storeroom', *The Age*, 16 February 2003.

Julian Huxley, ed., *T.H. Huxley's Diary of the Voyage of HMS Rattlesnake*, Chatto
and Windus, London, 1935.

'How Amalie Dietrich's Lonely Years in State's Outback Aided Science',
The Courier-Mail, 12 January 1939.

'I Light Upon Treasures', *The West Australian*, 18 December 1948.

'John Gilbert: Naturalist and Explorer', Liverpool Museums, http://www.
liverpoolmuseums.org.uk/wml/collections/zoology/john-gilbert/about-john-
gilbert.aspx.

E.B. Joyce and D.A. McCann, *Burke and Wills: The Scientific Legacy of the Victorian
Exploring Expedition*, CSIRO Publishing, Melbourne, 2011.

Joseph B. Jukes, *Narrative of the Surveying Voyage of HMS Fly, Commanded by
Captain FP Blackwood RN in Torres Strait, New Guinea, and Other Islands of the
Eastern Archipelago During the Years 1842–1846 Together with an Excursion into
the Interior of the Eastern Part of Java*, vol 1., T. and W. Boone, London, 1884.

John MacGillivray, *Narrative of The Voyage Of H.M.S. Rattlesnake, Commanded by
the Late Captain Owen Stanley, R.N., F.R.S. Etc. During the Years 1846–1850.
Including Discoveries and Surveys in New Guinea, The Louisiade Archipelago, Etc.
To Which is added the Account of Mr. E.B. Kennedy's Expedition for the Exploration
of The Cape York Peninsula. By John Macgillivray, F.R.G.S. Naturalist to The
Expedition*, vol. 1, T. and W. Boone, London, 1852, via Project Gutenberg,
http://www.gutenberg.org/files/12433/12433-h/12433-h.html.

Hannah McPherson, 'The Australian Botanical Collections of 19th Century
German Naturalist Amalie Dietrich', Australian German Association Inc.
in conjunction with the Goethe Institute, 2009, http://www.aga.org.au/
wp-content/uploads/2011/10/AGA-Report-Hannah-McPherson-20-August-
2009LR.pdf.

'Murder of Mr Strange and Three Others', *Sydney Morning Herald*, 21 November
1854, p. 4.

Patrick Noonan, 'Sons of Science: Remembering John Gould's Martyred Collectors',
Australasian Journal of Victorian Studies, vol. 21, no. 1, p. 28–42, July 2016.

Penny Olsen, *Glimpses of Paradise: The Quest for the Beautiful Parrakeet*, National
Library of Australia, 2007.

Roslyn Russell, *The Business of Nature*, National Library of Australia, Canberra, 2011.

Ray Sumner, 'Photographs of Aborigines in North East Australia: A Collection of
Early Queensland Aboriginal Photographs, made by Amalie Dietrich for the
Museum Godfroy', Aboriginal History, vol. 10, no. 2, 1986, at http://press-
files.anu.edu.au/downloads/press/p71821/pdf/article14.pdf.

Ray Sumner, *A Woman in the Wilderness*, University of New South Wales Press,
Kensington, 1993.

'The Late Mr Kennedy', *Sydney Morning Herald*, 7 March 1849, p. 2.

Marjorie Tipping, *Ludwig Becker: Artist and Naturalist with the Burke and Wills Expedition*, Melbourne University Press, 1979.

Isabella Tree, *The Bird Man: The Extraordinary Story of John Gould*, Barrie and Jenkins Ltd, London, 1991.

Chapter 4

'Australian Museum', *Sydney Morning Herald*, 17 April 1875.

John Cann, *Snakes Alive! Snake Experts and Antidote Sellers of Australia*, Seymour Lansing, NSW, 2001.

John Cann, 'John Cann, the Last Snake Man of La Perouse, Tells Story with Bite in New Book', *Sydney Morning Herald*, 24 January 2018.

Thomas Darragh, 'William Blandowski: A Frustrated Life', *Proceedings of the Royal Society of Victoria*, vol. 121, 2009, pp. 11–60.

Colin Finney, *Paradise Revealed: Natural History in Nineteenth-Century Australia*, Museum of Victoria, Melbourne, 1993.

Rosemary Fleay-Thomson, *Animals First: The Story of Pioneer Australian Conservationist and Zoologist Dr David Fleay*, Petaurus Publishing, Nerang, 2007.

George B. Halford, *The Treatment of Snake-Bite In Victoria: Being a Paper Read Before The Medical Society of Victoria*, Stillwell and Knight, Melbourne, 1870.

Peter Hobbins, 'Spectacular Serpents: Snakebite in Colonial Australia', in *Venom: Fear, Fascination and Discovery* (online exhibition), Medical History Museum, University of Melbourne.

Murray Johnson, 'Fangs and Faith: The Search for an Effective Antidote against Snake Envenomation in Australia', *Journal of the Royal Australian Historical Society*, vol. 95, no. 2, November 2009, pp. 125–143.

Philip Jones, *Search for the Taipan: The Story of Ram Chandra*, Angus and Robertson, Sydney, 1977.

Gerard Krefft, *Snakes of Australia: Illustrated and Descriptive Catalogue of All the Known Species*, Thomas Richards, Sydney, 1869.

'Mackay's Taipan Man', *AM*, ABC Radio, 31 July 1999, https://www.abc.net.au/am/stories/s40470.htm.

Kevin Markwell and Nancy Cushing, *Snake-bitten: Eric Worrell and the Australian Reptile Park*, University of New South Wales Press, Randwick, 2010.

Kevin Markwell and Nancy Cushing, 'From Snake-handlers to Wildlife Entrepreneurs', in *Venom: Fear, Fascination and Discovery* (online exhibition), Medical History Museum, University of Melbourne.

Peter Mirtschin, 'The Pioneers of Venom Production for Australian Antivenoms', Venomsupplies.com, http://www.venomsupplies.com/assets/Pioneers-published-paper.pdf.

J.P. Murray, 'Notes of a Case of Successful Treatment of Snakebite', in *Australian Medical Gazette,* Clarson, Massina and Co, Melbourne, 1869.

James Murray, *Venom: The Heroic Search for Australia's Deadliest Snake*, Echo Publishing, Richmond, 2017.

Roy Norry, *Australian Snake Man: The Story of Eric Worrell*, Thomas Nelson, Melbourne, 1966.

'"Pambo" Bitten by Snake', *The Argus*, 16 March 1933.

Julie Power, 'Australian Museum Puts Spotlight on Controversial Darwinist Gerard Krefft', *Sydney Morning Herald*, 13 October 2017.

'Snake Poison and Its Antidotes', *The Argus*, 8 November 1861.

'Taipan Victim Dies in Hospital', *Cairns Post*, 29 July 1950.

Brownyn Watson, 'Krefft's Chair: Museum Director Took Sacking Sitting Down', *The Australian*, 8 February 2019.

David Williams, 'The Death of Kevin Budden', Kingsnake.com, http://pandora. nla.gov.au/pan/107967/20110506-1206/www.kingsnake.com/aho/species/ extras/budden.html.

Chapter 5

'Baby Platypus Born at Healesville', *The Argus*, 5 January 1944.

Charles Darwin, *Complete Works of Charles Darwin*, Delphi Classics, London, 2015.

'David Fleay Nature's Gentleman', YouTube, 8 April 2013, 44:43, https://youtu.be/W-VooQwjiHQ.

David Fleay, *Paradoxical Platypus: Hobnobbing with Duckbills,* Jacaranda Press, Milton, 1980.

David Fleay, *Living with Animals*, Lansdowne Press, Melbourne, 1960.

David Fleay, *We Breed the Platypus*, Robertson and Mullens, Melbourne, 1944.

Rosemary Fleay-Thomson, *Animals First: The Story of Pioneer Australian Conservationist and Zoologist David Fleay*, Petaurus Publishing, Nerang, 2007.

Adrian Franklin, *Animal Nation: The True Story of Animals and Australia*, University of New South Wales Press, Sydney, 2006.

Carol Freeman, 'Is This Picture Worth a Thousand Words? An Analysis of Harry Burrell's Photograph of a Thylacine with a Chicken', *Australian Zoologist*, vol. 33, no. 1, June 2005.

Fred Ford, *John Gould's Extinct and Endangered Mammals of Australia*, National Library of Australia, Canberra 2014.

Brian K. Hall, 'The Paradoxical Platypus', *BioScience*, vol. 49, no. 3, March 1999, pp. 211–21.

Angela Heathcote, 'Fake or Real? This Photo of a Thylacine Has Caused a Lot of Controversy', *Australian Geographic*, 10 January 2018.

'Historic Newsreel David Fleay Platypuses New York 1947', YouTube, 23 March 2009, 1:19, https://youtu.be/SUt3w7mrwC4.

Natalie Lawrence, 'Churchill's Platypus', *BBC Wildlife Magazine*, September 2017.

Natalie Lawrence, 'The Prime Minister and the Platypus: A Paradox Goes to War', *Studies in History and Philosophy of Biological and Biomedical Sciences*, 2011.

Peter Macinnis, *Curious Minds: The Discoveries of Australian Naturalists*, National Library of Australia, Canberra, 2000.

'Memories of West Burleigh with Stephen Fleay', YouTube, 31 March 2013, 29:55, https://youtu.be/qjYfoUsF8p4i.

Ann Moyal, *Platypus: The Extraordinary Story of How a Curious Creature Baffled the World*, Allen and Unwin, Crows Nest, 2001.

New York Zoological Society news, 3 June 1958, http://www.wcsarchivesblog.org/wp-content/uploads/2014/03/1958-06-03-NYZSNews-AustralianPlatypusExpedition.pdf.

Abby Ohlheiser, 'The Platypus Is So Weird that Scientists Thought the First Specimen Was a Hoax', *Washington Post*, 1 April 2015.

Penny Olsen, *Upside Down World: Early European Impressions of Australia's Curious Animals*, National Library of Australia, Canberra, 2010.

Tony Perrottet, 'How Australia Put Evolution on Darwin's Mind', *Smithsonian Magazine*, January 2015.

Libby Robin, 'Paradox on the Queensland Frontier: Platypus, Lungfish and Other Vagaries of Nineteenth-century Science', *Australian Humanities Review*, vol. 19, September 2000.

George Shaw, 'The Duck-billed Platypus', *The Naturalist's Miscellany*, no. 10, 1799, plates 385–6.

Chapter 6

C.A. Bacon, 'A Brief History of the Jane River Goldfield', Tasmania Department of Mines report, 1989.

C.A. Bacon, 'Notes on the History of Mining and Exploration at Adamsfield', Mineral Resources Tasmania report, 1992.

E.A. Bell, 'Tigers Were Her Hobby', *The Australian Women's Weekly*, 10 May 1967.

George F.J. Bergman, *The Hermit of Cradle Mountain*, 1955.

C.J. Binks, *Pioneers of Tasmania's West Coast*, Blubber Head Press, Sandy Bay, 1988.

Michael Charles Byers, *Tourism and Bushwalking in the Cradle Mountain-Lake St Clair National Park: Context, Characteristics and Impacts*, University of Tasmania, Hobart, 1996.

John Cannon and Grant Dixon, 'Gordonvale: Ernie Would Approve', *40 [degrees] South*, no. 68, Autumn 2013, pp. 64–70.

Simon Cubit and Nic Haygarth, *Mountain Men: Stories from the Tasmanian High Country*, Forty South Publishing, Cambridge, 2015.

Lindsay D. Crawford, 'Gordon Vale, Launceston Walking Club', *Wild Life*, 1953.

Fred Ford, *John Gould's Extinct and Endangered Mammals of Australia*, National Library of Australia, Canberra, 2014.

'Gordonvale World Heritage Area Reserve Background Report', Tasmanian Land Conservancy, 2015.

Kathleen and Ralph Gowlland, *Trampled Wilderness: History of South-West Tasmania*, Regal Publications, Launceston, 2004.

Nic Haygarth, *A View to Cradle: A History of Tasmania's Forth River High Country*, Canberra, 1998.

Francis R. Hrdina, 'Marsupial Destruction in Queensland 1877–1930', *Australian Zoologist*, March 1997.

Timothy Jetson, 'Almost a Walker's Paradise: A History of the Cradle Mountain-Lake St Clair Scenic Reserve to May 1922', PhD thesis, School of History and Classics, University of Tasmania, Hobart, 2005.

Simon Kleinig, *Frenchman's Cap: Story of a Mountain*, Glass House Books, Brisbane, 2012.

Keith Lancaster, 'With the Hermit of Gordon Vale', Bushwalking diary, 1947, http://dveltkamp.customer.netspace.net.au/KeithLancaster/071HermitofGordonVale.htm.

Christobel Mattingley interview with Robyn Williams, 'King of the Wilderness – The Life of Deny King Part One and Part Two', ABC Radio, 16 February 2003.

Christobel Mattingley, *King of the Wilderness: The Life of Deny King*, Text Publishing, Melbourne, 2001.

Mary Roberts, 'The Keeping and Breeding of Tasmanian Devils (*Sarcophilus harrisi*)', *Proceedings of the Zoological Society of London*, 1915, https://www.biodiversitylibrary.org/item/98466#page/357/mode/1up.

Ned Terry, *Pioneers and Their Memories of Tasmania's High Country*, Artemis Publishing Consultants, 2007.

Gustav Weindorfer, 'Wild Life in Tasmania: Read before the Field Naturalists Club of Victoria, Dec 8, 1919', *The Victorian Naturalist: The Journal and Magazine of the Field Naturalists Club of Victoria*. March 1920, https://archive.org/stream/victoriannatural3536fiel#page/n5/mode/2up.

Chapter 7

Damon Adams, 'The World According to Alby', *South Florida Sun-Sentinel*, 22 May 1995.

'A Flower Hunter: Mrs Ellis Rowan's Travels', *The Argus*, 10 December 1904.

Alby Mangels' World Safari 1: The Adventure of a Lifetime!, Home Cinema Group, Australia, 2009.

Alby Mangels' World Safari 2: The New Adventure, Home Cinema Group, Australia, 2009.

Nicole Alexander, 'The Brushmen of the Bush: Jack Absalom', blog, 14 July 2019, https://www.nicolealexander.com.au/2019/07/14/the-brushmen-of-the-bush-jack-absalom.

David Allan-Petale, 'Legendary Aussie Explorer Alby Mangels on What Drove Him to Adventure', *WA Today*, 19 October 2017.

'A Painter of Flowers: Mrs Ellis Rowan Interviewed', *Barrier Miner*, 3 November 1906.

'Australian Story: Ask the Leyland Brother', *Australian Story*, ABC, 6 March 2015.

Malcolm Bodey and Mark Dodd, 'Legacy of TV's Original Croc Hunter Malcolm Douglas', *The Australian*, 24 September 2010.

Harry Butler, *In the Wild*, ABC, Sydney, 2000.

Brendan Borrell, 'John Young Rediscovered the Australian Night Parrot, but Did He Lie about His Later Findings?', Audubon.org, 4 April 2019, https://www.audubon.org/news/john-young-rediscovered-australian-night-parrot-did-he-lie-about-his-later.

'Episode 8: Alby Mangels: The Adventure Documentary Pioneer', *The Thread*, 14 October 2017, https://www.youtube.com/watch?v=CK_pdtrP2qs.

Escape: World Safari 3, Home Cinema Group, Australia, 2009.

'Flashback: Malcolm Douglas on 40 years of adventure', ABC News, 23 September 2010, https://www.youtube.com/watch?v=_hYws3P9w5w.

Gideon Haigh, 'Donald Macdonald', Australian Media Hall of Fame, https://halloffame.melbournepressclub.com/article/donald-macdonald.

Gay Hawkins and Ben Dibley, 'Natural History on TV: How the ABC Took Australian Animals to the People', *The Conversation*, 20 November 2019.

Interview with Harry Butler, *In Conversation*, ABC Radio National, 27 July 2006, https://www.abc.net.au/radionational/programs/archived/inconversation/harry-butler/3322176#transcript.

Ann Jones, 'Jack Absalom: The Painter, Author, Desert Survivalist on His Unconventional Outback Life', ABC News, 10 March 2018, https://www.abc.net.au/news/science/2018-03-10/jack-absalom-life-of-a-renaissance-bushman/9523960.

Ann Jones, 'The Night Parrot: A Mystery as Old as Our Country', ABC News, 10 February 2019, https://www.abc.net.au/news/2019-02-10/night-parrot-chase/10612496?nw=0.

Donald Macdonald, *How We Kept the Flag Flying: The Story of the Siege of Ladysmith*, Ward, Lock and Co, Melbourne, 1900.

Donald Macdonald, 'Death at Black Rock, Nature Lover and Journalist', *The Argus*, 24 November 1932.

Peter Macinnis, *Curious Minds: The Discoveries of Australian Naturalists*, National Library of Australia, Canberra, 2012.

Norman McCance, 'Donald Macdonald Memorial: Tributes to a Great Naturalist', *The Australasian*, 23 December 1939.

Russell McGregor, 'Alec Chisholm: Bush Naturalist and Benign Nationalist', State Library of NSW, https://www.sl.nsw.gov.au/stories/alec-chisholm-bush-naturalist-and-benign-nationalist.

Russell McGregor, 'Encyclopedia for a Nation', *SL*, State Library of New South Wales magazine, winter 2017, https://www.sl.nsw.gov.au/sites/default/files/4918_sl_magazine_winter_2017_210wx265hmm_aw_spreads.pdf.

Russell McGregor, 'Mateship with Nature: Nationalism and Conservation in the Writings of Alec Chisholm', 2019, http://www.whpress.co.uk/EH/papers/1757-McGregor.pdf.

Peter Menkhorst and Edward Ryan, *C.H. McLennan ('Mallee Bird') and His Aboriginal Informant Jowley: The Source of Early Records of the Night Parrot Pezoporus occidentalis in Victoria?*, Memoirs of Museum Victoria, vol. 73, pp. 107–15, 2015, https://museumsvictoria.com.au/media/4235/107-115_mmv73_menkhorst_3_web.pdf.

Louisa Anne Meredith (Mrs Charles Meredith), *Notes and Sketches of New South Wales; During a Residence in That Colony from 1839 to 1844*, John Murray, London, 1844, and Penguin Books, Ringwood, 1973.

Dorian Moro and Isobel McAulay, *A Guide to the Reptiles and Amphibians of Barrow Island*, Chevron, https://australia.chevron.com/-/media/australia/publications/documents/nature-book-reptiles.pdf.

Martin Mulligan and Stuart Hill, *Ecological Pioneers: A Social History of Australian Ecological Thought and Action*, Cambridge University Press, Sydney, 2001.

'Obituary: Harry Butler, the Bushman who Brought His Love of the Outback into living Rooms', *Sydney Morning Herald*, 14 December 2015.

Graham Pizzey, *Crosbie Morrison: The Voice of Nature*, Victoria Press, Melbourne, 1992

Larry Schwarz, 'White Fella Bushman Back in the Saddle', *The Age*, 19 February 2009.

Joanne A. Smith, Lisa J. Wright and Keith D. Morris, 'An Annotated Bibliography of the Natural History of Barrow Island 1622–2004', Department of Conservation and Land Management, 2006, https://www.dpaw.wa.gov.au/images/documents/about/science/cswa/articles/111.pdf.

Valerie Taylor and Ben Mckelvey, *Valerie Taylor: An Adventurous Life – The Remarkable Story of the Trailblazing Ocean Conservationist, Photographer and Shark Expert*, Hachette Australia, Sydney, 2019.

'Valerie Taylor interview', *Conversations*, ABC Radio, 19 August 2015.

Sally Wilson, 'Ellis Rowan: Plant Hunter', *The Planthunter*, 26 October 2015, https://theplanthunter.com.au/culture/ellis-rowan-plant-hunter/.

Epilogue

David Coates, 'Undocumented Plant Extinctions are a Big Problem in Australia – Here's Why They Go Unnoticed', *The Conversation*, 13 June 2019.

Ken Eastwood, 'Beauty Rich and Rare', *RM Williams Magazine*, October/November 2015, https://www.rmwilliams.com.au/bush-blitz/Outback_Stories_Bush_Blitz.html?lang=en_AU.

James Fitzsimmons, Sarah Legge, Barry Trail and John Woinarski, *Into Oblivion: The Disappearing Mammals of Northern Australia*, The Nature Conservancy, Melbourne, 2001.

Mike Foley, 'Why Is Australia a Global Leader in Animal Extinctions?', *The Sydney Morning Herald*, 20 July 2020.

Fred Ford, *John Gould's Extinct and Endangered Mammals of Australia*, National Library of Australia, Canberra, 2014.

James Gill, 'Genesis of the Australian Whaling Industry: Its Development Up to 1850', *Journal of the Royal Historical Society of Queensland*, vol 8, no. 1, 1966, https://espace.library.uq.edu.au/view/UQ:212779.

Frances C. Hrdina, 'Marsupial destruction in Queensland 1877–1930', Queensland Department of Environment and Heritage', *Australian Zoologist*, vol. 30, no. 3, March 1997, https://publications.rzsnsw.org.au/doi/pdf/10.7882/AZ.1997.003.

Page Jarreau, 'Not Your Everyday Rats', *Science Next, Official Blog of the LSU College of Science*, https://lsuscienceblog.squarespace.com/blog/2017/5/19/not-your-everyday-rats.

Samuel Mossman, *Our Australian Colonies: Their Discovery, History, Resources and Prospects*, Religious Tract Society, London, 1866.

Sara Phillips, 'Slender Root Rat: New Mammal Species Discovered by Scientists on Indonesian Island,' ABC online, https://www.abc.net.au/news/2016-04-19/slender-root-rat-discovered-on-indonesian-island/7339184.

John Pickrell, 'There's a Lot We Don't Know about Echidnas', *Australian Geographic*, 6 November 2020.

Augustus Rudder, 'Sixty Years a Settler', *Town and Country Journal*, 1902, cited in Bruce Elder, *Blood on the Wattle*, New Holland, Sydney, 2020.

Sue Taylor interview with Robyn Williams, 'John Gould's Extinct and Endangered Birds of Australia', *Ockham's Razor*, ABC Radio National, 2 December 2012, https://www.abc.net.au/radionational/programs/ockhamsrazor/john-gould27s-extinct-and-endangered-birds-of-australia./4404118.

Andrew Trounson, 'Speeding Natural Selection in the Name of Conservation', *Pursuit*, 28 May 2018, https://pursuit.unimelb.edu.au/articles/speeding-natural-selection-in-the-name-of-conservation.

B.A. Wintle, N.C.R. Cadenhead, R.A. Morgain et al., 'Spending to Save: What Will It Cost to Halt Australia's Extinction Crisis?', *Conservation Letters*, vol. 12, no. 6, 2019, pp. 1–7.

John C.Z. Woinarski, Andrew A. Burbidge and Peter L. Harrison, 'Ongoing Unravelling of a Continental Fauna: Decline and Extinction of Australian Mammals Since European Settlement', *Proceedings of the National Academy of Sciences of the United States of America*, 9 February 2015, https://www.pnas.org/content/112/15/4531.

John Woinarski, Brett Murphy, Dale Nimmo, Michael Braby, Sarah Legge and
    Stephen Garnet, 'Scientists Recount Australia's Extinct Species: The Results
    are Devastating', *Australian Geographic*, 2 December 2019.

Index